BEETHOVEN AND HUMAN DESTINY

The Bourdelle Beethoven. Musée Bourdelle, Paris

Beethoven and Human Destiny

BURNETT JAMES

ROY PUBLISHERS · NEW YORK

© Burnett James, 1960

Library of Congress
Catalog card number 61–11045

Made in Great Britain at the
Aldine Press, Letchworth, Herts, for
Roy Publishers, 30 East 74th Street, New York 21, N.Y.
U.S.A. edition 1961

Contents

Plates

Preface

FOR SUCCESSIVE generations the music of Beethoven, like the plays of Shakespeare, presents a new challenge. And it is not only—perhaps not principally—to scholarship and musicology that the challenge presents itself, but to the human spirit and imagination with which it comes constantly into contact. Just as biographers discover new facts about Beethoven's life and arrive at new interpretations of the established facts, and just as each new generation of musicians and executants must discover for itself a fresh approach to Beethoven's music, so the commentator and musical critic must come to it with a fresh mind, yet one matured by contact with and imaginative understanding of the past and its own attitudes and assumptions. This book is an attempt to interpret the music of Beethoven in relation not only to our own times, but to the developing consciousness of mankind.

The idea that Beethoven's music goes far beyond mere patterns in sound, that music was for him, in a very real and precise sense, a language through which he communicated his deepest experience of life and art, is by no means new. Its ethical and idealistic, and later on its mystical, quality has always been sensed, and many attempts have been made to expound it. But no exposition can be final, any more than any particular performance of a particular work can be final. The inquiring mind has to seek anew.

Beethoven stands at the centre of human consciousness. In him, as with a few others—artists, philosophers, saints—are summed up the inner impulses that have gone into the historical and spiritual development of the human race. That he was a partially (but only partially) unconscious agent of the life forces is readily demonstrable, though he was never a passive one. But through the blending of the conscious and the unconscious in his extraordinarily deep and comprehensive experience of the farthest mysteries of this life, and above all in his overwhelming ability to embody in music the essence of that experience, Beethoven bears witness to the destiny of man.

In these precarious days an understanding of the life-forces revealed to us by those who have experienced them to the full is a task not to be shirked. It may in the end be the one chance of salvation of the world in which we live. 'If I understood him as I feel him', one of Beethoven's close friends once said, 'then I should know everything.' Such knowledge is not only invaluable: it is essential. We must seek it always. This is a book which makes one more effort to do so in terms of philosophy as well as in terms of music.

B. J.

July 1960

ACKNOWLEDGMENTS

The author and publishers are grateful for permission to quote from copyright material to the following:

George Allen & Unwin Ltd, for *The History of Western Philosophy* by Bertrand Russell; A. & C. Black Ltd, for *Civilization and Ethics* and *J. S. Bach* by Albert Schweitzer; Geoffrey Bles Ltd, for *Solitude and Society* and *Freedom and the Spirit* by Nicholas Berdyaev; Doubleday & Co. Inc., for *Beethoven: the Man who freed Music* by R. H. Schauffler (copyright 1929 by R. H. Schauffler. Copyright 1929 by the Outlet Company); Faber & Faber Ltd, for *English Poetry* by Leone Vivante, and *Little Gidding* by T. S. Eliot; The Hogarth Press Ltd, for the Standard Edition of *The Complete Psychological Works* of Sigmund Freud; The Oxford University Press, for *Beethoven* and *Essays in Musical Analysis* by D. F. Tovey; and the Editor of *The Sunday Times*, for contributions by Ernest Newman.

The author wishes to thank J. E. Caleinar of Deutsche Grammophone (Great Britain) Ltd for obtaining photographs from the parent company.

I

The Prelude

EXACTLY HOW far heredity and early environment influence the formation of character and the subsequent development of men of genius, we still do not know. How much is genius made, or at least directly conditioned, by external circumstance, and how much is it a free, spontaneous, and in a sense miraculous growth? Probably it is in something of an inverse ratio—the stronger, more autonomous the power of genius, the less is it 'made'. If we knew more about the childhood of Shakespeare it is possible that some further illumination might be thrown on Shakespeare the poet and dramatist; but it is doubtful, to put it no stronger, if a different childhood would have produced a substantially different Shakespeare. So with other men of the highest genius; and so, unquestionably, it is with Beethoven. We know a certain amount about Beethoven's earliest years, and although particular incidents, to some extent, and the broad general pattern can legitimately be held to account for an intensification of certain of Beethoven's characteristics in later life, it is not safe to seize with a too disingenuous simplicity on the material circumstances. All the same, we cannot nonchalantly flout the findings and theories of modern psychological research, led principally by Freud and Adler, and so ignore the obvious effects of a childhood fraught with bitterness, suffering, and perplexity on the one hand, and the influences of the social and cultural atmosphere of Bonn on the other. On the contrary, one of the most profound elements in Beethoven's hold over the human mind lies precisely in the way in which his creative personality emerges triumphant from an evil destiny.

From the beginning Beethoven was called upon to suffer greatly— he neither inherited the primrose path nor throughout his life was he able to make it for himself, except for a few rare and passing moments.

Whatever he achieved, the one thing that always eluded him was human happiness as the world understands it. He constantly illuminated the dark and sinister corridors of existence; but the cost to himself was one that few men would willingly pay, even if it were within their power to pay it. And there is perhaps an enduring lesson in that alone for the world which is always seeking short cuts to felicity and unfailingly demands the blessings without taking full cognizance of the underlying tragedy.

It is tempting, following Adler at a respectable distance, to attribute Beethoven's lifelong aggressiveness in social and personal relations to the frustrations and difficulties of his childhood—a sort of defence mechanism, the seeds of which were sown by the gradual break-up of the Beethoven family life, the father's lack of moral fibre and addiction to alcohol, the adored mother's tragic death, the incessant financial stringency, all of which led to Beethoven's being obliged to assume full family responsibilities at the age of barely eighteen. Certainly all the ingredients were present, and no doubt they had their lasting effects on the character of the grown man and on a mind of extreme sensibility and perception. It is doubtful, though, whether the whole explanation can be found there, or even the major part of it: there was something deep-seated in Beethoven's nature—something unique and altogether apart from circumstance—that made him what he was. Nor can we properly attribute it to the personal tragedy of deafness; for Beethoven's special characteristics were well in evidence before that catastrophe overtook and all but overwhelmed him.

It is necessary, therefore, to tread with some care before treating Beethoven as a sort of psychological case-history in the light of current theory. The theory applies, no doubt, in so far as it has basic and universal validity; but it must not be allowed to dictate terms on its own, especially as there are other and equally potent factors in Beethoven's mental temper which have to be put into the balance and weighed judiciously with the rest.

We are probably nearest to truth if we understand that, although the ordinary man is profoundly influenced and conditioned by environment and early associations, genius possesses, in fact is, an extra quality which liberates it to some extent from external circumstance—makes it more independent, more autonomous and less susceptible to influences from the outside. Genius is in a very real sense a miracle, and it is the element of the miraculous that defies analysis and sets it apart from the

BEETHOVEN'S BIRTHPLACE. BUST IN THE BEETHOVENHAUS, BONN

common laws of cause and effect. Genius is as unaccountable in origin as it is unpredictable in development; and although men of genius are as likely to have strongly conventional streaks in their make-up as irrational or revolutionary tendencies (and even the professed revolutionary is as often as not conventional), the *quality* of their genius remains free and inexplicable. Beethoven in fact provides a fascinating study in the way in which the human mind can, by constant and conscious effort under the impulse of the fire of genius, free itself from determinism and the material world.

When we set ourselves face to face with the creative life of Beethoven we suddenly understand the meaning and reality of transcendence. We cannot explain Beethoven away by reference to prevailing psychological and scientific theory, even though we shall be helped along the road to comprehension by a knowledge of the external circumstances of his life—especially his early life—and the primary data with which he set out on the long and arduous journey: by placing him, that is, in historical and social perspective.

There is, for example, a fruitful line of thought to be followed in connection with Beethoven's already mentioned social and personal aggressiveness. The so-called 'power complex' is familiar to psychologists, who usually define it as the desire to compensate for feelings of inferiority and insecurity first apprehended in childhood. The child's sense of dependence turns into the desire to wield power over others in one form or another. Generally speaking, this lust for power means a desire for domination. In its most extreme forms it manifests itself as outright gangsterism, military conquest, the abuse of political and economic power, or the psychological effects of the more blatant forms of propaganda, which is a domination of the mind. Its less obvious manifestations are many and various—parental tyranny, officiousness at work and in the home, a general attitude of censoriousness towards one's fellows, even the harsh-handed domination of animals. Often it passes off under the blessed name of 'discipline'. It is a large and complex problem; but stemming from the theories of Freud and Adler it strikes at the roots of human conduct.

At first it seems as though Beethoven provides an admirable example of the lust for power generated by early environment and conditions. His frequently overbearing attitude; his tendency to ride roughshod over obstacles, whether human or material; his expressly stated sense of superiority—these and other attributes of the man in his day-to-day life fit, once the basic information is at our disposal, very well with the theories of psychology. But deeper investigation reveals another and, in the long run, more convincing side to the picture. Although unusually conscious of his own power, Beethoven, with one or two important exceptions, was strikingly free from the desire to exercise his power in the worldly sense—that is, to use it as a weapon to dominate others.

The principal exception was his pathetic but high-handed efforts to interfere in the domestic affairs of his brothers—especially his precipitate taking up of arms in an attempt to sever the liaison of brother Johann with his mistress Therese Obermyer—an attack that Johann countered in the most effective way by clinching the union with marriage lines. Here Beethoven was completely off his own ground, and was lured into trying to use his internal strength for external ends. He tried to dominate, became almost bureaucratic, and suffered immediate, summary, and entirely foreseeable defeat. No doubt this aspect of his behaviour had its roots directly in his youth, and can be explained by the promise to his dying mother that he would all his life hold himself responsible for the family welfare. He carried fraternal duty to excess, for he was deep down a man for whom moderation was impossible; but even here his actions tell us much about what manner of man he really was. In worldly matters his judgment was often at fault; but his heart was sound even though it occasionally led him into undignified, not to say ridiculous, situations.

On the other hand, what for want of a better word we must call the 'real' Beethoven—the Beethoven, that is, who lived and exercised his power in his art—was entirely devoid of the will to domination that characterizes the man of action—the politician, the financier, the warrior. His strength was of another kind and he knew it. When Castelli called Beethoven 'the personification of strength' he spoke perhaps more profoundly than he knew. And when Beethoven himself said, 'Power is the morality of men who stand out from the rest, and it is also mine', he also spoke truth, though ambiguously. For the 'morality of men who stand out from the rest' is also the morality of a Napoleon, a Hitler, a Dillinger.

It is, I suppose, possible to see the manifestation of power in artistic creation as another facet of psychological compensation. No doubt a school of psychology would assert it to be a species of 'sublimation' of the common will to power in the worldly sense. It is not easy in a few words convincingly to refute such an argument—nor in fact is it necessary so to do. There is no doubt that Beethoven turned constantly to his art as a bulwark against the miseries of his personal life, even if there is a great deal more to it than that. To rest for a moment on the more superficial plane, it is impossible to ignore the evidence that his music was the one compensation that made his life endurable at all—the Heiligenstadt Testament [1] makes that abundantly clear, to say nothing of the pronouncements in letters, diaries, and conversations. But where Beethoven differs is in the way in which he was so possessed by his genius that it eventually led him out of the domains of ordinary life altogether and became, in fact, the complete synthesis of his personality. For Beethoven his art was not merely an activity which 'compensated' for the trials and tribulations of his everyday life, but something which so completely absorbed him that the other aspect ceased to have any meaning.

We are familiar with the word-portraits of Beethoven at the very end of his life which make it clear that only in the most material and prosaic sense was he still an inhabitant of this world and concerned with its transitory affairs. Exactly where he had gone can only be discovered from long-standing intimacy with the last quartets and sonatas; and how he arrived there can only be learnt from the music of his so-called 'second period'.

The wise Donald Tovey once wrote: 'To study the lives of great artists is often a positive hindrance to the understanding of their works; for it is usually the study of what they have not mastered, and thus undermines their authority in the things which they have mastered. To undermine that authority is an injury much more serious than any merely professional technicality.' [2] This is not to argue that the study of biography is vain and useless—only that it ought to be put to its proper use and not be employed as a stick for moral or philosophical beatings. The trouble with biography is that it tends to prevent criticism from being properly disinterested, in the sense in which Matthew Arnold insisted that criticism should be—it tends to introduce ulterior motives into the assessment of artistic values. The study of a man's life, like the study of his technique, has to be used as a stepping-stone to final understanding, not as the be-all and end-all of critical inquiry.

Beethoven's biography, though of absorbing interest and entirely

[1] *See* Appendix.   [2] *Beethoven.*

B

essential, tends to be more tiresome than most because it contains so many irrelevancies. No doubt this is true of any artist (or, for that matter, of any man whose principal activity is not on the purely physical plane); but with Beethoven it is more than usually the case, because no man existed more completely in his art and is so little explicable outside of it. Whenever we seek to throw light on one of Beethoven's major works by examining the external circumstances of its composition we are led, often after preliminary excitement, to the conclusion that there is really little of substance to be learnt from the books of reference. At best all we find is perhaps the spark or chance stimulus which set the creative process in motion; but of the process itself, of the heart of the matter, we find almost nothing of interest. The broader picture gives us an occasional and sometimes illuminating insight into Beethoven's state of mind at a particular time or during the composition of a particular work; but again it is only an indication— a signpost, so to speak—and often a misleading one.

The question of the relationship between an artist's 'life' and his works is fundamentally moribund. In the overwhelming majority of cases his works are his life—at least the essential and interesting part of it. And with Beethoven this is particularly true. Indeed it is hardly an exaggeration to say that if we knew all Beethoven's music but nothing of his biography our understanding of him would be incomplete, but we should still have a vivid picture in our minds of the vital spirit, temper, and temperament of the man.

That Beethoven should have been called upon to overcome the terrible affliction of deafness seems at first sight to be wholly relevant; but even here we are on slippery ground—we can be too easily led into missing the cardinal point that Beethoven's sense of a tragic destiny was something deep-rooted in his spiritual experience and in no way dependent on personal disaster. The failure of his hearing accentuated that sense and gave it a focal point; but it did not create it. The triumphant emergence out of darkness into light of the finales of the Fifth Symphony and the third 'Rasoumovsky' Quartet would have sounded just as triumphant and, what is the real point, would still have been written even if Beethoven had never gone deaf or if we had never known about it. The details might have been different; but not the basic premises.

There are some men who probe—and must by their very nature probe—to the depths of human life; and there are others—certainly the majority—who even more persistently avoid such a probing. Beethoven was simply by nature, temperament, and spiritual intensity one of the former; and such was the power of his genius that he was both able and compelled to probe farther than any other artist except Shakespeare—certainly farther than any other musician.

Certain composers or poets may have gone as far as Beethoven in one particular direction; but what makes Beethoven unique among musicians is that he saw life big and saw it whole, and was enabled by the magnitude of his talents to leave an extraordinarily eloquent and complete account of his experience. Beethoven's art, like Shakespeare's, is not so much a criticism of life as a statement of it; and the extra-ordinary spiritual preparation of the music of his third period shows conclusively how little the details of his biography have to do with the revelation of his art. If anyone really supposes that the 'Hammer-klavier' Sonata was the outcome of lawsuits over Karl or the obstinate behaviour of domestic servants, then it must be regretfully concluded that he or she knows nothing whatever about the workings of genius.

To return for a moment to the observations of Tovey already quoted, it is necessary to see at the outset that we do not fall into an elementary trap. Beethoven never satisfactorily mastered the art of day-to-day living. Except for an unusual perspicacity in the matter of first principles, the man who emerges from the pages of Beethoven's biography is not remarkable. His views and opinions on the world in general were, though sound enough, not far out of the ordinary; and however much his forthright manner of living and his independent attitude may appeal to us they were seldom on a higher level than those of any good and courageous man, and occasionally not nearly so high. It is generally conceded nowadays that an artist is expected to occupy his position in society as a man, although there is no reason why he should bow to conventional behaviour and morality if it seems to him stupid or hypocritical. Beethoven was on the whole neither a better nor a worse citizen than the next man—only a more explosive one. His social and personal relationships were never on very sure ground and his domestic life was a mess. Much indulgence was needed to make him manageable, and it was generally felt that his genius and his personal difficulties entitled him to it. He could be impulsive, sus-picious, overbearing, and downright bad-mannered. Even if we make a show of apology on his behalf in the light of the increasing deafness and the consequent sense of isolation it caused him, we cannot in honesty say that the man who penetrated more deeply than any other to the heart of the eternal mysteries was a model of perfection and righteousness in his daily life. We can indeed be thankful that he was not, because his very faults and foibles bring him nearer to us as a human being and help us the better to understand the extent of his spiritual elevation. But Beethoven took himself not less seriously as a man than as an artist—his sense of responsibility and personal integrity was enormous both in life and art. He was essentially a man of principle, even though he did not always contrive to live up to his own ideals, and even though the ideals themselves occasionally went awry.

We are nowadays more or less free from the idea that our heroes must be perpetually whitewashed and turned into saints and martyrs. Some of Beethoven's earlier biographers, Thayer among them, went to pathetic lengths to gloss over or explain away the less savoury aspects of his behaviour and character. Such a procedure evidently springs from the curious notion that the man who wrote matchless music must have been a matchless individual—an idea which rather spoils the point of Beethoven's conquest of himself. A later age, one addicted to debunking everything and everyone, went to the opposite extreme by showing an apparently insatiable appetite for discovering and revealing what a poor specimen of struggling humanity he really was. But in the end neither exaggeration is in the least necessary, and both offer small compliment to their subject. Beethoven is quite strong enough to stand up to just and accurate criticism, and much too strong to suffer from misrepresentation. It is only necessary that the want of authority in his daily life should not be allowed to undermine the authority of his art.

Beethoven has often been called a true child of his times—and there is truth in it. On the other hand, it is another of those popular turns of speech all too open to misinterpretation. Beethoven's general attitude —his sturdy independence, his democratic outlook, his challenging spirit which looked constantly to a new and luminous future—appears to be typical of the age in which he lived, and indeed was typical of it. But it is unusually wide of the mark to imagine that the 'age made the man'. Although Beethoven was accustomed to make occasional forthright comments on the affairs of the day (and sometimes to put them into disconcerting practice, as in the famous incident at Teplitz when he scandalized Goethe by treating the Austrian royal family and assembled aristocracy of Europe as equals), there is little in his correspondence or his conversations directly related to the prevailing 'spirit of the age'. The French Revolution seemed to the mind of Beethoven, as to most other perceptive minds of the day, a magnificent gesture on the side of the human liberty and brotherhood he so greatly prized; and at one time Napoleon certainly appeared to him as the champion of those new ideals. But there is hardly any direct reference in Beethoven's recorded utterances either to the event or to the man; and he does not seem to have become very excited about it all. His feeling of resentment and disappointment at Napoleon's failure to be the hero depicted in the 'Eroica' Symphony was, though momentarily inflammable, short-lived. Indeed thereafter Beethoven's attitude towards the fallen Napoleon was one of philosophic indulgence.

The ideals liberated by the French Revolution influenced Beethoven to the extent that they animated the prevailing currents of thought and feeling, for he was the last man to live insipidly and wilfully divorced from the community of his fellow men and their aspirations. Beethoven in fact consciously spoke on behalf of all suffering and struggling humanity.

Beethoven came of a musical family. Both his father and his grand-father were capable musicians—especially the grandfather. I am not sure that much reliance should be placed on this particular piece of evidence. The habit is rather too prevalent among critical biographers of searching out by the most ingenious expedients some remote ancestral connection with the art practised by their subject—*any* connection, even though it be nothing better than a distant third cousin several times removed who once played the 'cello in an amateur string quartet. It is frequently forgotten that, in the eighteenth century, music was as much a craft as an art; and there is no more significance to be derived from the fact that a composer's family boasted a musician or two than that it contained a good mason, a carpenter, or a master baker.

Because of the paternal occupation Beethoven was certainly brought up in an atmosphere and environment strongly musical, and his boyish studies considerably advanced. I doubt, though, whether the honest competence of the father and grandfather in music can be held to have profoundly influenced the making of Beethoven.

There is, however, one aspect to Beethoven's heredity that has not received its proper attention. Marion Scott in her perceptive book on Beethoven [1] seems to have been the first English biographer to make direct reference to a possible, not to say probable, strain of Spanish blood in the Beethoven family. The Beethovens originated in that part of the Netherlands where Spanish occupation, influence, and internal absorption had been at their strongest. It is thus logical to think that the ancestors of Beethoven at some point in their history absorbed an influx of Spanish blood, and that it erupted in the character and temperament of Beethoven himself.

In his young days Beethoven was nicknamed 'the Spaniard', not, we may be sure, without reason. He had the dark, swarthy complexion of the South, an easily discernible Mediterranean look that is noticeable even in the indifferent portraits of him that have come down to us. But far more than physical features, though allied to them, he had the temperament, the fierce pride, the deep-rooted sense of personal dignity, the quick flashing anger at an insult, real or imagined, and the impulsive generosity so typical of Spain. We need not over-stress the inferences; but, as Miss Scott argues, a strain of southern blood might easily account for certain of Beethoven's characteristics not readily explainable in terms of his more usually accepted Flemish and German ancestry. Beethoven thought of himself as essentially German; on the other hand, if we accept the idea that 'the Spaniard' was something more than a clever nickname, does it not suggest that here are two vital and opposing forces of heredity which, placed in a state of constant action and interaction, throw some light on the qualities of mind and temper so familiar both in Beethoven's biography and in his music?

The childhood of Beethoven was not an enviable one. He adored and revered his mother; but his father was a bully, a weakling, and a petty tyrant who trusted in alcohol to offset the frustrations of everyday life. Gottfried Fischer, a neighbour of the Beethovens in Bonn, remarks that 'the Beethoven children were not brought up with kindness: they were often left to the servants; the father was very severe with them'. No doubt it is easy to over-estimate paternal failings in the Beethoven family. In all probability Johann van Beethoven was not a positively vicious or evil man, only a weak one. The first part of his married life appears to have been reasonable enough; but as the years passed, the blocking of his ambitions due to an inherent lack of moral fibre caused him to fall into drinking habits and general loose living.

[1] *Beethoven.*

The effects of his father's cruelty and shortcomings were especially severe on a sensitive child like Beethoven, as much because of the suffering it caused his mother as on his own account. It seems probable, to say the least, that Beethoven's lifelong dislike of excess and his rigid moral code (even though he did not always manage to live up to it) were the direct outcome of his early memories. It is likely too that his conviction that mortal fallibility could be mastered by conscious effort on the part of the individual had its roots in the failure of his own father to make that effort.

The harshest tragedy of Beethoven's early life was the death of his mother at the age of forty—an old woman already, worn out by struggle and suffering, and defeated by the long fight to keep the family on an even keel. Her death took from Beethoven the one human being he really loved and who in any way understood him, and removed the only influence that made home life endurable at all. After the passing of Frau Beethoven the father went rapidly to pieces, and by the time he was eighteen Beethoven, as the eldest surviving child, was obliged to take over the status of both moral and legal head of the family.

But the picture was not all black. If one of Beethoven's early music teachers, Tobias Pfeiffer, was, though a fine musician, cruel, a bully, and one of Johann van Beethoven's most disreputable drinking companions, Christian Gottlob Neefe, another and later instructor, was a good and kind man. Beethoven owed much to Neefe, both as a teacher of the art of music and as a respected figure in the court of Bonn, whose good offices were ever at the service of the young genius newly trying to spread his wings. Then there was the first visit to Vienna and the meeting with Mozart; there were friends good and staunch, prominent among them the Breuning family and Franz Wegeler, who not only helped to draw the sting out of the misery of Beethoven's home life, but who did so much to show him that the world was bigger, more bountiful and generally a better place than he had at that time reason to think it. It was the Breunings who rubbed the rough edges off the raw, unpolished youth who came among them and gave him whatever social presentability he ever did achieve, so that when eventually he settled in Vienna he could move in society with some ease and self-confidence.

The Bonn period was by no means unfruitful for Beethoven, whatever may have been the domestic difficulties he encountered. He was soon in service as a musician at the Elector's court; and although the hidebound atmosphere of the first years, before the spirit of the new age got to work on it, and the servitude of musicians in court service must have irked a spirit so independent and free-ranging as Beethoven's, he was at the centre of musical activity and already gaining valuable experience. There is reason to suppose that, after he had recovered from the shock of his mother's death, life was not unattractive for the young Beethoven. He was finding his feet in the world, and the future was beginning to open before him in several directions. He had already tasted the bitterness of suffering and personal tragedy; but even at this early stage his courage was immense, and a superb confidence in his own power was already becoming the unshakable main pillar of his life on this earth. When towards the end of 1792 he left Bonn for Vienna, never to return, all that was to go into the making of the mature man was already revealed. The disaster of his deafness was yet some way off in the future; but when it came he had already tasted enough of the cup of life to be able to meet it and, after fierce struggle with himself, to overcome it.

2

The 'Eroica' Symphony and *The Ring*

THE YEAR 1802, the year of the Heiligenstadt Testament, marked a physical and spiritual crisis in Beethoven's life. The deafness which already bid fair to wreck his hard-won social and professional position in Vienna and which seemed to threaten the whole basis of his living turned him inward on himself, and called forth all his inherent steadfastness and courage to meet the tragedy. This crisis, with its calling into question of everything on which his life and hopes were built, wrought in Beethoven not only a spiritual but also an artistic rebirth. 'I am not at all satisfied with my works so far, and I mean to make a fresh start from today,' Beethoven said to Krumpholz in the year 1803 or thereabouts. It was a portentous, prophetic saying, looking forward to and ineffably linked with a similar remark he made to Cipriani Potter some fourteen years later. Now Beethoven stood on the threshold of the development of his personality as expressed through the medium of his art. The external circumstance of physical disaster was the immediate, though not the comprehensive, cause of a new revelation of the great force of his genius; and, as was to happen again later on, the impulse given to his deepest spiritual experience was to result also in a great expansion of his technical resources.

The 'Eroica' Symphony, which was the most complete and immediate outcome of this combined spiritual and technical expansion, was only nominally occasioned by the suggestion of General Bernadotte that Beethoven should compose a symphony in honour of Napoleon Bonaparte. At that time Napoleon was striding victoriously across the face of Europe as First Consul of France and champion of a new social order arising out of the ideals of freedom and brotherhood newly liberated by the French Revolution. But while it is true that at the turn of the century Napoleon appeared to young, eager hearts as the champion of awakening humanity, and that Beethoven himself both saw and felt him in that light during these years, the heroic ideal was by no means a new element in Beethoven's imagination. His own struggle with his destiny from childhood, and his consequent realization that only through the temper of his courage and the strength of his will could he live at all, had already made him actively aware of the ideal of heroic endeavour. One way or another the 'Eroica' would have been written without any external promptings, and even if Napoleon had never existed, because it was not the celebration of a public event or the laudation of a public figure, but the expression of compulsive forces at work inside Beethoven himself.

When it first burst upon the struggling consciousness of the world the 'Eroica' suffered from much misrepresentation and spurious programmatic commentary. So vast was its conception, and so dynamic the life-forces that surged through it, that it could not hope to escape from a crop of literal interpretations which sought to confine its boundless vision within the limits of the known and generally acceptable. Beethoven's genius was always prophetic. The technical expansions and revolutions he wrought on the body of the musical art were a symbol of his forward-looking vision. The creative spirit is always prophetic—it looks forward, not back; its consummation lies not in the past but in the future, although it calls upon the spirit of the past to give life to the new synthesis. The search for the ideal which looks only to the past is retrogressive, even though some aspect of the past may be used as a sort of springboard from which to jump forward to a higher and more complex order of being which can only exist in the future.

The spirit of revolution is not, however, dynamic or creative, and it is not the cardinal element in Beethoven. The essence of creativity is not revolution but revelation. Nicholas Berdyaev has written: 'Revelation is a catastrophic transformation of consciousness, a radical modification of its structure, almost, one might say, a creation of new organs of being with functions in another world.' [1] But Berdyaev goes on to say: 'Revelation is not evolution but revolution.' This is certainly true of revelation and evolution: but there is a further distinction, that between revelation and revolution. Revelation is revolutionary in its impact but is not in itself the same thing. Revolution in its primary sense is materialistic and naturalistic: it is an affair of means rather than ends; it is essentially destructive rather than creative.

[1] *Freedom and the Spirit.*

Beethoven was the greatest revelationist of modern times. He showed that he was perfectly aware of his own position when he described music as a higher revelation than all wisdom and all philosophy, and himself as 'the Bacchus who presses out this glorious wine for mankind and makes them spiritually drunken'.[1] Confronted with his own words Beethoven is reported to have replied: 'Did I say that? Well then, I had a raptus.' But there is nothing particularly strange in that, and certainly nothing invalidating. Beethoven was not surprised by it: he made no protest and expressed no astonishment. He was evidently accustomed to being possessed by a 'raptus'. Indeed, the whole act of creation is in itself in the nature of a 'raptus': every time Beethoven wrote one of his major works he was in that state—a state, that is, in which the consciousness becomes extended above and beyond its normal and everyday level. Beethoven's self-knowledge in itself partook of the nature of revelation.

The spirit of revelation and the visionary faculty comprehend reality at a higher and more complex level than that of day-to-day consciousness. But they do not as a rule embrace the whole of it at one and the same time. Before reality can be apprehended as a whole, successive stages of development are necessary during which its various aspects are dealt with individually. The achievement of personality, the realization of the Divine Image in man, is a long and hard task and leads us along the road of tragedy and loneliness—the more so since we know that it has no end and brings us no peace until we have reached the final consummation; until we are completely at one with God. But however far we may be from the ultimate goal, we only admit defeat if we are content to rest finally when we have progressed only a little way. It is neither personal disaster nor plain error which marks death in life: it is the inertia which symbolizes spiritual stagnation.

It is the great revelational power of Beethoven that each successive stage in his development, each conflict lived through and each problem tackled, was not an end but a new beginning. Even at the very end of his life, when he had passed altogether beyond the accepted limits of human consciousness, there is no suggestion of finality, of a spiritual dead-end from which no further progress is possible.

In the 'Eroica' Symphony Beethoven gave expression to an ethical ideal of heroism in the most forthright and uncompromising terms.

[1] *See* Appendix.

But he did more than that. The 'Eroica' is not just an 'idea'—certainly not a piece of musical dialectic. Indeed, so little is it logical exposition or systematic argument that, apart from the first movement, its grand design has been a bone of hard contention for each successive generation. Why did Beethoven place the Funeral March directly after the first movement? What in its context is the meaning of the Scherzo and, even more, of the Finale? Its first hearers could envisage precise incidents depicted throughout: the clamour of war and the roar of cannon in the first movement; the groans of the wounded and the lamentations of suffering humanity (or an elegy for the death of some general or admiral) in the Funeral March—and so forth. But as the symphony became more completely assimilated and experienced as a whole these naïve explanations could no longer be thought adequate, even if they did not verge on direct misrepresentation, as we today can see that they did. One thing is now certain, and is not denied even by Beethoven's detractors: the 'Eroica' Symphony is conceived according to some vast yet wholly unified poetic idea. What is that idea and where does it lead us? What, as the symphony draws to its tremendous conclusion, is the ideal which Beethoven has made articulate in items of music, and what part does it play, not only in Beethoven's own development, but, more important still, in the developing consciousness of mankind? These are questions which we have to try to answer, each for himself, because the 'Eroica' is the first full-scale composition in which Beethoven truly 'spoke out', and because it treats of an aspect of experience with which Beethoven is especially associated.

The idea of heroic aspiration has attracted man's imagination ever since the first stirrings of human consciousness. The hero in one form or another appears constantly in myth and legend from the dimmest recesses of antiquity, and continues right up to the present day. The search for the heroic ideal, whether as a personal or a communal force, has come down to us most directly from ancient Greece, and passed through the vicissitudes of the life of the world in the aspiration towards a higher and richer order of being. In our own times it has emerged as a driving force in Hitler's Germany, where it was a communal rather than a personal ideal. Like all dynamic ideals, heroism can be distorted and put to the service of evil, as in Germany—it can turn either way because, being dynamic, it cannot be confined to any one channel or manifestation but must have freedom to move in any direction at any time. No ideal that cannot be distorted, be made to serve good or evil,

God or Devil equally, is dynamic. It is the freedom to turn either to creation or destruction that gives an ideal its dynamic quality. Most of history's heroes have been evildoers—enemies of the spirit and servants of the blind forces of destruction. It is easy to be heroic at someone else's expense, and the historical hero has usually emerged as a conqueror and self-glorifier. This is certainly true of Napoleon, and it gives added weight to Beethoven's summary action in tearing the title-page off the score of the 'Eroica' when Napoleon proclaimed himself Emperor. It was not simply that Beethoven was politically a republican —that in itself was never of much importance. Napoleon's action was symbolic to Beethoven who did not misjudge it. It was nothing less than the death of the ideal hero which Beethoven later declared with truth he had already portrayed. Napoleon died by his own hand in Beethoven's eyes, and in so doing freed the 'Eroica' for ever from all connection with his own spiritually impotent career. It is as well he did it, and did it just in time, else the 'Eroica' would have become even more the victim of muddle-headed literalism than it has already.

The opening Allegro con brio of the 'Eroica' enshrines Beethoven's heroic ideal in terms that can hardly be misunderstood. This hero is no vainglorious conqueror lusting after power and domination, no self-seeking monster ready to destroy with fire and the sword all who stand in his way. Nor is he a mere benefactor in the generally accepted sense of that term. He is essentially the creator, one who realizes in himself and, through himself, in others, the Divine Image in man. He is pure in heart—therefore he does not seek to dominate, to impose his will by force. His power is not of this world; it is the power of the creative spirit, which effects rebirth both in the individual and in society. The assertiveness of the first movement is not directed against mankind, but against psychic and naturalistic forces which constrain and devitalize the will to live richly, fully, and expansively. It has nothing whatsoever to do with terrestrial warfare or embattled hosts—a fallacy which has led to much confusion of thought over the meaning and form of the three subsequent movements.

So far we are on familiar ground. The heroic ideal of the first movement is now universally apprehended. But the Funeral March brings us up against a very real problem, and one which is not solved more than a hundred and fifty years after its composition. At first sight the context of this movement seems at least enigmatic. Why, we must ask again, did Beethoven place it immediately after the first movement, and, if it is not merely formal but integral to the poetic idea of the symphony as a whole, what is its meaning? There have been any number of explanations, but not all of them have grappled with the dual question of form and context. Crudely put, the question is simply this: why was the death of the hero apparently celebrated before the work in which the heroic ideal is enshrined is more than half completed? Is not the death of the hero the proper ending for the symphony, in which case do not the two following movements come as anticlimax? Many have felt this to be the case, in spite of a willingness to concede Beethoven his mastery of both form and content in music. And this in its turn has led to further theories which reduce the visionary oneness of the 'Eroica' by trying to account from the outside for what can only be apprehended by the inward power of imagination.

It is impossible to believe, as Wagner among others intimated, that Beethoven used the form of the Funeral March as no more than a technical device—as one form among many in which a slow movement could be written—without attaching to it some particular significance. It is even more impossible to think that he placed the slow movement before the Scherzo in deference to established symphonic practice. The 'Eroica' was the first full-scale work to emerge from Beethoven's 'fresh start'; and it is inconceivable that he should have been influenced either by convention or by technical convenience.

As a matter of fact Beethoven had already used the form of the Funeral March in the Piano Sonata in A flat, Op. 26, where it is placed after the Scherzo and so disposes of any idea that he would be afraid to offend tradition by disturbing the accepted order of movements. We cannot, therefore, explain either the form or the context of the 'Eroica' Funeral March by reference to musical custom. (Incidentally the A flat Sonata with its *Marcia funèbre sulla morte d'un Eroe* is further support for the contention that the heroic idea was a major force in Beethoven's consciousness long before Napoleon, via General Bernadotte, served to ignite the spark of creation that produced the 'Eroica' Symphony. The A flat Sonata is a more significant pointer to the mental background of the 'Eroica' than Napoleon Bonaparte or anyone else.)

In all Beethoven's music there is an overwhelming simplicity and directness. He had the disconcerting simplicity of the child who asks questions and will not be put off with evasive answers. This childlike directness is a pristine quality which belongs inherently to the creative process. It is the worldly who circumscribe spiritual values by a resort to ingenious complexities. Sophistication is a social attribute that consists in having a ready-made answer to all questions, and thrives on the turning away from reality; and Beethoven was the least sophisticated man who ever lived. In his music as in his life he showed a blunt directness of thought and action that confounds those who live largely in the dimensions of social and political manœuvring. His most profound and far-reaching visions come with the force of revelation because they are unencumbered by conventional trappings. It is thus with the 'Eroica' Funeral March. Only by accepting it literally does its meaning become clear; only by accepting the death of the hero in the context which Beethoven gave it do the three other movements reveal the full scope of the heroic ideal.

The death of the hero which is mourned in the great march is real and exactly as depicted—no more and no less. After the titanic life-affirmation of the Allegro con brio, death comes in all its stark and bitter reality. There is here a parallel with the death of Jesus on the Cross. We need not give the 'Eroica' a specifically Christian interpretation in order to see in it something of the symbolic significance of Christ's suffering and betrayal. But it is quite possible that Beethoven was conscious of the Crucifixion when he composed the Funeral March. Not long before the composition of the 'Eroica' Beethoven had written the oratorio *Christus am Oelberge* (*Christ on the Mount of Olives*).[1] It is not one of his best works, although it contains a few noble passages. It has the appearance of an occasional piece and seeks too obviously after effect and a conscious 'modernity' in its oddly theatrical conception. On the other hand, it was never Beethoven's habit to approach a serious subject without taking thought; and although in this case it did not strike from him the true creative fire, there can be little doubt that he was profoundly aware of his text.

Although in no way an orthodox churchman, Beethoven was essentially religious. The immanence of God was a constant driving force of his inner life and became more so as he grew older.[2] No doubt at this time the figure of Christ did not produce an overwhelming effect on his artistic imagination; but he probably did see Jesus as a liberator of mankind and as a creator—in fact, as a hero after his own heart.

[1] The opus number, 85, is misleading: the work dates from 1800.
[2] *See* Appendix.

In any case it is not necessary to think of Christ alone in this context. There is the same symbolic significance to be discerned in the life and death of Socrates—the good man betrayed and cast down by the malignant forces of the world. Beethoven's general education was not comprehensive in the modern sense; but he was familiar with Plato and the Greek world in general, and in view of the evident Greek affinities of the 'Eroica' it could easily be that the death of Socrates was also not far from his mind when he composed the Funeral March. All the same, it must be insisted that we are concerned only with symbolic implications and not with literal exposition. Beethoven knew intuitively that the ideal, non-self-seeking hero must inevitably be destroyed by the hostile forces of the world. He knew that the world uses the instrument of death to destroy and overthrow what it cannot contain and assimilate. The death of the hero, therefore, marks his material defeat at the hands of the material world. But Beethoven knew also that this death is only final on the naturalistic plane; that the fact of the hero's death releases new and still more potent creative forces into the life-stream of the universe—forces to which he has given birth but which can only be consummated in the spiritual regeneration which follows on the heels of death. The world can never be the same again after a great creative spirit has lived and suffered in it—a radical transformation has taken place and the revelation has quickened its sensibility. To this extent one might say that Beethoven himself was the hero of the 'Eroica' Symphony.

The deaths of Jesus and Socrates symbolize the refusal to compromise with the destructive forces of the world; while Napoleon's self-death merely reveals an inherent inferiority and lack of the true heroic quality. In death is life reborn, and only after the severance from all material limitations does the complete creative and regenerative spirit go forth unfettered to combat and in the end conquer the powers of evil and destruction. The freedom of evil in the world is endemic, and no less essential than the freedom of the creative spirit: therefore Christ suffers on the Cross and Socrates is poisoned. But after the betrayal the forces of creation gather themselves up anew to reveal the impotence of death and of those who resort to it as an instrument of policy. Even in the Funeral March itself there are deep-sea surgings that presage rebirth, the resurrection to come, in the great C major expansion.

As the last bars of the Funeral March move to their solemn ending we wait expectantly for the resurrection through which the heroic ideal will become for ever and indestructibly a vital factor in the spiritual life of mankind. If the Funeral March had indeed ended the 'Eroica', the whole spiritual content would have been distorted, for there would have been nothing more to come from it. As it is, the two subsequent movements, by coming after the Funeral March, unify and give ultimate meaning to the entire conception.

Berlioz's interpretation of the Scherzo is very near the mark. Berlioz sees in it 'play of a funeral kind, at every instant clouded by thoughts of mourning—a kind of play, in fact, recalling that which the warriors of the Iliad celebrated round the tombs of the chiefs'. And, we might add, akin to the mingled joy and sorrow in the Christian heart immediately after the Crucifixion. But again, such interpretations are only of value so long as they are not taken literally and in a naïvely pictorial sense, but are used as symbols through which our own minds are enabled to stretch out to meet Beethoven's by a process of imaginative identification.

The dynamic energy of the 'Eroica' Scherzo is pregnant with new life and the reawakening of the will to live and create. The rich tone of horns in the trio is an imperative call to renewed activity. There is no mistaking the command and authority of this passage; and its contrast to the rhythms of the Scherzo itself, which seem to echo the pulse of some gigantic dynamo or generator beneath the earth's surface, only serves to emphasize its character. In the midst of sorrow life waits for its renewed answer; formal patterns of the dance give a sublime impression of the new life to come. The Scherzo is an intermediate movement—the recharging of creative energies between life and resurrection. Then, in a sudden burst of light through the full orchestra, almost blinding in its intensity, rebirth becomes accomplished. The age of regeneration and creativity, to the initiation of which the hero has given both his life and his death, is made reality.

The Finale is a remarkable example of imaginative creativity. Beethoven's use of his own Prometheus theme was not fortuitous. Now it is the Promethean spirit transfigured which surges through the last movement of the 'Eroica' and provides the clue to the whole symphony. The hero represents the Promethean idea transmuted in Beethoven's mind and imagination. Berdyaev again has written: 'There is a Promethean principle in spirit, a rebellion against the natural gods, against determinism of human destiny, an aspiration to a higher,

C

freer world.' It is an extension of the spiritual aspects of Prometheus which informs the 'Eroica'; and it is from this point of view that we can speak of its Greek affinities. But the world had travelled far between the mythology of ancient Greece and Europe at the turn of the eighteenth and nineteenth centuries, so that the Hellenic ideals were no longer sufficient in themselves. None the less, they could still be used as starting points.

The form of the 'Eroica' Finale is symbolic in itself. Not only does the main theme—or, to be precise, thematic combination—present a fertile duality; but of all musical forms those of variation and fugue are the two most adaptable for the varied deployment of musical fertility. The kaleidoscopic colours and technical diversity of this movement arise as much from the form as from content. Beethoven's unerring judgment led him to find exactly the right technical formula through which to project a vision of the creative spirit functioning unfettered in the reborn life of the future. Thus the poetic idea of the symphony is unified in the Finale. Those who think it too light in weight and too diverse in form to balance the power and bulk of the first movement entirely miss the point. The Finale of the 'Eroica', seen in its proper light, is not less adequate emotionally, psychologically, intellectually, and poetically than the Finale of the C minor Symphony.

Such is the manner of the 'Eroica' Symphony—but only the manner. As an indication of essences these words may lead us to a closer identification with the creative mind of Beethoven; but they cannot in the nature of things do more. Like all great manifestations of genius, the 'Eroica' belongs in its totality not to this world but to a renewed and revitalized life in the future. Our explanations and subjective interpretations can only direct us to follow on the path of Beethoven's own exploring spirit. If they do less than that we become snared in the fatuities of fanciful programmes and the weaving of irrelevant fairy-tales.

The search for the heroic ideal was a dominant motif in nineteenth-century Romantic thought. It appears in one form or another throughout Romantic literature and Romantic philosophy, and it finds one of its most potent expressions in Wagner's musico-dramatic tetralogy *The Ring of the Nibelung*. In the form of Siegfried the Romantic idea of the hero became articulate in music just as it became articulate in literature and philosophy in Nietzsche's Superman. Both Wagner and Nietzsche belonged essentially to the nineteenth century—they were the embodiment of the spirit of that age and gave the most vital expression to its impulses and aspirations. They took the new currents of thought and feeling and crystallized them in art-works of immense splendour and significance.

By going back to northern mythology for the dramatic substance of *The Ring* Wagner acted in complete accordance with Romantic thought. The Romantic generations looked back to a lost innocence in the distant past and an identification with the natural world in an effort to free the human spirit. They exalted primitive, natural man and sought liberation as well as consolation in communion with nature and in the conception of a social order based on 'natural law'. They called on the old heroes of mythology to help lead them to salvation at a time when European society was undergoing drastic reorganization under the impact of newly discovered technical and scientific knowledge. 'Back to Nature' is essentially a Romantic cry—a cry from the heart of humanity which was losing its way and becoming divided from the natural world. The eighteenth-century sense of security and reason was gone; and although the new dawn promised untold riches, it left a void which could not readily be filled—in fact has not been adequately filled to this day.

Because it sought to reinstate the individual against the objective and hostile forces of the world the Romantic movement touched fundamental truth; but it was retrogressive rather than prophetic. It postulated the return to a lost Elysium rather than spiritual transcendence, and so did much to invalidate the element of truth in its own tenets. The weakness of Romanticism lies in its dependence on nature and natural law—on those very forces from which the developing consciousness of mankind had tried to free itself ever since the legendary days when Prometheus wrested fire from the gods. While its value lay in its elevation of human personality, it remained incapable of breaking out of the impasse created by its own reliance on the primitive and the elemental. That is why there is such a poignant undertone of loneliness and isolation in Romantic art and thought. But this isolation and this loneliness were not between man and man socially considered: they were the result of a schism in human consciousness. Through the idealization of nature and the insistence on the observance of natural law, man found himself divorced from the world of the spirit and isolated in a cosmos of which he felt himself no longer a part.

If 'classical' ethics insisted on the subservience of the individual to reason, logic, and the dictates of society, Romanticism found itself bogged down by its elevation of the natural and by its reliance on primitive instincts and impulses. If Romanticism brought in its wake a fresh wind of freedom and emancipation on the social plane, it nevertheless failed to release the power of the creative spirit. It made a great and partially successful effort on the side of human liberation; but it raised questions which it could not answer, and in the end it could only counter the yawning gulf of isolation which surrounded the individual —largely created by a return to social rather than personal values, albeit in a different form. The predominance of social and communal ideals in today's thought and politics is the outcome of the Romantic movement's failure to answer its own questions.

But Romanticism, even if it failed ultimately to bring about a re-fusion of the natural and the spiritual, opened up new channels and released new currents which had a profound and revolutionary effect on human consciousness. The Age of Reason was overthrown and the way seemed open for a fresh advance in mankind's constant search for reality and a new and higher world-view. Inadequate though it was, the Romantic movement was necessary in its historical context.

In *The Ring* Wagner presents us with the Romantic hero struggling against the forces of evil and denial. It is the fashion nowadays to decry Wagner's thought while extolling his music; but it is doubtful if such a distinction can legitimately be made—or, if it can, whether it does not bring the whole of Wagner's art into question. The idea that Wagner's political and philosophical doctrines now mean nothing and that only his music remains is at bottom a fallacy. The problem of the expression of concrete ideas or doctrines in a work of art is a large one in itself; but it is nonsense to pretend that we can arrive at full understanding of art-works which are informed through and through by a specific idea or philosophy without at least some working knowledge of those ideas and that philosophy. Whether the fusion is complete and satisfying; whether the ideas are absorbed into the art and so become spontaneously expressed through it, or whether they are merely superimposed on it from the outside is another matter.

Didactic art is usually considered to be bad art, justifiably for the most part. But our distaste is concerned more with the common failure to achieve a proper fusion of form and content, so that the ideas stick out like sore thumbs and do not arise from the inner compulsion of the form, than with the artistic articulation of ideas as such. In the end we cannot separate the form and execution of a work of art from its content, emotional and intellectual, although our enjoyment of the one is by no means dependent on our acceptance of the other. All that matters is whether or not the ideas come to us as authentic and dynamic experience of life and reality, or merely as a piece of intellectual cleverness. It is artistic pamphleteering that is indigestible.

In the case of Wagner it is clear that his ideas did spring, in part at least, from within. Wagner was capable of authentic experience, but he was not always capable of purifying his experience from external and devitalizing influences. In *Tristan* and again in *Meistersinger* the note of authenticity is unmistakable. Indeed, *Meistersinger* might have been no more than a pamphlet if Wagner had had his original way. But his genius took a hand in the matter and decided, without his full knowledge or consent, that it should be nothing of the sort. His genius took hold of him and compelled him to fill *Meistersinger* with warmth, life, and vitality, and even to treat Beckmesser with indulgence.

As well as being a great musical genius, Wagner was also a conventional revolutionary with a mind little more distinguished than a hundred others of his day and age. It is typical of Wagner that he should have been more interested in destroying old fallacies than in creating new values. Like Don Quixote he had to be tilting at windmills. But whereas Don Quixote's gestures were noble and generous, if foolish, Wagner wasted much of his substance on conventional posturings and rhetorical flourishes more fitting for minor politicians than for major artists. It is a labour of love and self-sacrifice to extract the authentic experience of Wagner the artist from the philosophizings of Wagner the nineteenth-century revolutionary.

There is in Wagner little of the almost nuclear compression of essence that makes Beethoven's every utterance so much vaster and more significant than it seems at first sight. *The Ring* says too little and says it for too long: the 'Eroica' Symphony says so much that it seems almost cryptic and foreshortened by comparison.

A comparison between Siegfried and the hero of the 'Eroica' reveals at once the gulf that separates a romantic revolutionary and a visionary revelationist. Siegfried answers to Wagner's heroic ideal—he was created for that very purpose; but how puny he appears beside the

'Eroica' hero! And he appears so not only because Beethoven was a greater composer of music than Wagner—which is a disputable point anyway—but because Beethoven's spiritual stature was so much greater than Wagner's.

There is no revelation in *The Ring*. It is complete and sufficient unto itself. Siegfried is really no more than a healthy young animal. Because he is strong and young, and because he has immense courage and bravura, he overwhelms the forces of evil and corruption. But having done that he is more or less at a loss. Siegfried's most significant creative act is his understanding of the bird's song; and this at once places him firmly as a nineteenth-century Romantic, for it is nothing less than a symbolic identification with nature. But Siegfried can progress no further. He represents in himself (and therefore in Wagner) the Romantic idea of a healthy, vital young pagan, with his sex repressions removed, his psychological inhibitions cleared up, and his natural instincts given free reign. Such an ideal of heroism is in itself valuable; we have not yet so organized our society that we can do without our Siegfrieds. It may even be that we shall all have to become Siegfrieds—or something like it—before we can elevate ourselves to the stature of Beethoven's hero. In any case, we all keep a Siegfried inside us, even if we take some pains to conceal him.

Siegfried's struggles and aspirations represent those of modern man faced with subservience to the machine and tyrannical social forces. The consciousness of the twentieth century is still very much an extension and modification of the consciousness of the nineteenth century. But the emergence of Siegfried is finite; it belongs to this world only and to the objective impulses of this world. It leaves the spiritual problem not only unsolved but at bottom unstated. The finiteness of *The Ring* lies in the identification of the final pages of *Götterdämmerung* with the opening of *Das Rheingold*. At the end the Rhine overflows and obliterates all trace of Valhalla and the preceding squabbles and conflicts. We are back where we began, with the river and the Rhine-maidens. Nature is pristine, unsullied, and beautiful again. The earth can accommodate a race of Siegfrieds; but nature is not transubstantiated. And in plain truth there is no valid reason why the squabblings and arguments should not begin all over again: there is nothing to stop someone else making a pass for the gold and so setting the whole process in motion, not once more but *ad infinitum*. The creative spirit is still confined within the natural world.

Where have all Wotan's stratagems got us? He has given us Sieg-fried; but Siegfried is dead and has his funeral march. We are returned to nature, to Mother Earth; but we are not given a new birth, only a return to the old, for Siegfried's death does not release new creative forces as the death of the 'Eroica' hero does. Adam and Eve may walk again, but, because Siegfried has spent his life knocking old fallacies and evils on the head instead of creating new ideals, the basic conflict remains and the struggle towards a higher spiritual consciousness has to be undertaken all over again from the beginning. We are one with nature but we are not one with God. All our aspirations, our sufferings, our struggles, are null and void. We have gone back to where we started: we are still like the squirrel in the cage.

In so far as Wagner's ideas and ideals no longer have validity for us today, they reveal a fundamental limitation in his consciousness. Because he belonged to the world in which we live, his premises, had they been vital and creative instead of merely revolutionary, would be as potent for us today as they were in his own time. But in truth Wagner now offers us very little except enchantment to the senses and stimulus for the musical faculties.[1] He belonged to a passing phase in European thought and feeling, but not to the universal historical struggle of man-kind to achieve a fusion with truth and reality—not in *The Ring* at any rate. There is no new life to come out of *The Ring*: it is complete in itself. It leaves us with no unexplored regions of experience, and it gives us no help towards discovering those new regions. From the spiritual standpoint *The Ring* is empty. It will continue to enchant, divert, and delight us; but Wagner intended that it should do more than that.

The spiritual inferiority of Wagner to Beethoven is most con-vincingly revealed in Wagner's descent into the devitalized, sentimental, and ritualistic floundering of *Parsifal*. To set Wagner's last opera beside Beethoven's last quartets is a devastating experience. There is no dynamism in *Parsifal*; no spiritual revelation or authenticity of experience. However subtle Wagner's organization of musical material may be in *Parsifal*, it is at bottom little but the ruminations of a man grown old in heart and soul, and seeking some respite from the rigours of a world he can no longer command by a return to the conventional trappings of religiosity. Wagner has grown old; the spirit of Siegfried has departed, and there is no tomorrow.

[1] No doubt there are many who will assert that we can expect no more from a composer of music; but that is not what we are talking about.

The hollowness of Wagner's heroic ideal is here made manifest, for it exists only in and of this world. It was obsessed with the idea of domination—as was Wagner himself—and now it has grown tired and emaciated because it has no life in the future. It belongs not to the spirit but to the whims and tyrannies of nature. The iconoclastic Siegfried, strong in heart and limb, collapses in *Parsifal*, which is not Christianity but a monstrous omega, deforming and distorting Christian vitality and dynamism. There is no forward-looking aspiration—the symbols have become the reality. Siegfried is dead and Tristan is dead, and in Wagner's world there is no resurrection. Wagner has turned his back on reality. Prometheus has returned fire to the natural gods without fight and without hope.

I am not trying to decry Wagner either for my own pleasure or to puff up the reputation of someone else. But Wagner overtly set out to do certain things, and we are therefore obliged to inquire whether or not he did just those things. Wagner set out to give musical life to his heroic ideal no less than Beethoven did; and it is therefore permissible to set the one beside the other and to draw what conclusions we may from the comparison. If the hero of Wagner appear less complete and less satisfying than the hero of Beethoven, we may find some reason to explain the difference by taking into account the subsequent life and compositions of each of them, where we should logically expect to see the proper continuation of that ideal in one form or another. The fact that Wagner retreated into empty rituals while Beethoven actually carried out in himself the prophecy of the 'Eroica' Symphony and achieved the spiritual elevation of the last quartets is as much a musical as a metaphysical matter. And those who resent the dragging of philosophical or metaphysical speculations into the discussion of art can, I believe, find all the evidence they need in the late music of Wagner and Beethoven to support these contentions without bothering themselves with spiritual issues at all.

Although the 'Eroica' is the record of an authentic and dynamic experience, it was only a beginning. Its Greek affinities were a starting point and not an end in themselves. Beethoven was not content to rest with the ideas and ideals of antiquity. But what were these affinities of which we speak so freely apart from the direct connection through thematic reference to Prometheus? I quote Berdyaev once again, in a passage that will throw light on the heroic background of both Beethoven and Wagner.

In ancient Greece, where for a moment the lost vision of Eden was recaptured, man was exalted for the first time in the pagan world and his image found expression in plastic forms of undoubted magnificence. For a long time the limits of human nature were not clear. The image of man was still confused and was not separated from the image of gods and that of animal nature. There is yet no precise differentiation between man the hero and the god. The hero is not simply a man, he is demigod. An anthropological process took place in ancient Greece through the creation of gods and heroes. In order to rise above the state in which the human and the animal image were confused, man had to receive in himself the image of the god and the demigod, a principle regarded as superhuman.[1]

Beethoven's hero has some of the attributes of the Greek demigod. But because Beethoven lived more than two thousand years after the pinnacle of Greek civilization, his hero has passed from the comparatively straightforward ideal of the Greeks and become directly related to modern experience. Whereas the Greeks were concerned to free the human image from the images of nature, Beethoven's hero approaches more nearly to the image of man in God. But Beethoven's apprehension of reality was not at this time so fully developed as it became in later years. There was still a good deal of the Greek spirit in him, whether consciously or not. All the same he launched his hero forward to the new order of being and not back to the old. It is here that the difference between the heroic ideals of Beethoven and Wagner become apparent. Siegfried is a throw-back to antiquity, but without the expansive and prophetic elements that frequently lay behind those ideals. As a matter of fact Siegfried goes back beyond ancient Greece to the days before the images of man became separated at all from the images of gods and animals.

Ancient Greece is of such importance and value to modern civilization because it was the first era in mankind's historical development, at least in the western world, of which we have a comprehensive record, and which exploited the forward-looking creative spirit. It was this spirit which Beethoven took up and cast out into the future.

In all creative activity there is an unconscious element at work. Images come involuntarily to the mind, and impulses not consciously apprehended drive the creative energy forward. Whilst we, from our superior position in time, can discern the relationship between the Greek and the modern currents of thought and feeling in the 'Eroica', it is unlikely that Beethoven himself was more than dimly aware of

[1] *Freedom and the Spirit.*

them. The spiritual apprehension of reality comes to the subjective personality of the artist whole and unified at one time and in one particular direction, and works its way through his imagination to produce the finished work of art. The conscious part of the process comes in organizing the vision of reality into manageable and significant forms. Beethoven's own sufferings had produced the effect of quickening his sensibilities and thereby of illuminating ideas that were already stirring in his mind. But the fact of the experience remains; and because it occurred in the personality of Beethoven it took the form of musical expression. The fusion of the experience itself is unique and unrepeatable. Beethoven took the impulses and energies of his imagination and organized them into the form of a symphony, which we now analyse and ourselves experience in our own terms.

It is impossible to define the exact province of the conscious and the unconscious in the creative act: they are complementary but variable. Occasionally one has the impression that the spiritual experience or illumination at a given moment is almost too intense for the conscious mind to be able to organize it. In some of his earlier music, and in fact at certain points right up to that long period of silence which preceded the third period, Beethoven's conscious technique was not always equal to controlling and directing the passion of his creative vitality—there is sometimes a sort of excess of amperage that threatens to overwhelm the capacity of the fuses. The sheer dynamism of Beethoven's personality nearly wrecked the material framework in which his music was, or sought to be, contained. There is no vagueness, no groping after imperfectly assimilated ideas; there is no mistaking the authority of a Beethoven masterwork. The uneasiness one feels is analogous to the discomfort wrought in the mind by an elemental outburst over which we have no control: or perhaps one might say nowadays, to a nuclear explosion which is only just held in scientific check. Beethoven, we feel, might annihilate us in spite of himself. This was the sensation experienced by Goethe when he refused to listen to the Fifth Symphony, because it threatened to bring the whole house tumbling about his ears. It is also what Beethoven himself intuitively understood when he said, on the threshold of the third period, that his earlier music 'lacked art'—that is, the perfect equation between form and feeling.

The 'Eroica' Symphony sprang from the imaginative consciousness of Beethoven at a particular point in his life. It is, in its physical organization, chronological but not biographical. It is concerned not with a particular hero but with the heroic ideal, although it is legitimate to speak of 'the hero'. It is a spiritual event of immense significance both in Beethoven's own consciousness and in the developing consciousness of mankind. It does not shut the door; rather does it open portals on to new fields of experience. It actively demands further development of its postulates. In this sense the Funeral March is the nodal point of the entire symphony. In my end is my beginning. In few other musical compositions do we feel more strongly the gigantic force of resurrection. In few other works of art have we a greater feeling of vast realms of experience explored and still vaster realms left unexplored. Through the technical resources of fugue and variation Beethoven reveals the power and creative passion of the free spirit. New vistas open before us, as before Beethoven himself: the journey leads us towards but not to the ultimate goal. We know instinctively that we must go forward, no matter what it may cost in toil and suffering and tragedy (this surely is the true and only meaning of 'progress'); and we know, unmistakably and ineffably, that—

> It may be we shall touch the happy isles
> And meet the great Achilles whom we knew.

The heroic ideal becomes fused in past and future; Beethoven's prophetic vision unifies time in a single focus—an existential point. The old legends are transubstantiated and a new race of men born into the world. Out of the Promethean idea of ancient Greece grew, in the course of time, the 'Eroica' Symphony: it will have its fulfilment in the life of the future.

3

Eros and Ethics

TO BECOME involved with Beethoven's love life is to enter a laby-rinth from which one can only with difficulty escape. And yet love, marriage, and the ideal relationship between man and woman is central to Beethoven's life and thought. His erotic escapades tell us less than half the story: in a sense they are misleading, because they direct inquiry away from the heart of the matter, which is not so much Beethoven the man, frequently, and often a little pathetically, under the romantic spell, but Beethoven the visionary poet and seeker, probing with imagination at white heat to the core of a great mystery and towards another and equally compelling ideal. In several compositions Beet-hoven gave us different facets of the ideal of heroism (all stemming from the same root), and in others the heroic conquest of personal destiny. The two are often closely linked. In still others he gave us in one form or another an ideal of love, also branching out from a single growth in the imagination.

The trouble is, of course, that it is difficult to disentangle, not so much the wheat from the tares among Beethoven's romantic attach-ments, but the susceptibilities of mortal flesh from the visionary ideal. It is easy to relate Beethoven's heroic ideal to his heroic music. The 'Eroica' and C minor symphonies, the 'Rasoumovsky' Quartets, *Fidelio*—these great and heroic compositions abide no question, nor ever have done. But when we try to isolate the imaginative ideal from the ephemeral infatuation and the passing fancy in Beethoven's emotional attractions, and then relate them to certain individual compositions, we begin to lose our footholds in fact and logic. That Beethoven wrote a quantity of love music in every way as authentic and passionately idealistic as his more familiar heroic music is, I believe, conclusively proved by the internal evidence. But—and it would be idle to deny it—the evidence is less clear-cut and is more dependent on imaginative identification. In short it is less tangible, more elusive.

Beethoven's attitude to women has seldom been understood, because his conception of love and the sexual relationship has been imperfectly assimilated. He appears to have been constantly in and out of love. He was highly susceptible to feminine charms, and for much of his life he desired marriage above all else—outside his art, that is. But despite his susceptibility and his dreams of conjugal bliss, his attachments, which were frequently hot and inflammable, never came to anything. Although there is reason to believe that on one occasion he actually went so far as to become engaged, and on another proposed marriage but was rudely rebuffed, there seems always to have been some barrier which held him back and prevented him from taking the final and irrevocable step. Was it due simply to his old spirit of vacillation, so disconcerting to his contemporaries, or to external circumstances? This I do not believe. Temerity was not a quality known to the heart and mind of Beethoven. His vacillation, though real enough, only afflicted him at those moments and in those circumstances when no paramount issue was involved. But to Beethoven love and marriage were nothing if not paramount issues. The truth is almost the exact contrary. It is the nature of the barrier inside him, the true reason why he never married, that gives us the key to Beethoven's ideal of romantic love.

Beethoven was too forceful a character ever to allow considerations of social position, financial insecurity, or conventional suitability to stand in his way if he had once made up his mind to marry any woman whatsoever, noble, plebeian, or honest bourgeois. That he remained unmarried is certainly not due to social or material difficulties, any more than to his 'vacillation'. That spirit of seemingly endless pro-crastination which so infuriated his friends when they urged the advisability of giving concerts, making journeys, or entering into business contracts, disappeared when he was faced with a situation that affected either his artistic or his moral integrity. His biography is full of instances which make the distinction clear. Not once did he waver when the issue was fundamental. He procrastinated when he did not care; but when he did care his decision was prompt, abrupt, and un-compromising.

Beethoven did not marry because there was no woman to whom he

felt, at the last ditch, he could give himself completely and uncon-
ditionally; and to have indulged only a part of himself would have
been a betrayal of that personal integrity to the preservation of which
his life was dedicated. We know that Beethoven was virile enough and
that he desired greatly a share of common domestic happiness. But
always the impenetrable barrier of his ideal rose up before him, so that
rather than compromise it he had to forgo—not from conscious
choice so much as from inner necessity—the thing he intensely longed
for. Late in his life he came to realize the inevitability of it all, and so
renounced finally the prospect of marriage. But for years he thought
the problem not insoluble, and in the search he knew moments of hope
and happiness, mingled always with foreboding and reactions into
periods of acute despair. And because the prospect meant much to him,
and because the ideal involved was fundamental to his life as man and
artist, something of it spilled over into, and became articulate in, his
music.

Such is the basic proposition: the analysis of it must be undertaken
on two complementary planes—the musical and the psychological.

Before tackling the problem at the source it is necessary to deal
briefly with the theory that Beethoven's celibacy was due to the
presence of a venereal disease—the legacy of some indiscretion in early
manhood. If indeed Beethoven did suffer from syphilis, and if that
alone dealt the mortal blow to his hopes of domestic happiness, then
much would be readily explained. If the destiny of personal loneliness
was in fact self-inflicted, the result of an act of self-indulgence in youth,
it would account for Beethoven's bitter heartache as revealed in various
letters and jottings in his journal, as well as for his passionate hatred
of loose living. The external problem at least would be easily solved.

Unfortunately, however, the syphilis theory, though a convenient
weapon in the hands of the professional denigrators, rests on the
shakiest of foundations. And those foundations become shakier still
when they are made to serve as supports for the cause of Beethoven's
deafness. If syphilis was the cause of deafness, it cannot reasonably
have been the cause of celibacy as well, since Beethoven became deaf at
the age of twenty-eight, and his marital ambitions lasted until some
twenty years later.

Again, leaving aside the cause of deafness, if Beethoven suffered
from syphilis as a young man, it is difficult to see how he continued to
entertain hopes of marriage until well into middle age. On the other

hand, if he only became aware of it (or actually contracted it) late in his life, it does not explain why his early amorous adventures came to nothing. Of course, it is quite possible to explain the whole situation on the basis of pure chance; to argue that he did not marry as a young man simply because the proper opportunity was not to hand, either because he did not find the right woman or, to be more brutal, because he did not find a woman who would have him. The long arm of coincidence stretches far and into the most unlikely places, especially at a distance of more than a hundred and fifty years, and it is possible that many factors, syphilis among them, worked to keep Beethoven single despite his private ambitions and inclinations.

However, as late as 1818 there appears a stuttering prayer in Beethoven's journal imploring God to let him find one 'who will be lawfully mine'. The existence of this entry lends small support to the idea that the cause of his celibacy was an incurable disease, although it does contain implications that may give a clue to his sexual behaviour at some previous time. But for the present it is sufficient to note that even at this late date Beethoven did not feel himself unable to realize himself as a man, biologically rather than artistically speaking.

Perhaps the heaviest evidence against the theory that Beethoven suffered from syphilis, either inherited or acquired, is on the negative side and consists in the total absence of any reference to it among his contemporaries. It seems inconceivable that if this fearsome malady and the consequent personal suffering it caused him really had been at the root of so many of his troubles, no one should have known about it, and having such knowledge would not have made it public, either during Beethoven's lifetime or after his death. He was not, at least for the first two-thirds of his life, a particularly reticent man, and it seems hardly credible that he should have kept, or even wanted to keep, such a secret to himself, even as a guilty secret. Yet no one seems to have an inkling: not Ries or Schindler or Stumpff or any of his closest associates; more remarkable still, neither Dr von Malfatti nor any of his physicians. Surely one or other of these must have known the truth, and could not have been expected, individually or collectively, to have taken it undisclosed to the grave. Beethoven was not so universally loved that all who came into contact with him should have felt obliged to keep to themselves a piece of information which might be thought to reflect discredit on him and in some way tarnish an artificially preserved reputation. Indeed, Beethoven was generally recognized as a difficult and erring human being, albeit one whose genius entitled him to indulgence. His lapses and foibles are frequently revealed and commented on by his contemporaries, both by apologists and detractors. But of syphilis there is no mention.

Dr von Malfatti in particular occupies an interesting position. Beethoven became enamoured with, and probably proposed to, his niece Therese. It is said that the good doctor put his foot down; but if one of the reasons was his special knowledge of Beethoven's health, with syphilis as the chief trouble, he keeps suspiciously quiet about it. And yet, as Beethoven's doctor, Malfatti must have known the truth. As I say, it is possible that there was a conspiracy of silence, even a remoter possibility of a coincidence of silence. But on the available evidence it does not ring true.

I do not intend to be dogmatic about Beethoven and syphilis, but have to give it as my opinion that it is probably no more than a myth. I do not believe that Beethoven suffered from an incurable venereal disease, not because I think him too 'good' and 'pure' to have fallen from grace, but simply because there is not one good reason for accepting it as true but plenty for rejecting it as false. It has all the appearance of something that was foisted on to his biography after his death as an easy way out of a dilemma. It might account for both his deafness and his celibacy; it might also explain the abnormally diseased state of Beethoven's internal organs when he died at the comparatively early age of fifty-six. And yet at forty Beethoven was known to be physically virile, with the appearance of a man ten years younger. The syphilis theory, though a poor one, is not impossible. But taken in the round, the most generous verdict that can be brought is one of 'not proven'.

Beethoven formed innumerable romantic attachments—probably a good many more than are actually recorded. He was undoubtedly sexually potent to an unusual degree; just how frequently he indulged the sexual passions we do not and cannot know. His celebrated remark about sensual enjoyment without a union of souls being bestial and leading to nothing but regret has the flavour of experience, authentic and practical. But if he knew the temptations of the flesh and paid the price of human frailty, he also knew elevation of the spirit and the aspiration towards the ideal. Just as in the 'Eroica' Symphony Beethoven expressed a vision of ideal heroism without being himself every day and hour of his life the ideal hero; just as in the Finale of the Ninth

BUST BY FRANZ KLEIN (1770–1840)

Symphony he gave expression to a great vision of human brotherhood without ever seeing that brotherhood fulfilled on earth, so too he expressed in music his ideal of romantic love without ever being able to make it a condition of his own life.

The work in which Beethoven most perfectly projected his ideal of romantic love is the Fourth Symphony, in B flat, Op. 60. He originally intended to follow the 'Eroica' with the symphony in C minor, the Fifth, but he suddenly turned aside when the latter was partly finished to write the gay, gracious, and lyrical Fourth. It is possible, looking into Beethoven biography, to find external reasons for this change of direction.

To inquire why the Fourth Symphony should be taken as Beethoven's musical embodiment of his ideal of love is to ask a fundamental question. It has no title-page or caption like the 'Eroica' or the 'Pastoral'; and Beethoven made no direct references to it either in his journal or in his conversations with his friends and interlocutors. It is, however, little more difficult to define the provenance of the Fourth Symphony—certainly no more difficult than it is to define the provenance of the Fifth. Leaving biographical linkages aside, the music itself has an unmistakable cut and quality of its own, a particular temper that leaves small doubt in the mind as to its intentions. Although at the time of its composition Beethoven was in an unusually happy frame of mind, and he was then deeply and, for the moment at any rate, hopefully in love with the woman whom of them all he came nearest to marrying, that is at bottom only incidental.

Edwin Evans speaks plain truth when he says, 'We do not, for instance, need to trouble about Beethoven's love-affairs to discover that this symphony is essentially romantic. The character of its melodies, the apparently extemporaneous flow of its ideas, and its long-drawn harmonies are quite sufficient to tell us that.' [1]

Standing as it does between the more obviously heroic proportions of the 'Eroica' and the C minor, the symphony in B flat has been over-shadowed both critically and historically. It has experienced some difficulty in overcoming the oppressive dominance of its companions. It has always been, and to some extent still is, the habit of criticism to write off the Fourth as something of less than momentous importance,

[1] *Beethoven's Nine Symphonies.*

D

and to regard it, along with the Eighth, as in some way inferior to the ubiquitous 'odd-numbers'. Despite the irresistible claims of its gaiety, its grace, its effervescence, and good humour, it has usually been felt that in this work, as in some others of a broadly similar type, Beethoven turned for momentary relief away from the conflicts of his more overtly 'superhuman' music to warmer but less exalted, one might almost say more mundane, values. This, we are told, is charming and gracious music, but it is not the 'greater Beethoven'. Its felicity has been allowed, but it has been largely denied its place in the higher canons of the Beethoven metaphysic.

Such is the reputation of the Fourth Symphony. We are, however, entitled to ask whether a reputation, even though it has been built up over a period of a hundred and fifty years, is necessarily final; whether or not it may yet be found to be based on false premises; whether in fact a work of art is necessarily inferior for being itself rather than something else. For my own part, I am convinced that the Fourth Symphony has been the subject of more misrepresentation than any other major work by Beethoven. For one thing, it is charged with being to some extent a reversion to the type and style of the eighteenth-century symphony, notably of Haydn, and therefore of being a species of backsliding on the part of the creator of the revolutionary 'Eroica'.

However, there is a confusion of thought here. The 'Eroica', from the point of view of form, is more closely related to the earlier form of the symphony than is generally recognized, while the Fourth is one of the most thoroughly 'Beethovenish' of all his symphonies. Weber, who wrote scandalous nonsense about the B flat Symphony, is nearer the mark than the common run of criticism; for at least Weber did recognize its unusual and individual qualities. The truth is, of course, that in this composition Beethoven was dealing with something different in content from both the 'Eroica' and the C minor symphonies. Therefore its form, its texture, and the manner of its speech are also quite different. What remains is that the Fourth Symphony, no less than the others, is an expression of Beethoven's experience.

How was it that this symphony in B flat came to interrupt the apparently continuous creative process that led from the 'Eroica' to the C minor? There are two probable answers. To begin with, the continuity between the Third and Fifth symphonies is not so direct as it appears on the surface to be, despite a quality in both that may be broadly styled 'heroic', and despite the probability that both originated, in a loose sense, from the same basic experience; and secondly, Beethoven always had several ideas at work in his mind at one and the same time, each awaiting some spark to set the flame of creation alight.

We have seen how the suggestion of General Bernadotte that Beethoven should compose a symphony in honour of Napoleon Bonaparte acted as the spark which led to a symphony dealing not with Napoleon but with a visionary ideal of heroism. Napoleon was only the match in the powder magazine. And in the same way it seems probable that the circumstances of Beethoven's life at the time of its composition acted as a similar motivating force for the creation of the Fourth Symphony.

The commission from Count von Oppersdorf had little to do with it. The Count simply wanted a symphony; he did not specify what sort of a symphony it should be—the C minor, or any other, would have done as well. But immediately after Count von Oppersdorf had asked for his symphony something happened in Beethoven's life which may be held to account, from the external point of view, for his turning from one composition to one of an entirely different type. In passing we may dismiss the idea that Beethoven followed the 'Eroica' with the B flat Symphony instead of the C minor for no better reason than that he wanted to give his public some light, not to say comic, relief between two large and strenuous compositions. The idea is so incongruously unlike Beethoven that it is little more than laughable—on a par with the idea that he placed the Funeral March in the 'Eroica' where he did in deference to established practice. The conventional grouping of Beethoven's symphonies by odd and even numbers is largely superficial and nonsensical anyway.

The year 1806 saw Napoleon's soldiers in occupation of Vienna and environs. It was a time of trouble and uneasiness. Beethoven heartily disliked the invaders; also he was already in an explosive state of mind, due to the failure of his opera *Fidelio* on two occasions, the failures being in part due to the presence of the occupying forces who crowded the theatre and were not impressed. Because of the invading soldiery Beethoven could find no peace in his favourite haunts outside Vienna. Then his old friend Count Brunswick invited him to visit the family estates at Martonvasar in Hungary; there Beethoven went and there he became enamoured of the Count's sister Therese. It is supposed that Beethoven and Therese actually became engaged. Talk of an engagement and projected nuptials at Martonvasar is inclined to annoy the more hard-headed Beethoven critics; but there seems no reason to believe that they were not momentarily contemplated. The matter is complicated, however, by the fact that Therese had a pretty sister, Josephine, whom Beethoven is also alleged to have adored at one time or another. That too may well be so, although it does not affect the central argument. I have insisted already that it is not my purpose to disentangle Beethoven's numerous and frequently mysterious love-affairs. I am looking only for points of bearing on Beethoven's creative life as an artist. And here, in the love of Beethoven and Therese at Martonvasar, there very definitely appears to be one. It is no use suggesting that the Fourth Symphony (or the 'Appassionata' Sonata) is 'about' Therese, that either is a direct transcript in music of a particular romantic attachment. But it is possible to suggest and defend the proposition that Therese in 1806 played a role in respect of the Fourth Symphony similar to that played by Napoleon to the 'Eroica' in 1803.

If we accept that the Fourth Symphony enshrines Beethoven's ideal of romantic love, we need no longer ask why its style and form are precisely as they are. Obviously the language of the 'Eroica' will not do for this purpose. Also, we need no longer trouble our consciences about the apparent lack of stature of this work in relation to the more familiar Beethoven metaphysic. Only if we are prepared to assert roundly that the ideal relationship between man and woman is of small importance to the human race shall we be able to write off the Fourth Symphony as being of lesser moment than the Third, Fifth, and Seventh. In miserly and deliberately anti-romantic ages—and such from time to time do occur—it may be temporarily possible to make such an assumption. But it will not endure as a permanent proposition. Because his sensibility to the major life forces was universal and all-embracing Beethoven himself knew better. He understood that in the life of the future, ideal love, no less than ideal heroism, must find its ultimate expression. And the two are inextricably linked together—a hero who cannot love is a mere impostor, a monster of egoism; while love that has not in itself an inherent heroism is a mockery, leading to nothing but promiscuous gratification and indulgence. It is possible to maintain that no compositions throw more light on each other than the Third, Fourth, and Fifth symphonies of Beethoven.

Schumann spoke of the Fourth Symphony as a 'slender Greek maiden between two Norse giants', and in one sense he was right. But Schumann belonged to the new Romantic generation whose ideas followed more or less the Byronic conception of wan and fainting females surrounded by hirsute, swashbuckling but essentially brainless warriors; and there is nothing frail about any music composed by Beethoven. Beethoven does not belong to the Romantic generation proper; like Shakespeare he stood outside time; he was conditioned but not determined by the age in which he lived; his genius was autonomous. He lived to become not the expression of an age but of eternity; and as such he contained in himself much that was typical of both the 'classical' and the 'romantic' ages—broadly if inaccurately so called—without being tied to either. In one sense he stands at the turning point of human development—he was, at least in the middle period of his life, the culmination of one age and the prophet of another. And for this reason his love music, like his heroic music, was romantic in the spiritual but not in the historical sense. The romantics proper could never have understood Beethoven's ideal of love, which is as far beyond the understanding of the common run of mankind as it is outside normal experience—a love that is transcendent and unself-seeking; a love that would deny its own fulfilment rather than compromise itself.

Only the pure in heart can fully understand the Fourth Symphony, just as only a man pure in heart could have written it. This is true of all Beethoven's major compositions, each in its own way and following its own particular direction, even though it is a saying hard to write, and harder still to communicate, in an age of scepticism and self-doubt. But in spite of unfortunate popular connotations, and risking various charges ranging from sentimentality to hypocrisy, one cannot forbear to use the word 'purity' in connection with Beethoven's music. Purity, innocence, chastity—such terms and qualities are not in general favour nowadays; but they none the less arise and demand their rightful place after analysis has removed the dross which misuse has gathered around them.

The purity, the innocence, of Beethoven's music, and of the Fourth Symphony in particular, is not a prim, Victorian-young-ladyish quality, anaemic and half inclined to swoon at the first breath of reality—it is on the contrary masculine and robust, with frequent tendencies to be openly rough-handed. The sheer gusto of Beethoven the man overflows continually into his music. It is not in any way sexless, but rather what may best be called trans-sexual.

Wagner gave us, in *Tristan*, the apotheosis of sexual love and the complete expression of the erotic impulse in the nineteenth century. But the inevitable end of *Tristan* is death. The *Liebstod* is not merely good theatre, it is profound psychological truth. Nor is Brangane's exchanging of the Death Potion for the Love Potion simply a theatrical twist—it too is a 'moment of truth' psychologically apprehended with the overwhelming force of Wagner's genius. The French, with a remarkable capacity for realism, call the sexual act 'the little death', and when Brangane makes the change of potions she condemns the lovers to an agony so great that in the end there is literally nothing left for them but oblivion. Throughout *Tristan* Wagner's orchestra ravishes the senses with the deep-sea surgings of sexual love, which leads on with ever-increasing momentum to the climax of the *Liebstod*. There is nothing left for the lovers but death, for the power of sex has overwhelmed the power of life.

The preoccupation with death is a characteristic of the romantic generations. Shelley had it to a remarkable degree. We find amid the rapturous lines of *Epipsychidion*,

> She met me, Stranger, upon life's rough way,
> And lured me towards sweet Death;

and again, in a passage not included in the final draft:

> To the oblivion whither I and thou
> All loving and all lovely, hasten now
> With steps, ah, too unequal! may we meet
> In one Elysium or one winding-sheet!

Elsewhere the death motive in Shelley's poetry is stronger still—even in his most exalted flights he remains profoundly conscious that 'The shapes of Death haunt Life'. This is something endemic to the Romantic movement as a whole. Keats gave perhaps the most poignant and certainly the most celebrated summary of it:

> Now more than ever seems it rich to die,
> To cease upon the midnight with no pain . . .

This is a predominantly adolescent attitude—it is the tragedy of passion as the young feel it. But the entire Romantic impulse in the nineteenth century was largely adolescent, as Matthew Arnold intimated without being quite sure what it entailed. Wagner merely pushed the whole thing to its inevitable culmination with unequalled tragic power and intensity. *Tristan* may be 'Schopenhauer set to music', but it is also a great deal more. The hand of truth lies on *Tristan*, as upon all great art.

All the same, I am convinced that Beethoven would have found the metaphysic of *Tristan* repulsive, whatever he might have thought of the music. *Tristan* represents just that naturalistic truth in psychological determinism that Beethoven rejected and subsequently replaced by higher and harder won spiritual truth. There is no death in Beethoven's music—it is a life-giving force welling up from the deepest founts of being and leading at the end, in the third period, to spiritual heights unsurpassed in the whole field of human endeavour. Just as *The Ring* contains much truth from the Romantic standpoint and from its context in historical time, and yet is found wanting when placed beside the 'Eroica' Symphony, so *Tristan* contains deep and searching truth of its own and yet cannot stand in the eyes of eternity beside the love music composed by Beethoven. And the reason why both *The Ring* and *Tristan*, though each is a triumph of the creative imagination and each contains profound truth, fail in the end to support the ultimate spiritual analysis is because individually and collectively they preclude anything in the nature of a third period.

There is nothing analogous in Beethoven to the sex-neurosis of Tchaikovsky or the fantasie-neurosis of Chopin, to cite two obvious examples. There is no self-indulgence: when Beethoven speaks it is with the voice of the whole man. Whether he is speaking of heroism, of love, of personal destiny, we know that the idea and the experience have been completely assimilated in the mind and imagination. And his capacity for this assimilation was probably greater than that of any other man—certainly greater than that of any other musician. Beethoven shirked nothing, took no short cuts to felicity; he is the least bogus of all creative artists. That above all is why with Beethoven we are seldom at one and the same time enchanted by the music that was written and haunted by the music that was not written. 'Heard melodies are sweet, but those unheard are sweeter' may be, and often is, all too true. But Beethoven more than any other, again with the exception of Shakespeare, reached nearer to the heart of unheard melodies. He left less unsaid, less drafts of poems instead of real poems than anyone else.

Since the musician is a poet in sound, there has always been a great deal of love music. But very little of it has the exact quality of Beethoven's. Brahms is often making love in his music. But because, after the first hot flush of youthful passion, he is for the most part sentimental, middle-aged, and cautious, Brahms's love music has often a pawing quality about it which can be repellent after the pristine freshness and directness of Beethoven. The celibacy of Beethoven and of Brahms stand poles apart. Neither early mishaps and misadventures of an unwholesome and psychologically destructive sort, nor a tendency to play safe in love and life and art, either had or could have had any determining influence on Beethoven's single state. Brahms remained single through caution and timidity, and, one must admit, through a certain lack of depth which all his sternness of beard and tenderness of heart, genuine enough though both were, cannot entirely hide.

There is plenty of love music in Richard Strauss too, and there is certainly nothing timid or devitalized about it. But with Strauss's love music, as with Wagner's, there is always a bed in the offing, and that means that it is first and foremost a sexual love. We need not be hypocritical about this, or turn up refined and supercilious noses. It is not a subject for high-minded disdain. Most love as we know it is predominantly sexual, and we only indulge in sentimentality if we deny it.

If the Fourth Symphony speaks largely of joy and happiness, that seems to be because Beethoven realized that on one plane, through ideal love between man and woman, one great conflict might be resolved and one split in the cosmos healed. But only on one plane. It is not the whole resolution of the spiritual problem any more than ideal heroism is the whole resolution. J. W. N. Sullivan in his revealing book on Beethoven says, apropos of the Adagio introduction, that it 'has all the effect of an escape, not of a victory'. But Sullivan has already committed the common error of supposing this to be one of Beethoven's less important compositions. As a matter of fact, the B flat Symphony is as much a victory as the C minor—or rather, its victory is comprehended as part of the victory of the C minor. It represents a fusion of experience in one direction, just as the 'Eroica' and the C minor also represent fusions of experience as facets of the whole at this particular time in Beethoven's life.

The Fourth Symphony is among the most masterful and aesthetically satisfying of all Beethoven's works. He never wrote music which falls more gratefully on the ear, and seldom did he reveal a more complete mastery of the techniques of composition. The dark, mysterious Introduction, which seems as though the mind is slowly awakening from some primeval chaos of the unconscious, burgeons suddenly forth into an Allegro vivace of extraordinary athletic grace and energy. There is not much of Schumann's 'slender Greek maiden' in this movement: it is full of fire and lyrical passion, of humour and exultant well-being; it is compact of the strength and vigour of a man with a vision of an ideal that has assumed reality.

The ensuing Adagio is by contrast a sustained flight of tender lyricism which no musician before or since has surpassed. The simplicity of its form and the perfection of its execution make us sometimes forget the sheer technical mastery that underlies it. Beethoven wastes nothing. The rhythmic figure of fourths serves as a springboard from which arises a strain of pure and serene melody, sinuous and infinitely tender, as much in the second subject as in the more familiar principal theme. It is a great song of love which for all its grace and innocence is surcharged with strength and singleness of purpose. This 'scarlet rose' of a movement, as Schauffler calls it, is one of the most perfect of all Beethoven's extended slow movements before the heavenly Adagios and Andantes of the third period. The melancholy which Berlioz sensed in it arises from the sadness of the human heart as it contemplates its own severance from felicity; it is a melancholy similar in kind to that which all but overwhelms us in certain movements of Mozart, and which Eric Blom described as 'the poignancy of perfection'.

The Scherzo, remarkable for the double repetition of its two parts, is again full of energy and humour, while the Finale is a bubbling study in orchestral texture, almost at times bucolic in its rumbustious humour and rhythmic verve. This is a fascinating movement, a sort of explosive consummation that has the force of a volcano and the humour of a Bacchus. Beethoven in love is no less disconcerting than Beethoven executing cosmic dances, as in the Seventh Symphony. That is another reason why the sentimentalists will never understand the Fourth, and why they will continue to prefer for their love music either the comfortable sentimentality of a Brahms or the neurotic posturings of the minor romantics. That too is why those who bow their heads at the tragic beauty and overpowering intensity of *Tristan* may feel some quality of cold abstraction in Beethoven's love music. But because it is the music not of death but of life, the B flat Symphony is perhaps the greatest love music ever written. It is, like the 'Eroica', music for the future, for the time when ideal love as well as ideal heroism will be no longer simply visions in the mind but living realities.

It is now necessary to ask why, if Beethoven had such a full and penetrating vision of ideal love, he yet never managed to translate that ideal into actuality in his own life. One might as well ask why despite the 'Eroica' he was not unswervingly the perfect hero from day to day and year to year. But that is to beg the question. Beethoven did not succeed in making the dream reality simply because he found no woman to whom he could give himself entirely, and because the nature of his ideal acted as a barrier which he could not overcome without compromising its integrity.

Freud, among others, insists that some barrier is essential between the lover and the loved one if love is not to degenerate into promiscuity:

> It can easily be shown that the psychical value of erotic needs is reduced as soon as their satisfaction becomes easy. An obstacle is required in order to heighten libido; and where natural resistances to satisfaction have not been sufficient men have at all times erected conventional ones so as to be able to enjoy love. This is true both of individuals and of nations. In times in which there were no difficulties standing in the way of sexual satisfaction, such as perhaps during the decline of the ancient civilizations, love became worthless and life empty, and strong reaction-formations were required to restore indispensable affective values.[1]

On the other hand, artificial obstacles and barriers are no more than makeshifts; they are necessary only to counteract the individual's, and society's, lack of integrity. They are objective and external, and to the man of spiritual freedom and personal integrity they have neither meaning nor compulsion. For a Beethoven freedom is absolute. But absolute freedom is only possible to someone of Beethoven's spiritual stature. For humanity at large it is only possible to live in some degree of order and harmony by the surrender of a part of individual freedom. But the ideal remains, and it is through such ideals and examples that mankind may hope to move forward.

Beethoven could dispense with conventional ethics and the artifices

---

[1] The Standard Edition of *The Complete Psychological Works*, vol. xi.

of society; the sheer strength of his personality entitled him to do so. He won the right to absolute freedom by hard and persistent effort—and anyone who is not prepared to make that effort has to pay the price of a certain moral and intellectual servitude. Beethoven violated conventional behaviour in many ways; but he refused to compromise with himself and to violate his own integrity. This most passionate and warm-hearted of men remained celibate for no other reason than that he could not surrender his own ideal and indulge only a part of himself in a union to which he could not give himself entirely. His ideal was his barrier: he had neither need nor use for any other.

Late in his life Beethoven stammered in his journal: 'Love alone—yes, only love can give you a happier life—O God—let me—let me finally find one—who will strengthen me in virtue—who will be lawfully mine.' We may be sure that the last words here do not refer to 'lawfully' as being in consideration of any known legal system. Beethoven never had much use or respect for the law of the land as dispensed by magistrates or judges of the High Court. He was speaking of the 'moral law' as he saw and understood it; he was praying for a union which would not violate his ideal. In 1820 he copied out Kant's dictum, 'The moral law in us, the starry sky above us'. It was one of those gleanings from the world's thought and philosophy that he liked to keep before him as symbolic of his own inner life.

When we say that Beethoven in the end found no woman to whom he could give himself entirely, we have to be very careful to know exactly what we mean. What emphatically we do not mean is that he never found a woman 'good' enough for him in the ordinary sense. Beethoven was no humbug—no Pecksniff looking down a supercilious nose at mortal and fallible humanity as from a height of self-satisfied elevation. His idea of women was very romantic and probably a little unreal. He tended to deduce a beautiful nature from a beautiful face—certainly his natural susceptibilities were excited by physical attractiveness. But this was only superficial. Once the external attraction was obliged to support a more profound and more spiritual attachment, it was found wanting and the barrier began to take shape. Usually the issue was at once too clear-cut—the barrier had no difficulty in obstructing the sensual desire. That is why Beethoven had many love-affairs of the normal and superficial kind, and why he was able to look back on them with a sort of cavalier good humour. But as soon as the attachment became more than mere infatuation with a pretty face and a charming disposition the conflict immediately assumed larger and more ominous proportions.

We are faced here with what is known as the element of degradation in erotic life. Sexual desire alone implies a lack of respect in relation to the object of that desire. On the other hand, when the desire is not predominantly sexual the degradation associated with sexual gratification usually acts as a psychological barrier to final union. Beethoven's romantically inclined view of womanhood undoubtedly reacted against his strong sexual desires. Freud again wrote:

> There are only a very few educated people in whom the two currents of affection and sensuality have become properly fused; the man almost always feels his respect for the woman acting as a restriction on his sexual activity, and only develops full potency when he is with a debased sexual object; and this in its turn is partly caused by the entrance of perverse components into his sexual aims, which he does not venture to satisfy with a woman he respects.[1]

Only when the strains of tenderness and sensuality are fused into one does the ideal union become a possibility; and Beethoven never experienced this. He might have made a marriage which would have given him sensual satisfaction and some measure of spiritual community without being quite the whole and undivided ideal, but this would have been a compromise, and he could not accept it. When he wrote that 'sensual enjoyment without a union of souls is bestial and will always remain bestial; after it one experiences not a trace of noble sentiment but rather regret' he was only saying what Freud put into more reasoned and scientific language:

> It is the fate of sensual love to become extinguished when it is satisfied; for it to be able to last, it must from the beginning be mixed with purely affectionate components—with such, that is, as are inhibited in their aims —or it must itself undergo a transformation of this kind.[2]

Thus sex, as always, becomes the point of fatal conflict. Beethoven resolved it in his music but not in his life. And perhaps the final resolution is impossible without some diminution or compromise in the present life of the world. And yet in the regenerate life of the future the complete resolution must be found. Indeed, it is one of the essential

---

[1] Ibid.
[2] Ibid., vol. xviii.

requirements of the new spiritual life to which the music of Beethoven is an imperative pointer.

To the ordinary man such an explanation of Beethoven's continence must seem fantastic. To remain celibate, not through lack of desire or want of opportunity but through the sheer quality of an ideal, is something quite beyond and outside normal human experience. But to Beethoven it was the only possible course. It was the price he had to pay to his destiny, and it was a heavy one, next to unbearable at times. When he wrote, 'Submission, absolute submission to your fate . . .' this, in part, is what he meant. He had to summon heroic fortitude on more planes than one in order to remain true to himself. To have compromised anywhere would have been to compromise everywhere. He was put to the test, and, although he prayed often that the cup might pass from him, he was not in the end found wanting. That is why there is victory here as much and as well as anywhere else in his creative life.

One question remains. Was there then no woman in Beethoven's life with whom he might have made the perfect union? Probably not, although he had the acquaintance of many fine women and the intimacy of some. But I believe that Therese von Brunswick came nearer than all others to becoming the ideal partner. Therese, as I have already suggested, seems to have acted as the igniting spark for the Fourth Symphony, and it was to her that Beethoven later dedicated one of the most perfect of his smaller compositions, the Piano Sonata in F sharp, Op. 78.—the one which provoked him into a remark about a visitation from his 'good angel'. Again, a portrait of Therese was one of the very few mementoes of his many women friends found among his possessions after his death.

I do not propose to enter into the argument whether or not Therese von Brunswick was the recipient of the famous letters to the 'Immortal Beloved'. Those letters [1] are priceless documents; but they are so for the insight they give us into Beethoven's mind rather than as points for biographical disputation. These passionate outpourings, clumsy though they are, are among the most touchingly sincere ever uttered. They were obviously written to someone whom Beethoven loved passionately, and who loved him in return. They are, like all Beethoven's efforts to express himself in words, awkward and often incoherent— they are not unlike what his music might have been if he had never

[1] *See* Appendix.

achieved his exceptional mastery of technique. And if there is no exact counterpart to them in Beethoven's music—as there quite obviously is not—then that is because music, not words, was his proper medium, and because the letters have particular reference whereas his music has universal reference.

Therese von Brunswick appears as the most likely to endure of all Beethoven's beloveds, mortal or immortal, largely because she seems to have been the most Leonora-like of them all; and in Leonora Beethoven enshrined something of his ideal of perfect womanhood. In *Fidelio* Beethoven, among other things, shows us the inevitable relationship between love and heroism. That this relationship is partially disguised in theatrical 'business' must not be allowed to obscure its meaning. The victory of Florestan and Leonora is much more than cosy domestic fidelity: it too has its ideality and its universal truth. *Fidelio* is another of Beethoven's misunderstood and misrepresented compositions, principally because it is unique among his major works in that from time to time his technique fails him.

Beethoven was not a clever man, but he did understand the human heart and saw into it as into a deep, mysterious, and troubled pool. Those who think that he drew human character according to convention should look again into the score of *Fidelio* with something less than the usual critical inattention. Note with what subtlety he differentiates between the love of Leonora and the love of Marcellina. The composer of conventional nineteenth-century melodrama could never have made that difference so touching and so true to life. And take the case of Rocco the jailer. Early in Act I Rocco sings his celebrated stanzas in praise of gold; and then, before we have forgotten them, and certainly before Rocco has forgotten them, comes Pizzaro with his vile purse, as bribe or incentive to the murder of Florestan. Rocco is sorely tried. He is a simple soul, earthy and acquisitive; the one thing he really wants to fulfil a lifetime's ambition is gold, in large quantities— and here it comes for the taking.   The chinking of Pizzaro's pieces is nearly too much for him. But Rocco has a conscience too. He has his price, no doubt; but every man not a monster must draw the line somewhere, and to murder old Rocco will not stoop, not even for all that gold. So in the end the man in him wins the day, and with much trembling and knocking of the knees he resists temptation and Pizzaro has to do his own dirty work. The situation is so packed with insight and psychological truth that one can only gaze in astonishment at those who in performance even contemplate the omission of the 'Gold' aria.

The key to *Fidelio* is perhaps to be found most readily in the 'Prisoners' Chorus'. This wonderful creation with its passionate human sympathy is of the same order of imagination as Van Gogh's picture *The Prison Yard*. Indeed, Van Gogh's credo, 'I want to paint humanity, humanity, and again humanity', might well have served also for Beethoven's almost superhuman humanity and breadth of sympathy.

The dramatic subtleties of *Fidelio* are germane to a discussion of Beethoven's ideals of love because they help to reveal the universality of his vision. It was Aldous Huxley who once said that if it be true that 'all the world loves a lover', then it is equally true that a lover loves all the world. Love is indivisible. Although in his everyday speech Beethoven tended to deal with the world around him in a satirical tone, this was only because he was conscious that the mass of mankind obstinately refuse to realize their own potentialities. He tended to regard them as a pack of fools who could scale the heights if only they had the mind and will to try—and he had good reason to know what can be achieved by personal endeavour. But he did not hate them; he wished to be remembered as one who had served his fellow men and loved God equally well.

To return to Therese von Brunswick, Beethoven's later biographers seem to have convinced themselves that the relationship is little more than a legend. But the internal evidence suggests more strongly that here at least was a deep and not short-lived attachment. Therese never married; she took the secret of it to the grave with her; she even indicated that Beethoven's real *amour* was not for her but for her sister Josephine. None the less the figure of Therese persists. It may be a mirage; but it looks and sounds pretty substantial.

Modern research has also propounded a theory that a child born to Josephine at a later date may have been Beethoven's. It could be true—we shall never know for certain. Personally I am unwilling to grant the prosecution its case, not because Beethoven was above moral lapses and indiscretions, but simply because it has lain quiet rather too long. Either Beethoven was not the father or he never knew about it—that much is beyond question. If he had known he was the father of any child it is beyond doubt that he would have made a great fuss over it. For one thing he passionately desired a child—as poor Karl found out to his cost—and for another he was a man always ready to shoulder his responsibilities. It does not sound true—unless, that is, Beethoven knew nothing about it, which is not impossible.

I am not at all convinced either by the idea that Beethoven remained single through an act of fate which worked to save him for his art alone and against all his private inclinations and ambitions. Should we really have been denied his greatest music if he had taken unto himself a wife? It is possible, but by no means likely. The chaos of his private life was enough as it stands to have checked the flow of his creative powers had any external force been able to do as much. Would a little good management at home and some care for his private needs have resulted in more waste of substance than his interminable struggles with bad housekeeping, pathetic attempts to make a good guardian for Karl, and persistent worry over lodgings and servants? On the surface it seems improbable.

It is true that there appears to be a conflict between love and the creative spirit. However, real and tragic though the conflict can be, there is the possibility of a misunderstanding here. Often the conflict manifests itself as a spurious one between creativity and 'love' taken as synonymous with marriage and the family. But love is not so synonymous. On the contrary it would be more true to say that ethical and spiritual love is incompatible with marriage and social family life. Love is in essence an integral part of creativity and is only opposed to it when conditioned by determinism from without, as in love objectified and socialized. Love between man and woman can only exist between two autonomous and independent personalities. The oft-expressed desire of conventional lovers for 'oneness' is meaningless: love is an expression of active personality, not a negation or submergence of it. Love cannot exist where personality is obliterated.[1]

The tragedy of love is bound up with the tragedy of freedom and creativity. The incompatibility of ethical creative love and socialization lies at the heart of the human tragedy. It is probable that in the end it was the distinction between socialized and ethical love which kept Beethoven single against all his warmest inclinations. Whether or not he was aware in his conscious mind of the distinction is an open question. He appears from his sayings and writings to have been at best

[1] 'The essence of love, its original value and power, lies in the ever-new discovery and realization of the intrinsic or eternal character of self-activity.'—Vivante.

PALAIS RASOUMOVSKY, VIENNA

dimly aware of it, or of something like it. But his music suggests unmistakably that deep down he did know and recognize it for what it was.

If we believe, as we must believe, that all great art is the outcome of man's passionate thinking and feeling in respect of life and love and death, then we cannot logically hold Beethoven's love music to be of less moment than his heroic music, unless at the same time we believe that on that subject he spoke with less authority. But we know, both from his life as revealed by his biographers and in his letters and conversations, as well as from his music itself, that the subject of love and the ideal relationship between man and woman continually occupied his mind, alike from the personal and from the metaphysical points of view. We know too that for Beethoven personal love was one of the major elements in the integration of all vital experience which formed the basis of his creative life. We cannot, therefore, deny the authority of his speech on that subject without at the same time destroying that whole spiritual foundation which gives him his place as one of the most potent forces in the development of human consciousness.

The Fourth Symphony represents a projection from the inside of Beethoven's vision of ethical-ideal love in the same way that the 'Eroica' represents a projection from the inside of his vision of ethical-ideal heroism—no more and no less. The two works are complimentary, exist eternally side by side and throw perpetual illumination on each other. They represent projections of two separate ideals from the same standpoint. If we deny the Fourth its parity with the 'Eroica', or with the C minor or the Seventh, then we deny Beethoven his universality. The world could be redeemed by the spirit of the 'Eroica'; and if love were really to become what the Fourth Symphony is, what a transformation would have taken place in the spiritual experience of mankind!

E

4

The Everlasting Yea

'TEMPTATIONS in the Wilderness!' exclaims Teufelsdröckh:

> Have we not all to be tried with such? Not so easily can the old Adam, lodged in us by birth, be dispossessed. Our Life is compassed round with Necessity; yet is the meaning of Life itself no other than Freedom, than Voluntary Force; thus have we a warfare; in the beginning, especially, a hard-fought battle. For the God-given mandate, *Work thou in Welldoing*, lies mysteriously written, in Promethean, Prophetic Characters, in our hearts; and leaves us no rest, night or day, till it be deciphered and obeyed; till it burn forth, in our conduct, a visible, acted Gospel of Freedom. And as the clay-given mandate, *Eat thou and be filled*, at the same time persuasively proclaims itself through every nerve—must there not be a confusion, a contest, before the better Influence can become the upper?

There are several points of contact between Beethoven and Carlyle. Beethoven, it is true, had little of Carlyle's didacticism, obtuseness, or puritanism—neither had he the temperament of a martinet. But they were alike in the recognition of the omnipotence of genius and intuition, in an ennobling worship of the ideal of heroism, and in a volcanic energy and vital power, although Carlyle's volcano tended to smoke opaquely where Beethoven's flamed heavenwards. They were much alike in kind, and it seems to me that the passage above from *Sartor Resartus* has direct relevance to Beethoven's consciousness during the middle years of the decade 1800 to 1810.

After the completion of the Fourth Symphony, Beethoven returned to the half-written one in C minor, the one which, as the Fifth, was to become the most familiar of all his symphonies. The postulates of the Fifth were imperative—they could not be side-tracked or evaded. As a matter of fact the preliminary sketches for the C minor Symphony date as far back as 1800. The real work on it was begun in 1805; but then, as we have seen, Beethoven broke off at a tangent to cope with another aspect of his basic experience in the Fourth Symphony.

There are some interesting speculations to be drawn from the existence of drafts of the C minor Symphony as early as 1800—before, that is, the expressed crisis contained in the Heiligenstadt Testament and before the conception of the 'Eroica', which is generally thought to be Beethoven's defiant riposte to the heavy questions posed by that bitter document. If General Bernadotte had not sparked Beethoven's imagination with a focusing point for a symphony enshrining the ideal of heroism, and if the happy associations at Martonvasar had not inspired him to do the same for ideal love, the C minor Symphony might well have been, not the fourth as at the time intended, but actually the third in the series.

It is true that even before 1800 Beethoven was becoming haunted by a gnawing apprehension in respect of his hearing. But he had for the moment no reason to believe that it was more than temporary, and thus he did not feel himself compelled to come immediately to terms with it. Then came the interlude of the first to be recorded of his really passionate love-affairs—that with the Countess Giulietta Guicciardi. Some have argued on behalf of Giulietta's being Beethoven's one and only 'Immortal Beloved'. Perhaps Giulietta did at least prepare the ground in which the seed planted five years later by Therese von Brunswick was to flower musically in the Fourth Symphony. If we are to be honest we must even admit the possibility that she and not Therese really planted the seed.

The reason for bringing Giulietta into the present discussion is to be found in a letter written by Beethoven to his friend Franz Wegeler in November 1801. It is in this letter, in which all the fear and bitterness of his mind in the face of his deteriorating hearing is mixed with hope for his 'dear, fascinating girl who loves me and whom I love', that there occurs the significant remark, 'I will take Fate by the throat; it shall not wholly overcome me'. Already Beethoven was moving into deep and ominous regions, and the necessity of finding himself as man and artist was becoming imperative to him, quite apart from the conditions of his everyday life and from his material fortunes. The Fifth Symphony was in fact shaping in his unconscious as well as in his conscious mind, as it had to do and as it would have done, deficient hearing or not, Giulietta or no Giulietta, he being Ludwig van Beethoven and no other.

The C minor Symphony is one of the most dramatic and highly charged documents in music. Not only musicians but the world at large have had no difficulty in recognizing that essential truth. That it is a faithful transcript of Beethoven's central experience during the earlier part of his life, and that it represents a victory won after fierce striving and heavy labour is also too self-evident to require extended comment. What is more important, and what is by no means beyond dispute, is the precise nature of that conflict and that victory, and the metaphysical premises on which both are founded or from which both derive.

An assertive challenge, both to the art of music and to the human mind, rings out with dramatic force in the 'signal' of the opening bars. Beethoven's remark to Schindler that these hammer blows represented fate knocking at the door has led to trouble in plenty. Ever since it was first uttered it has caused critical heads to knock together with an impact that echoes yet through the musical world. Some have thought it to be just one of Beethoven's little jokes. But Beethoven, although a man of plentiful humour and often a bitingly satirical tongue, was not in the habit of making little jokes about things that meant much to him. On the contrary, that remark is just the sort of key which Beethoven would sometimes use to open momentarily the door on to the inner mysteries of his music—the sort of key that could easily be seen to open the door, then slam it again for the wrong sort of interpreter. But, as so often, it is safest to begin by assuming that Beethoven meant what he said in words, just as he meant what he said in music. When he was composing Beethoven invariably had in his mind a *Bild* (picture, image, or idea—the German word comprehends all three), although it was not his practice to disclose its exact nature.

Schauffler, in a laudable effort to free the C minor Symphony, along with practically all Beethoven's music, from the attentions of moronic programme-spinners, gets into some intricate difficulties with the knocking on the door:

> Even if it conveys to the mind of Smith such a Goethean conception as fate supplanting the traditional wolf at the door, it may quite as reasonably convey entirely different things to a group of creative listeners unbiased by program annotations.
>
> To Brown it may signify a fierce conflict with a sexual obsession. To Jones a desperate campaign against an inferiority complex. To Robinson an old-fashioned pitched battle *à la Paradise Lost* between the forces of

good and evil. To a victim of hysteria it may depict a war between sanity and bedlam. To a neurasthenic the struggle between those two mutually exclusive objectives: 'To be, or not to be?' To an evolutionist it may bring up the primordial conflict of fire and water, of man with beast, of civilization with savagery, of land with sea.[1]

There is obviously a confusion of thought here, and for the simple reason that the whole argument omits the preliminary definition of 'fate'. Just as Schauffler argues elsewhere, and correctly argues, that music may mean all things to all men, so fate manifests itself in one form to one individual and in another form to a different one. If Brown suffers from a sexual obsession, then to Brown conflict with that obsession is 'fate'; if Jones has a persistent inferiority complex then 'fate' to Jones is the campaign against that complex—and so on. It is a too restricted and over-specialized conception of fate that is at fault, not its relevance to the Fifth Symphony as such. We are nearer the mark if we follow Beethoven's intimation that what is really involved here is a conflict between free will and determinism, between freedom and necessity, for here at least are no constricting and falsifying categories. Brown's conflict, Jones's campaign, Robinson's pitched battle —these and all the rest are comprehended by that one overriding definition. And so far as Beethoven is concerned it is probably still the most generally applicable.

Because Beethoven's sense of the fundamental life forces and his understanding of essential issues were more all-embracing and comprehensive, his conception of fate was at once simpler and more complex than that of the ordinary man—simpler because it could admit more easily of one universal definition, and more complex because it embraced the whole and did not deal in aspects only. Beethoven's idea of fate as represented in the opening movement of the Fifth Symphony is inclusive, not exclusive; that is why a simple statement of the eternal strife between freedom and necessity most aptly sums it up in one phrase. To Beethoven this was the pivotal issue, from which all others stemmed. It is the basic theme, and it lasts right through his life. The triumph of freedom over necessity is the victory, not only of the Fifth Symphony, not only of the assertive and challenging second period taken in the round, but of the whole outcome of his life. Beethoven's personal motto was 'Freedom above all'; as Paul Bekker wrote: 'The sum of his message was freedom, artistic freedom, political freedom,

[1] *Beethoven, the Man who Freed Music.*

personal freedom of will, of art, of faith, freedom of the individual in all the aspects of life.'

We have seen while studying the 'Eroica' that there is a strong element of the unconscious in the act of creation, and that it exists to a varying degree. Generally speaking the more potent and autonomous the power of genius, the greater is the element of the unconscious. The greater genius is more 'possessed', more freely and undeliberately motivated, less dependent on the will in its origin; but also, as a corollary, often more demanding on the conscious faculties and requiring great conscious effort to give it external organization.

Of course, genius varies in type as well as in degree. The facility of a Mozart must frequently have been envied by Beethoven struggling with sketch after sketch to give his basic material enduring form. But Mozart was not faced with the same problems; he could take more on trust; because of the nature of his genius and the age in which he lived and which he accepted, Mozart was seldom obliged to cope with inherently intractable material. Mozart's art was based on order—Beethoven's basically on chaos. Mozart had to infuse life into established forms; Beethoven had to invent new forms in order to organize material that was also new because profoundly subjective. Not that one type of genius is superior to another; but given a Beethoven in the first place it does mean that the struggle is bound to be harder in the long run.

Before we can progress much further in an analysis of Beethoven's personal development, and through it his universal significance as revealed in his art, it is necessary to turn aside for a moment to consider the validity of experience as such. And that leads us towards the science of epistemology and to Kant and German idealism. Beethoven, it is necessary to insist, was not a systematic philosopher, and no amount of juggling will turn him into one. He made his position clear and unmistakable when he called music, and his own music in particular, 'a revelation higher than all wisdom and all philosophy'. His great value to mankind is, and it is in the end the most potent and fructifying value of all, the direct communication of a vital experience of the life-forces that he gives us through the medium of his music. At the same time, before we can put a proper value on Beethoven's life and art, we must, from the inherent nature of the postulate itself, clarify the position of experience as valid in the spiritual life of personality.

The validity of experience is not seriously challenged once it is understood that experience goes beyond mere sense perception. Experience is not only sensory, but imaginative and spiritual as well. What is needed is an enlargement of the bounds of experience so that it can be freed from the objective world. There is, of course, another form of knowledge—*a priori* knowledge which is independent of experience and exists outside it. Certainly all knowledge is not derived from the senses—the laws of cause and effect, of Euclid and mathematics, are not dependent on sense perception, although they fertilize imagination and so give rise to imaginative experience. The discovery of the laws of mathematics, before their truth could be verified by direct observation—by sense perception, that is—and their universal application to the material world 'proved', was one of the most remarkable developments in the consciousness of the human race. Those laws do not in themselves constitute experience: they were perhaps the most brilliant achievement of the process of deduction and pure reason. But when through the development of applied science those laws were found to be the very ones on which the material universe depended, immense new potentialities opened before the human mind.

What do we mean by imaginative and spiritual experience? In all experience there is a fertile duality—a conflict between the perceptible and the imperceptible, the material and the immaterial. And it is this duality which gives rise to creative activity. It is the conflict between realism and idealism (in its largest and most comprehensive sense). Monism is passive and static—dualism is active and positive. But the conflict is internal, not external. Dualism is the energizing principle, and it is through its eternal strife that the personality passes from the passive to the active state of being. Freedom implies dualism, for without the existence of duality there can be no vital conflict out of which freedom can develop. There is no freedom in fixed causality—that way leads to determinism, to the slavery of personality and the denial of spiritual transcendence. It is only by opposing determinism with freedom that denial and the triumph of impotence can be overcome. But freedom demands the acceptance of tragedy. To quote Berdyaev again: 'The admission of a fundamental opposition between freedom and necessity, spirit and nature, subject and object, personality and society, the individual and the general, postulates a tragic philosophy.' [1] Freedom implies primary choice. A man is free either to

---

[1] *Solitude and Society.*

choose or to reject a tragic philosophy, and experience can be fulfilled or denied.

But is the choice free in the first place? Much philosophical thought denies it vigorously. Materialists and determinists believe that all human actions are in the nature of 'conditioned reflexes', after the manner of Pavlov's dogs, only more complex. According to this school of thought we are asked to believe that all activity is dependent on material and psychological conditions; that, in fact, freedom is an illusion and choice non-existent except to a very small and unimportant degree. The history of art and philosophy, however, does not support this restricted view of man's potentiality. Determinism is at bottom unintelligible because it leaves out of account the most potent factors in human consciousness: it destroys the will and the intellect no less than it destroys ethics and creativity. It runs contrary both to spiritual experience and to sense perception. It is only by opposing determinism with freedom that we can properly account for mankind's endless struggle towards an ethical world-view, and for the fact of creative activity as made manifest not only through art but in all aspects of life. But what is the origin of this freedom which makes choice both a possibility and a necessity? Or, to put it another way, what is the element in personality that frees it from the natural world, from sense experience only and from the circumscribing power of materialism? The answer lies in the active subject.

It is a central argument of Kant's *Critique of Pure Reason* that the human mind is not a passive substance which can only receive objective imprints of sensation, but an active organism which selects, correlates and organizes the impressions it receives into significant ideas and forms. The method by which this is achieved is one of the pillars of Kantian philosophy and the primary fact of the distinction is one of the great forces in philosophical thinking.

The thesis of positive activity leads at once to the question of ethics as a pivotal point in human thought. If mind is truly active then it must be free to choose, for activity without freedom is meaningless. And as soon as there is freedom of choice ethics become of paramount importance. So long as mind is regarded as passive the will is paralysed and all activity, all art, all philosophy is moribund. Kant realized the mysterious and supranatural origin of ethics and saw it as an act of volition which releases man from the determinism of the natural world in a way that opens on to a higher and more comprehensive metaphysic.

It is true that Kant seems to deny the complete validity of experience; but he is mainly concerned with experience as sense perception. It is also true that in upholding the absolute ideal of moral duty Kant is ultimately faced with the necessity of arriving at some system of conduct which is finally binding, and therefore by implication he denies the essential liability of personality. But his insistence on the supranatural origin of ethics is of the first importance and leaves the way open for a solution of the metaphysical problem, even though he himself, and despite a bold assertion to the contrary, did not entirely achieve it.

The potency of Kantian philosophy lies in its assertion of a fundamental dualism and in its freeing of ethics from the natural world. In this sense Kant becomes one of the great historical liberators of human consciousness. The active subject in Kant overthrows the objectivist philosophies, and although he tends to deny the validity of experience, and therefore the primacy of freedom over Being, he none the less stands as a great ethical thinker who reveals new vistas to the development of the life of the world. The difficulty is that by erecting complex philosophical systems Kant depersonalizes philosophy and thereby creates fresh problems in place of the old ones.

The revelational impact of experience considered in its broadest sense is a cardinal element in human consciousness; but without the incidence of the active subject it cannot lead to creativity and to the integration of personality. When Kant insists that perceptions without conceptions are blind he effectively challenges the earlier theories of the passivity of the will. The active subject seizes on experience, moulds it into conceptual forms, and fashions it according to its own capability by a process of positive activity.

Sensitivity to experience and its organization into recognizable concepts is the supreme quality of the active subject, and varies as the qualitative sensibility and creative potency of the subject itself varies. Experience is not fixed and finite: it depends for its scope and intensity upon the quality of the active subject, so that the same root experience produces different effects and gives rise to different concepts in different subjects. And these variations postulate freedom of the will and free acceptance of the call to creativeness.

It is in the freedom of the creative faculty that the thesis of the active subject differs primarily from the unitarian theory of passivity. Experience cannot be accepted passively and absorbed deterministically

—it must be revealed, organized, and correlated by a free act of creativity. At the same time, *all* experience must be accepted: renunciation leads to a turning away from authentic experience and a denial of the creative spirit.

Experience is a spiritual as well as a sensory factor in the life of man, and it is through its spirituality that it becomes transcendent. Sense experience alone is incomplete and inadequate. Spiritual experience leads to a breaking down of natural and determinist barriers: it is in the nature of a revelation—indeed, revelation itself may be described as transcendental experience. Revelation emanates from freedom and therefore leads to tragedy. But it must be accepted if the destiny of personality is to be fulfilled: and, as a corollary, freedom can only be achieved through acceptance.

Here is the hard core of the conflict. To turn one's back on freedom and the acceptance of experience is one of the most potent of temptations in the wilderness; denial is at once inviting and the easy way out, since it leads to the avoidance of painful consequences and to a static state of being from which suffering is banished. But the spiritual cost is a heavy one. Just at the moment when the personality is emerging from the constraints of naturalism the tragedy of freedom looms up, dark and sinister. The lures of worldly happiness and easeful living set up a powerful and often determining contrary force, so that in the end freedom is denied and destiny remains unfulfilled. As Bergson intimates, human nature inclines to materialism, to the tangible and the objective. We exist in the material world and are conditioned from birth by its laws. Therefore we tend by nature to cling to that which is immediately perceptible to our senses—or to the extension of our senses by way of scientific instruments. We have small taste for the intangible and the immaterial, for the mysterious and the baffling. Our inclination is to play safe, to make the best of what is rather than to match ourselves, mind and sinew, against what might be. But the irony of it is that in the everyday life of humanity there is more poignant suffering and dull pain than ever arises out of the tragedy of freedom. For in the ultimate tragedy there is salvation, whereas in the resigned ache of denial there is none.

It is no coincidence that Beethoven's creative life overlapped the Kantian era of philosophy. We have seen that Beethoven copied out a dictum of Kant's and kept it by him as one of his private lodestars. But that in itself is not very significant. What is significant is that Kant made metaphysics fashionable. Everyone talked metaphysics; it permeated into the most unlikely corners and crannies. What Goethe said to Eckermann, referring to Kant: 'he has influenced even you, although you have never read him; now you need him no longer—for what he could give you you possess already', is no less applicable to Beethoven, who certainly had read him, in part at least.[1]

How deeply into Kant, or into any other philosophy, Beethoven had actually read is, however, not what we are looking for. The point is that the philosophical temper of Europe was ready for Kant, just as musically it was ready for Beethoven. Great men are not tied irrevocably to the age in which they live; but they flourish and grow to plenitude in a propitious soil. This is not to deny the autonomy of genius—simply to say that genius, like any other growth, needs fertilizing. Kant propounded the thesis of the active subject and in so doing enormously increased the scope of human consciousness: Beethoven for his part was perhaps the most formidable example of the active subject yet known to history, and he too opened doors on to whole new vistas.[2] For it is the element of positive activity, carried through to the end in the integration of all experience and the unrestricted acceptance of the tragedy of freedom, that metaphysically speaking stands out above all others. Freedom of choice and positive activity are made manifest in Beethoven—not in theory but in actuality—as nowhere else.

If we accept Beethoven's own indications that in the Fifth Symphony the conflict between freedom and necessity is brought to a head, then we can immediately begin to see it as it is from the inside. No more than with the 'Eroica' or the B flat symphonies need we concern ourselves with programmes and irrelevant details. We have our proposition, and we too must bring some positive activity of the mind to bear on it. It cannot be too often or too strongly reiterated that the understanding and appreciation of art is in itself a creative process. Passive contemplation yields a barren crop: the experience of a work of art in its impact on the mind and the imagination has to stimulate an active response.

---

[1] Kant's *Natural History and Theory of the Firmament* was found in Beethoven's private library.

[2] I do not want it to be thought that I am under the delusion that the thesis of the active subject was Kant's sole contribution to philosophy. Kant's theories of time and space are of enormous value to philosophic thought; but they are not germane to the present discussion.

The celebrated motif which opens the C minor Symphony had a profound significance for Beethoven. This figure of three short notes followed by a long one occurs again and again in his compositions, now in one form, now in another, sometimes direct and unmistakable, sometimes subtly transformed, and always in its pure or 'C minor' form it is associated with heroic aspiration. If it finds its most direct expression in the Fifth Symphony and is the underlying motif of the whole of that work, it is hardly less remarkable or less imperative in the 'Appassionata' Sonata, the Scherzo of the Harp Quartet, the *Egmont* overture and others, in all of which it has the true heroic ring. As a rhythmic pattern by no means always associated with one mood or root experience, it turns up in so many other compositions that it is neither possible nor desirable to catalogue them. It knocks at the door of the 'Pathétique' Sonata, invades the finales of both the D minor, Op. 31, No. 2 and the 'Moonlight'; it is present at the opening of the G major Piano Concerto and, with one note added, of the Violin Concerto; and it is even present, pure and unadulterated, at the lead-in to the Vivace of the Seventh Symphony. Indeed, it is possible to see the whole rhythmic basis of the Seventh Symphony as a sort of subtle and varied transubstantiation of this very 'fate' motif. Its introduction at the fifty-ninth bar on the violins, anticipated by flutes and oboes at the fifty-eighth, can hardly have been accidental at the point where the whole orchestra is pausing for breath before the eruption of the Vivace 6/8. It is as though in the mind of Beethoven at the moment of his greatest exultation in his creative power there had stirred a sudden memory of the conflict he had been called on to live through, and from which he was obliged to emerge victorious as the condition of the release of all this divine exuberance. But whatever its meaning here or in another specified place, it had for him a far-reaching significance.

That this motif was not original is a matter of very small consequence. Haydn used it in his Piano Sonata in E flat (Augner No. 3), and it makes internal gestures in his Sonata in E minor (Augner No. 2). But this is beside the point: all artists are pilferers, and the greatest artists are the greatest thieves. The borrowings of Shakespeare, of Milton, of Virgil—indeed, of any major artist—make a formidable list and lend poor support to those who think that genius must be original at any cost all the time. The language of the arts is common currency, and all we can really concern ourselves with is that the borrower is not at the same time a debaser of the coin. That this most famous of all Beethoven's motifs was not originally his own creation is not, therefore, remarkable; on the contrary, borrowing was his normal practice. Like all great geniuses Beethoven had no need to be always trying to stun by novelty. In this very C minor Symphony there occurs at the opening out of the golden triumph of the finale a progression that is no more than a student's exercise—and yet it remains one of the most astonishing examples of his art and one of the most Beethovenish passages in all his mid-period music. I refer of course to the plain C major triads, resonant with the splendour of trombones, which let everlasting light into the dark and sinister regions in which the Scherzo concludes.

The prevalence of the rhythm of the 'fate' motif in Beethoven's music is in no way surprising, because it symbolized for him the kernel of a fundamental conflict. In the Fifth Symphony this conflict is fought out in the open, and the triumphant outcome of the struggle thus becomes the corner-stone of Beethoven's creative life up till 1812, when he came to the threshold of his third period and when even this immense triumph was found to be insufficient. But for the whole of his creative activity during the second period the bitter struggle and final emergence expressed in the C minor Symphony gave him the subjective freedom that made the music of his middle years possible.

That the sketches for the Fifth Symphony date back as far as 1800 suggests that of all Beethoven's second-period compositions the content of the C minor Symphony fermented in his mind longer than any other. There is no igniting spark which sets off the creative faculty here, for this is in very fact the basic postulate of the mid-period Beethoven metaphysic. In this sense the Fifth is the most personal of all Beethoven's symphonies before the Eighth. Whereas the 'Eroica' and the Fourth were 'projections' of an ideal, and the Ninth a projection of a different order, the Fifth is the expression of Beethoven's own inmost experience. Although it is heroic in tone, it stands apart from the 'Eroica' in more senses than one; neither in content nor in form does it approximate to the states of mind that were behind the production of several compositions besides the 'Eroica' which are frequently coupled with it.

That the experience out of which the Fifth Symphony arose was fundamental to Beethoven's life as man and artist before it found its full expression in his music is made evident by the fact that the 'Eroica' and the B flat symphonies, to say nothing of several other compositions of hardly less import, were composed well before it; for if the basic experience of the Fifth had not been already a vital factor in Beethoven's life, none of those other works could have been composed at all. In this sense Sullivan is justified in implying that at least in its first three movements the Fifth Symphony represents an earlier stage of the experience which underlies the 'Eroica'. Even so, this is true only up to a point. Because the experience is fundamental in the sense that it is more comprehensive and less 'directioned', it both precedes and post-dates the 'Eroica' at one and the same time. It is an example of the basic and all-embracing experience at the heart of a man's life which probably arises only slowly from the unconscious; but when it arrives at its ultimate point of intensity it does so with an eruption of vital energy so comprehensive that it immediately puts all other facets of his work into a new perspective. Without the Fifth Symphony it would be impossible fully to understand practically all the works of Beethoven's second period. It sheds its light both backwards and forwards, and the world at large has not been wrong to see in it something quite exceptional and of overriding significance.

The first movement of the Fifth Symphony is an expression of internal conflict so dramatic, so overwhelming, so passionate, and an artistic triumph so masterful, that no amount of barefaced repetition or blatant misuse has ever been able to stale it. There is no need to ask why Goethe would have none of it and why its 'wildness' seemed to him to threaten to bring the whole house down around his ears; why it ruffled intolerably the bland self-assurance of Mendelssohn; or why Berlioz's Frenchman after hearing it was so distraught that on going to put on his hat he couldn't find his head! These various reactions and anecdotes have the touch of truth, for this is music which, more than any other, comes straight to the point without peroration, and catches up the imagination into its own rugged domains and will not release its hold. To the sensitive mind it is among the most disturbing music in existence, for it carries us to the root of one of life's great metaphysical problems and reveals it in all its stark reality and tragic power.

In point of form and technique this first movement is an artistic achievement that even Beethoven himself did not surpass until his third period. By stripping sonata form to its elements; by removing at a stroke all bridge passages, decorations, and mechanical contrivances, Beethoven broke away from the tradition of the classical symphony as it had come to perfection in the hands of Haydn and Mozart. And in so doing he achieved a miracle of matching form to content. Although among Beethoven's symphonies it is the 'Eroica' which in point of physical dimension and spiritual content broke new ground, the general idea that the C minor is the epoch-making symphony is justified. It is true that nothing like the 'Eroica' had been heard before—that for variety, eloquence, and organic unity it represented a completely fresh conception of the symphony. But technically the 'Eroica' is firmly anchored in the classical tradition, whereas the C minor breaks away from the fetters and introduces not only an enormously developed idea of symphonic style, but a new conception of sonata form itself. It is the precursor of those particularly Beethovenian conceptions, like the *Egmont* and *Leonora* overtures, in which an inexorable organic growth gives rise to an overwhelming compression of essence. We are confronted here with a first sampling of that instrumental music-drama which throughout his life Beethoven sometimes released on the world with an awful power that seems to resemble a species of spiritual and intellectual nuclear fission. The experience behind it is so intense and so imperative that there is no time for diversions or ornaments; every note contributes its essential part to the whole; every figure, however subsidiary, is vital to the music's organic growth; and from the first bar to the last it moves inevitably forward in one broad, masterful sweep.

It cannot be said that the variations, 'andante con moto', of the second movement maintain either the musical or the emotional heights of the Allegro con brio. It is a beautifully fashioned movement; but in its context it fails to justify itself. I am certain in my own mind that the reason why Beethoven later in his life preferred the 'Eroica' to the C minor was because of the inability of these variations to uphold the poetic idea of the symphony as a whole. The 'Eroica' is more completely realized all through, even though the C minor in three of its movements marks a clearly definable advance from the point of view of freedom of form. It is often the habit of criticism to take exception to the Funeral March of the 'Eroica'; but that, as we have seen, is more because of an inability to grasp the overall conception of that symphony than because of any failing in its particular parts. The same cannot be said of the slow movement of the C minor. Whichever way one looks at it the feeling that here is something of a formal gesture is inescapable. Perhaps the artistic problem of finding a suitable successor to the great Allegro was at this time beyond even Beethoven's powers to accomplish. In this third period he could have done it; but by then the problem itself had changed.

Beethoven's sketch-books are among the most illuminating documents in existence: no extant material gives us such clear insight into the processes of creative activity. The sketches for the variations of the Fifth Symphony are many and various. Beethoven evidently had great trouble in shaping this movement at all. In itself that is not unusual—most of his greatest music had to be ground into shape by sheer hard labour. But here one has the impression that Beethoven had no firm hold on the basic idea. The constant shaping and reshaping seems not so much devoted groping after the elusive ideal as conscious effort to make the best of something only too tangible. At least that is what the final result suggests. The note of authenticity that is one of the most remarkable features of this symphony is lacking in the slow movement. There had to be a slow movement—but was it in some way that there was really no place for one between the heroic conflict of the Allegro and the dark, awesome gropings of the Scherzo which had to lead, whatever else happened, into the open triumph of the Finale? At any rate, fine and beautiful and moving though the Andante is, the mind cannot entirely fit it into the poetic plan of the symphony as a whole. Perhaps it is in the nature of a tentative foreshadowing of the victory to come; but if so, it seems more or less superfluous and not germane to the central theme or argument.

With the opening of the Scherzo all doubts and critical uncertainties disappear. This is one of the most remarkable movements in any symphony. There is in it an element of the grotesque which is, I believe, fundamental to all superabundantly vital art. The lumbering of the double basses and the portentous gruntings of the bassoon towards the end produce an effect analogous to the grinning gargoyles on the medieval cathedrals. Beethoven avoided actual use of the word 'Scherzo' in relation to this movement, largely because at that time it was too closely associated with light comedy and jesting. Today, however, it appears as a supreme example of the orchestral Scherzo as Beethoven created it.

It is to Beethoven more than anyone that we owe musical conception of the giant grotesque, the kind of grim, desperately serious humour which is always hovering around and often breaks openly into the highest dramatic tragedy. It is the outcome of an exceptionally vital creative energy and an imagination so vivid that it comprehends life in its totality—warts, or gargoyles, and all. It is no coincidence that all the great masters of the grotesque have been those whose creative vitality has an essentially eruptive or combustible quality—it is never present in men of fastidiousness of mind and a predilection to live and work within the limitations of good taste and artistic refinement. Shakespeare possessed it to an extraordinary degree; so did Dickens and Balzac; while in music it is almost completely absent from Brahms but often near the surface in Wagner. Among later composers, Elgar, Sibelius, Vaughan Williams, and Richard Strauss—all men of outstanding vitality—have their visions of the grotesque and the fantastic. Verdi was a master of grim and often grotesque humour; so in certain moods was Chopin (who might appear to be the exception to the rule, except that critical attention is usually focused on his least instead of on his most characteristic compositions—in their context the scherzos of Chopin are in the direct line of Beethoven's most savage examples). But it appears not at all in Falla, Ravel, and their like, where an extreme fastidiousness limits and circumscribes the freedom of the creative vitality.

The Scherzo of the Fifth Symphony begins and ends in some mysterious depths. The conflict expressed here is almost more terrifying than in the first movement: it seems to grope upwards from some restless impulse of the unconscious; then bursts forth in an outburst of defiance; goes into the fantastic turmoil of the Trio; and finally sinks back with a ghostly menace to the farthest reaches, where it is only fitfully and spasmodically articulate before at last it is brought under the firm control of the conscious mind, and with a great uprising of the will reaches its enduring solution in the C major chords that usher in the Finale. The transition at the end of the Scherzo is an outstanding example of the human mind imposing itself on chaos. Spiritually and psychologically the victory is conclusive. It can also be seen to be inevitable, given the initial exposition of the conflict in the first movement. No other outcome was possible once the experience had been lived through to the full. But that is not to say that battle had not still to be fought out to the end: it was still necessary to pass through the valley of the shadows that is the Scherzo. There could be no short cut, otherwise the victory would be hollow—a sham, a mere gesture.

The simplicity of the Finale is typical of Beethoven. Most of his greatest triumphs emerge with the utmost clarity and directness. It

F

is a psychological concomitant of enduring victory that all the elements should be resolved and that the end should come without leaving a question mark at the foot of the final paragraph. In other words, the conclusion has to be conclusive. This is the secret of several of Beethoven's endings which have come in for unimaginative censure as being too 'obvious'. The choral ending of *Fidelio* and the Finale of the Ninth Symphony are two examples. It is only if one takes these conclusions at their face value that they can be seen in their right perspective.

In the Fifth Symphony the resolution is perhaps the most conclusive of all. By fighting the battle out in the key of C minor and then breaking away to a triumphant solution in C major Beethoven won victory on his chosen ground. The triumph had to be in C major—any other solution would have been survival by evasion. Not for nothing has Beethoven been called the most psychologically truthful of all musicians.

The victory is won, and in music of ceremonial splendour the creative spirit of Beethoven moves forward to freedom and plenitude. Never again will this particular battle have to be joined: the whole experience with its tragic implications has been accepted, lived through, and assimilated. All the same, it cannot be taken for granted. The master-stroke which brought back the theme of the Scherzo to interrupt the splendid procession makes that abundantly clear. But, like the Finale of the 'Eroica', it is a beginning as well as an end. By conscious effort the victory has to be fertilized and brought to fulfilment or it may yet turn barren.

In his symphonies Beethoven realized his fundamental experience in the open, so to speak. By confiding his ideals, his struggles, and his aspirations to the orchestra, Beethoven entered the common life of the world and spoke out as a man among men. But I do not agree with those who assert that in so doing he deliberately dramatized his experiences and consciously made, as it were, a public spectacle of them. An artist has the whole of his medium open to him: he uses it now in one way, now in another; the categories are not exclusive. A composer of music may turn from symphony to string quartet, from pianoforte sonata to opera, to express different facets of the same basic experience; and frequently one form of expression is complementary to another. If we affirm that the string quartet is a more 'intimate' form than the symphony, we have at the same time to be careful not to drive artificial wedges into the totality of the creative process. While on the one hand it is reasonable to say that the whole of Beethoven is to be found not in the symphonies or the sonatas, but in the series of seventeen string quartets, that does not mean that the quartets render the symphonies or the sonatas superfluous, or that the former are comprehensible without the latter.

With Beethoven the creative process is one and indivisible, although it manifests itself in different forms, not so much at different times or on different levels as from different angles, all of which converge towards a unified centre. If by some caprice of fortune we were obliged to forgo all but one category of Beethoven's compositions, it would inevitably be the string quartets that we should wish to hold fast to; and in so doing we should retain a picture of the mind and spirit of Beethoven, not complete but with gaps less unbridgeable than in any other. It is, therefore, clear that for further illumination of the experience that lies behind the C minor Symphony we must turn to the three string quartets dedicated to Count Rasoumovsky which share the Opus number 59. And as soon as we do so we find conclusive evidence that the kernel of the C minor Symphony is the Scherzo. If the first movement is a dramatic expression of the basic conflict, it is the Scherzo, via the 'Rasoumovsky' Quartets, that exposes the regions of consciousness in which the conflict originates. Although, apart from the Andante, the informing experience of the symphony is completely realized, it is the quartets that put it into final perspective and give us plainly to understand just how profound and fundamental it was.

The period during which the Fifth Symphony was written lies across several of Beethoven's most productive years; and it was during this period—in 1806 to be precise—that the 'Rasoumovsky' Quartets also came into being. Indeed, at this time in Beethoven's life a whole crop of compositions, including the C minor Symphony, the Op. 59 quartets, and the 'Appassionata' Sonata, appear to be centred round this one vital and overwhelming experience. And although other works of the years 1803–7 are in a sense related to it they are only so on a broad and generalized plane. It is inaccurate to suppose that the 'Eroica' and the C minor symphonies are more or less equal projections of the same basic experience; the real relationship is between the Fifth Symphony, the 'Rasoumovsky' Quartets and the

'Appassionata' Sonata, with the 'Eroica' and the B flat symphonies existing both stylistically and spiritually in a different dimension.

The correspondence between the C minor Symphony and the 'Rasoumovsky' Quartets is revealed in many ways. Besides the affirmative conclusions in C major of both, there are in the quartets those elements of giant grotesque and the mysterious gropings upwards from the deepest regions of the mind that are so prominent in the Scherzo of the symphony. If the proposition itself is nowhere stated with the overwhelming force of the symphony's opening bars, that is because the origins of the conflict rather than the conflict itself are being explored.

The spiritual content of the 'Rasoumovsky' Quartets is extraordinarily rich and varied; but it is all of a piece—each individual movement, as well as each quartet, plays its essential part in leading onwards to the consummation of the C major fugue. For these quartets, though three complete and separate works, are in the nature of a single composition. With the six 'Lobkowitz' Quartets of Op. 18 the grouping is largely objective and strategic: Beethoven simply followed established practice in issuing a group of compositions as a single opus, so arranged that they would set each other off to the best advantage, but without any pretence at internal or external relationship beyond that of sharing a common place in the catalogue. But Op. 59 is a different proposition. Here there is no arbitrary grouping, no marriage of convenience—the set is 'through-composed' and internally related. There is also an external connection in the presence of Russian folk-song melody or melody derived from Russian folk-song which Beethoven incorporated into these quartets, either as a gracious compliment to his patron or because Count Rasoumovsky expressly asked for such an inclusion, and Beethoven, sensing no outrage to the independence of his art, agreed and contrived that it should be so. Which way round it chanced to be is of no great consequence; but this accidental linkage is inclined to obscure the more potent and significant internal relationship—the relationship that makes the triumphant fugal conclusion not only the culmination and the crowning glory of a single quartet, but of the entire set.

So far as I know, the American scholar and critic Homer Ulrich was the first to lay bare and expound this inner connection between the three quartets of Op. 59 [1]—others may have dimly apprehended it,

[1] *Chamber Music: the Growth and Practise of an Intimate Art.*

but the majority have been led astray by the linkage of Russian folk-song. However, once one recognizes this internal connection the 'Rasoumovsky' Quartets take on an entirely new perspective in Beethoven's creative life. To see these quartets as three independent compositions which merely happen to share a common opus number, is not only to deny them their proper significance, but to cloud the outlines of the whole of Beethoven's creative activity at this period.

The 'Rasoumovsky' Quartets reveal a continuous line of development from the opening of the F major to the final conclusion of the C major. The F major opens with a broad melody for 'cello, itself derived from a Russian folk-song,[1] which is neither heroic nor assured but hesitant and speculative. It is hinged on the fifth degree of the scale and cannot, despite persistent endeavour, find a positive conclusion. In a musical melody the dominant is more often than not a strong pivot; but here the insistence on the fifth in denial of the tonic, and the initial point of rest which comes on an incomplete six-four chord, serves to produce an effect of indecision and more interrogation than affirmation. For Beethoven this tune, or rather his treatment of it, is markedly unassured—it poses questions and arises from spiritual uncertainties that are only resolved by C major fugue three whole quartets ahead.

In order to comprehend the provenance of this opening theme it is only necessary to place it side by side with the corresponding theme of the 'Archduke' Trio, a subject of basically similar curve and span but which has a serene, masterful assurance lacking from the quartet's exposition. The movement is also another example of Beethoven's reorganization of sonata form. The compression which is so marked a feature of the C minor Symphony shows its hand here in the lack of formal repetition and in the manner in which the recapitulation is both unprepared and passes far beyond mere restatement. If the traditional formal balance is thus disturbed, the intellectual and expressive potency of sonata form is also enormously enlarged. The correspondence with the Fifth Symphony, and the divergence from the predominantly classical outlines of the 'Eroica' and the B flat symphonies, as well as from the earlier 'Lobkowitz' Quartets, is thus immediately established.

The Scherzo, placed second in the ground-plan, is plainly capricious and has much of the giant grotesque and desperate, almost savagely serious, humour of the Trio of the C minor Symphony's Scherzo. The

[1] It appears in Rimsky-Korsakov's collections. Tchaikovsky used it in his Second Piano Concerto.

rumbling of the double basses in the symphony is directly related, both technically and psychologically, to the antics of the 'cello, with its celebrated one-note opening, and the grizzled, spiky rhythms of the movement as a whole. Its earliest performers were naturally outraged, just as many a double-bass player has sworn copiously and sweated profusely over the enormities of grotesque humour demanded of his instrument in the symphony.

The slow movement, by contrast, is a tragic Adagio of the most profound and sombre beauty. Not until the 'Hammerklavier' Sonata did Beethoven again write a movement more deeply tragic and more instinct with the sadness of resignation; and the slow movement of the 'Hammerklavier' occupies a place in Beethoven's third period analogous to that occupied by this F minor Adagio in his second period.

Into the Finale Beethoven introduces one of his Russian themes, marked as such. It leads directly out of the Adagio, and although externally boisterous and energetic, it is full of the undertones of melancholy so characteristic of the Slav races in their elemental songs and dances. It is clear that the questions posed in the opening bars of the first movement have as yet no conclusive answer, no enduring resolution.

The second Quartet, the E minor, is from several points of view an intermediate work. It too begins tentatively—the two abrupt opening chords have small relevance to the peremptory calls to attention that herald the 'Eroica'. This movement has much difficulty in getting under way at all; and when eventually it does, harmonic uncertainties and insecurity of rhythm prevent it from giving any deep sense of purpose and forward-moving confidence. The coda is admittedly more hopeful; but the E major Adagio that follows is more in the nature of a withdrawal to some starry eminence outside the central conflict than a confirmed resolution or extension of it. Commentators have not failed to note the celestial and unearthly atmosphere of this Adagio, which Beethoven once said he conceived while gazing at the sky. If many of the movements of the 'Rasoumovsky' Quartets seem to be drawing the essential experiences up from the deepest recesses of the mind, the E major Adagio appears to be a reversal of the process—a withdrawn, even aloof, contemplation of them from above and without. All three slow movements in these quartets have a particular quality about them; and those of the E minor and C major quartets have a strange elusiveness that sets them outside any other music composed by Beethoven.

The succeeding Allegretto is by turns wistful, moody, and reckless. It is neither broad comedy nor savage humour, and so is less a kind of scherzo than a psychological replacement for a type of movement that has no place in this pensive and largely undemonstrative quartet. The Trio introduces a further Russian melody, ineffably sad and mournful. The Finale, on the other hand, turns towards C major and makes determined gestures on the side of assurance. If this quartet stood alone, the note of triumph in its Finale might sound forced and arbitrary. But three 'Rasoumovskys' stand together and are only comprehensible in relation one to another. And in this light the ending of the E minor appears as a foretaste only of the victorious ending of the next quartet. It is not arbitrary because we are not yet done with the main argument; and it is not forced because what is to follow will make its meaning clear.

So far we have followed Beethoven through two whole quartets without reaching a positive conclusion. The question posed by the opening of the F major led to the tragedy of the same quartet's profound Adagio. But the answer to that tragedy has not yet been revealed. There is still much inquiry, much intense searching of the heart and mind necessary before that tragedy can be, not eliminated—for that in the context is neither possible nor desirable—but fused into the totality of experience.

The C major Quartet begins with a nebulous introduction which leads into the strong and athletic Allegro as from the deepest regions of consciousness. Sturdy and confident is this Allegro—it seems for a moment to justify the uneasy hopes aroused by the Finale of the preceding quartet. But at its close Beethoven returns us to the depths in an extraordinary and unique Andante, so unlike anything else in his music that most commentators have been unable to explain its existence at all. With the poignant sadness of its melodic line and its plunging pizzicato for the 'cello it inhabits a fantastic world all its own, with even a remote touch of the grotesque in some far-off way derived from the grotesqueries of the scherzos. 'What it is doing in this quartet', says Sullivan, 'we cannot imagine.' And yet, with a little inquiry, we can, so I believe, discover its relevance and justify it in its context.

The minuet emerges slowly from the depths plumbed by the Andante. It too is nebulous, unemphatic, unassertive. And here the 'fate' rhythmic figure makes its first appearance in these quartets—not dramatically and challenging, but with a quiet insistence, in the Trio. As in the C minor Symphony there is a sense of expectancy—a pregnant calm before the dawn. When it comes it is a huge, irresistible, all-conquering fugue whose supremely confident tones sweep aside all previous doubts and hesitancies, all insecurities of rhythm, infirmities of harmony, and uncertainties of melody. It was over the sketches for this movement that Beethoven scribbled the words—'Make no secret of your deafness, not even in art.' The outward sign of an inner victory.

Beethoven, then, tackled the fundamental problem at the centre and achieved victory over it in two different but interrelated ways in C major. Psychologically there is a difference between the two victories or conquests, because in the Fifth Symphony victory in C major grew out of dramatic conflict in C minor; while in the 'Rasoumovsky' Quartets victory, also in C major, was evolved over a long span out of preliminary doubt and speculation in F major and tragedy in F minor. By a reversal process the tragedy in F minor arose from the postulates of original inquiry in F major. It was subsequently necessary to work via a series of spiritual and psychological as well as tonal modulations to C major. None the less, the same 'root' experience lies behind the quartets and the symphony.

In relation to the Fifth Symphony Beethoven intimated that the core of the experience was the conflict between freedom and necessity. The knocking at the door was to be seen as the challenge of determinism and objectivity to the free activity. But in order to get to the heart of creative freedom it is essential to probe into depths of the mind and personality far below the levels of normal consciousness. The problem cannot be intellectualized and reduced to a series of propositions. It has to be fully experienced from the inside; and furthermore, the experience, whatever it be and however hard the road along which it leads, has to be accepted in full and realized in its totality. It is only thus that the spirit of affirmation can defeat the spirit of denial. At the same time, experiencing by itself is not enough—only through the application of positive activity to experience can freedom be achieved and the latent powers of personality realized.

Beethoven was true to his experience, whatever it was: he accepted tragedy as the price of freedom because to do otherwise would have been to deny his integrity as man and artist. Not every one who is capable of profound experience has at the same time the courage, the power of will, and the positive capability to remain true to that experience. But Beethoven knew from the beginning that only by remaining continually true to his experience could he fulfil himself.

A mind like Beethoven's, in which the capacity for experience is the driving force, is by definition more 'open' than others. That is to say, it is more sensitive and more receptive to experience at various levels and in various directions; and for that sensitivity and that receptivity to become operative in conscious activity it has to possess both the will and the ability to explore profound regions of the unconscious— to release into the level of consciousness impulses and experiences normally kept hidden beneath the surface and blind in respect of their impact on conscious activity. Modern psychology has revealed the existence of not only the unconscious itself, but also many different layers of unconsciousness, unknown both to themselves and to us.[1] Different minds, however, vary in their degrees of un- or sub-consciousness and in the number and extent of these layers which they can uncover and release into positive activity. A shallow mind is one which is activated only by a restricted layer of consciousness. Like an iceberg, the largest part of the mind lies submerged, and although the underwater part conditions the activity of the upper part, it does so without conscious direction and control. But it remains possible to explore downwards and so to enlarge the area of consciousness. Indeed, the capacity for experiencing and realizing experience itself postulates an enlargement of the area of conscious activity—of a substantial transference from the unconscious to the conscious mind.

There is no doubt that those individuals—poets, mystics, philosophers, saints—who appear to have revealed to us new regions of experience, or who seem to possess an unusually acute insight into the human mind and its motives and capabilities, have in the first place made this extension and transference. The experience or perception itself does not actually lie in the unconscious—for spiritual experience and penetration presuppose the existence of experience outside and independent of mind as such—but the capacity for significant experience and realization is dependent on a preliminary exploration of the deeper strata of consciousness. Vague and amorphous sensation related to genuine experience is possible to undeveloped minds; but not the

[1] *See* Freud's essay, 'The Unconscious', in the Standard Edition of *The Complete Psychological Works*, vol. xiv.

direct organization and realization of experience. The mind as active subject, no less than personality itself, is a task to be achieved by persistent endeavour.

That the mind of Beethoven, Shakespeare, Dante, Goethe, Plato, was each in its own way more 'open', more highly developed, more comprehensive than the average mind, is not a matter of dispute. One has to say 'in its own way' because these and other minds were in no sense alike and did not give rise to similar activity or reveal similar experience. The minds of Beethoven and Shakespeare may be regarded as most alike only because they appear as the most comprehensive. They seem to have probed deepest of all, to have released more essential energy, not on a single plane, but in many and various directions. The sense that we get from Shakespeare's poetry of a complete picture of life in all its rich and various manifestations can legitimately be paralleled in Beethoven's music. The degree of comprehensiveness and penetration appears remarkably similar. We have too meagre a record of Shakespeare's daily life to know much more than we can logically deduce about his actual creative processes. And in any case, because Shakespeare was Shakespeare and not Beethoven, we need not expect their respective processes to have been substantially alike. On the face of it, it looks as though Shakespeare was a more unconscious genius than Beethoven, less aware of his creative powers, and less aware of the path he trod. But here again the two men lived in very different ages and emerged against very different backcloths. What matters is the impression we retain that through both artists the full, unadulterated life-forces spoke with unique power and eloquence.

Beethoven's continual efforts to realize and organize his experience led him into far and complex regions. We have to remember that a completed work of art is a form of after-expression—it represents the basic experience after it has been assimilated in the mind and finally organized and realized by conscious activity. But there remains the beginning of the process, the first stirrings before the conscious mind starts its work.

There are one or two movements, or sections of movements, in Beethoven—the Introductions to the Fourth Symphony and to the third of the 'Rasoumovsky' Quartets, the ending of the Scherzo of the Fifth Symphony, are obvious examples—which seem to hover near the brink of chaos, and which in fact appear to express stirrings in the deepest regions of the mind. They sometimes seem difficult to fit into their contexts. But if one accepts the unusual depth and breadth of Beethoven's mind and the way in which he constantly went to the root of experience they immediately become more comprehensible.

Although it is impossible to arrive at a satisfactory definition of these elemental stirrings, it seems reasonable to suppose that they represent the roots of the experience at their farthest point from full consciousness. These strange, nebulous, groping passages give one the impression of a slow uncovering of the unconscious. Only the most highly developed minds can descend to these regions without toppling over the verge into incoherence. Much over-ambitious and imperfectly realized art does just that. But because in everything he composed Beethoven revealed an extraordinary capacity for realization we can accept these passages as a form of pre-conscious grappling with the root experience.

In the Scherzo of the Fifth Symphony there takes place a process that is practically unique. The whole movement is concerned with a most profound and intense aspect of experience. It begins with mysterious upward gropings, and although it brings matters to a head almost at once it never seems to come entirely to the surface. Its energy is throughout mysterious and confined to the shadows. Even the grotesqueries of the double basses seem related to dark forces in the unconscious. And towards the end it sinks deeper and deeper, to hover on the verge of articulation, as though the mind only just retained hold on the experience. But Beethoven does maintain hold, down and down into darker and darker layers, until only the croakings of a bassoon and the muttering of strings over a handful of notes remain. The transition also starts in the depths, but it soon begins to take a hold on rhythmic security, even if harmony is more nebulous than ever. But eventually harmony is clarified and melody returns, and with a gathering upward motion leads to the assertion of the Finale fortified by trombones as the mind answers its challenge and emerges into full consciousness.

In the 'Rasoumovksy' Quartets the emergence is not less convincing; but the road to it is longer and more complex. It is suggested but not achieved in the Finale of the E minor; and after a transition from darkness into light in the shifting introduction, it seems to be very near, if not actually reached, in the confident rhythms of the C major Allegro. But then there is a check, not a return to the old terrain, but a shifting to a new and unfamiliar region in the Andante. When an artist produces something apparently out of style and out of character, as this Andante is thought to be, there can be two possible explanations. Either it is a conscious experiment in technique, an attempt to organize material in another and unusual manner; or it represents the realization of an experience outside the regions normally associated with that particular mind. It seems to me that the latter is what has happened here. Beethoven, before finding his victory, has another realm to explore.

That this Andante stands outside the rest of the quartets, and outside any other music composed by Beethoven, is because here he found in the depths of his experience one further stone left unturned. And it was a stone obviously near to the regions of the unconscious. But where?—in what recesses of the mind did this strange, dark-hued, infinitely sad music originate? There is a tradition, supported by Marion Scott, that here is the Russian element which otherwise seems to be lacking from this quartet, in distinction from the other two. Though the actual folk-song, if any, used by Beethoven remains unidentified, the whole movement has a deeply tinged melancholy, a soulful turn of phrase, and a profound elemental sadness generally associated with the Slav temperament.[1]

The consciousness of Russia stands some way outside the consciousness of western Europe. It is strikingly apart from the consciousness of France, of Germany, of Italy, of Spain, or of the northern lands. Now Beethoven, either on his own initiative or in deference to the wishes of Count Rasoumovsky, was intent on working Russian elements into these quartets. They are easily recognizable in the other two. But here Beethoven is approaching the end of his interrelated triptych. May it not be that, with the breadth and depth of his sympathies and his profound natural insight, the influence of the Russian consciousness had seeped deeper into his mind than he originally intended or recognized? There would be much in the Russian outlook that would make a direct appeal to him—the awareness of suffering, the feeling for human community, the resentment of uniformity and regimentation, and the respect for the dignity of personality in conflict with individualism and collectivism alike. These are characteristics of the age-old Russian consciousness, whatever temporary political aberrations may have made of them. And they lay at the heart of Beethoven's own conviction and experience. That he, a man deeply sensitive to human

---

[1] The key to its origin in the completed sequence is probably to be found in the opening of the first quartet.

feeling and aspiration, was aware of them, if only dimly, would not be surprising. And the original conception of the quartets probably turned his mind towards Russia, and so introduced an element as strange as this Andante.

Perhaps after all the Russian element affords a closer and more significant relationship between these three quartets than is at first apparent. Perhaps through an association of ideas what began from the outside became near the end an internal tie in imaginative sympathy with and understanding of all humanity. And if it was some almost mystical feeling for the essence of the Russian consciousness which inspired the C major Quartet's Andante, then the realization of that aspect of experience would inevitably draw from Beethoven music unlike any he had composed elsewhere and in answer to other and more 'normal' experience. It is also arguable that the Russian consciousness lies lower beneath the surface than is customary with western civilizations—which would account for the impression this movement gives of existing deep in the complex regions of the mind and in some way isolated from the other and more familiar strata.

That the triumphant culmination of both the 'Rasoumovsky' Quartets and the C minor Symphony is joyous and exultant is because it is complete and arrived at through freedom. It is not an enforced victory; it is the triumph of fulfilment in free creativity.

The third 'Rasoumovksy' Quartet has sometimes been called the 'Hero' Quartet. The name is a misnomer, even more than most. If this quartet has to have a distinguishing label, its name should be 'Affirmation', just as the Fifth Symphony should be known as the 'Affirmation'. For that is the real meaning of the conflict and of the victory. Acceptance and affirmation—therein lies the vindication of the human mind and the human spirit, not only in adversity, but in the face of all experience and all perception. 'On the roaring billows of Time, thou art not engulphed, but borne aloft into the azure of Eternity. Love not Pleasure; love God. This is the EVERLASTING YEA, wherein all contradiction is solved; wherein whoso walks and works, it is well with him.'

5

The Call to Creativeness

HAZLITT WAS of the opinion that no really great man ever thought himself so: and the old question of whether or not genius is conscious of its powers is by no means satisfactorily answered. To argue that artists tend to misjudge their own productions is to talk aside from the point, because such judgments are too often entangled with personal difficulties. A man is often tempted to set the highest value on a work that has caused him great difficulty or obliged him to go into heavy labour in the accomplishment of it. All the same, a man who mistakenly overvalues a portion of his output may well have a pretty accurate idea of his general capabilities—an honest man, that is, one not puffed out with self-importance. There are plenty of noisy but essentially minor people who imagine themselves lords of the earth and the greatest yet cast up on the busy shores of history. But they are invariably alone in that opinion: it is not to inflated insignificance that we have to look for illumination and the clear radiance of truth. It is possible—though it by no means goes without saying—that the truly great man is always conscious of his powers and is confident in the knowledge that posterity will prove him correct. Indeed it might be more readily stated, and defended, that *only* the great man ever really thought himself so. When the highest order of genius takes hold it is not likely to be mistaken for the activity of common day-work. Even if, as Hazlitt argues and as we have already observed in these pages, genius acts to a great extent unconsciously and unostentatiously and is only to a limited degree dependent on volition, it is still likely to be recognized as such. When the true fire burns brightly it generates an authentic heat not easily passed over and mistaken for mere galvanic radiation.

However we may be disposed to answer the general proposition—

and there is room for argument and ample evidence either way if one chooses so to arrange it—it is clear that from his earliest days Beethoven had a vivid and accurate idea of his own powers. It is not only his cryptic words on the subject uttered from time to time throughout his life—to Zmeskall, 'Power is the morality of men who stand out from the rest . . .'; to a friend concerning a ring sent by Frederick William of Prussia, 'I too am a king'; to Bettina, remarks about kings and princes being able to create professors, privy councillors, and the like, but not great men, i.e. Goethes and Beethovens—it is not, as I say, only such remarks that illustrate Beethoven's consciousness of his genius, but even more his music itself. Only a man supreme in the awareness of his own powers could have exulted in them so openly and with such evident relish as Beethoven did in many a composition of the latter part of his second period. To look down the list of works of the crowning years of that period is to know at once that the man who composed them had no doubt of the road he was travelling or of the power lodged in him by Providence and brought to fulfilment by his own efforts.

It was the sure knowledge of that power that sustained Beethoven in the darkest moments of his life. In the Heiligenstadt Testament he had written, 'I would have put an end to my life, only art it was that withheld me . . .'—and it was not art as escape which withheld him, but the consciousness that he had urgent things to do, that he was born to greatness which transcended personal suffering and tragedy. If he had not been fortified by awareness of the demands of his genius he could never have lived to fight it out to the bitter end and to pit himself against an evil destiny with matchless courage and tenacity. It was because the power lodged in him had sustained his heaviest hours that in due time he came to exult in it with an unbounded joy and a Jovian omnipotence.

The nature of the difference between man and the animals—the inmost difference in kind, not merely in degree—is a subject that has troubled the inquiring human mind in most ages, and in none more than the present with its lack of a central faith and its uncertainty in the face of scientific developments, frequently destructive. The scientists, philosophers, and psychologists have advanced their theories and elucidated their propositions. But the doubts remain, not least in minds unable to accept without question a ready-made traditional answer. Man stands apart from the animals by dint of his possession of the power of reason; on account of an indigenous sense of humour; by reason of a moral or ethical sense, or a deeper complexity of ideal; by possession of this or that particular faculty—all sorts and kinds of argument have been put forward and earnestly debated. But none of them goes to the heart of the matter, and most are either of doubtful validity or from one point of view or another simply inadequate. Man certainly has both the power of reason and a sense of humour; but it cannot be definitely asserted and proved that at least some animals entirely lack the one or the other. The existence of a moral or ethical sense and a complexity of the ideal is certainly particular to man; but again, in neither case is the thesis sufficient. A moral and ethical sense and a complexity of the ideal do not exist by themselves and in isolation—they are symptomatic of something deeper and more differentiating. We have already taken note of Kant's insistence on the supranatural origin of ethics and on the emergence of ethics out of freedom. It is freedom not ethics which is paramount—the existence of an ethical sense postulates the basic fact of freedom. And freedom is at the core of personality.

Man has been variously called a political animal, a social animal, an economic animal—all categories more or less true, but superficial because materialistic and objective. In the end the old definition is probably the most completely satisfactory—Man is a being who bears within him the Image of God. And surely to say as much—that God created man in His own Image—means simply that the distinction between man and the animals lies in the possession by man of the power of free creativity. The image lies in the creative power. God the Creator gave to man an innate faculty of freedom and creativeness. From this all other distinctions arise. Because man is a creator who must in the end take on himself the burden of freedom, he can and must create new forms. He acts not simply as a member of the herd and according to rule and instinct, but as a freely motivated being and a unique, irreplaceable personality. Man is at bottom free to turn either to God or devil, to accept or renounce, to soar to the heights or sink to the depths—and therein lies his limitless potentiality. That is why man can range himself on the side of the angels or plumb depths of depravity and degradation. Man can elevate himself to within clear sight of God, or descend to a bottomless pit uninhabited by any animal. Creativity arises out of freedom and cannot exist without it. If man were not equally free to sink he could not soar. He can accept or reject the challenge of freedom; but only by voluntary acceptance of it can he fulfil his destiny.

Freedom of the creative spirit—the ability to achieve oneness with God the Creator—is the central message of Christianity, transcending and illuminating all others. As Dostoevsky clearly perceived, Christ lay the intolerable burden of freedom on men and thereby showed no pity towards them. There is no burden as pitiless as freedom—freedom spiritual, ethical, and creative. And man alone can accept that burden and carry it into a far country, out of the range of materialism and objectivity. If we do not believe in the ultimate reality of freedom we are less than the animals, haunted by perceptions without conceptions, and obliged to go all the days of our lives blindly down a road which leads we know not where.

As the first decade of the nineteenth century drew on, Beethoven felt that he had accepted the tragedy of freedom to the full and had triumphed over it. He could feel that he had faced his destiny and become its master. And he had every reason for that feeling. He had emerged from the crisis symbolized by the Heiligenstadt Testament; he had found himself as a man and was well on the way to fulfilling himself as an artist. In the Third, Fourth, and Fifth symphonies, the 'Rasoumovsky' Quartets, and a number of other compositions, he had faced the deepest problems of his spiritual life and brought them to apparently enduring solution. He was free now to create new works from the point of vantage won by his own earlier struggles. He was essentially a man who had come through, and so could give free rein to his creative powers. He had in fact freed his art from the forces of denial which had once sought not only to circumscribe but actually to destroy them. He could think that he had gone to the heart of the mystery of this life. He had good and just cause to think of himself as a king among men; not in a spirit of boastful vanity, but of one conscious of his own capability and ready to put it at the service of the universal spirit of the call to creativity.

No man who had not a truly godlike consciousness of, and confidence in, his powers could have produced the compositions that Beethoven gave to the world in the second half of his middle period. Especially is this true of the Seventh and Eighth symphonies, the 'Emperor' Concerto, and the 'Archduke' Trio—all works of spacious and confident power and a truly Olympian grandeur. But hardly less remarkable is the quality of some of the smaller pieces of this time—

G

the A major 'Cello Sonata, the F sharp major, E flat major (known as 'Les Adieux') and E minor Piano Sonatas, and the G major Violin Sonata, all of which have a sureness of touch, a quality of lyrical expressiveness without aggression, and an inner serenity that could only come from the sense of absolute certainty of a man who could bring great creative powers to a comparatively small task without overwhelming it.

It is true, of course, that these qualities are present in many of Beethoven's compositions of the preceding years; but now there is a more equable flow, a freer flexing of the muscles, a more perfect integration of the conflicting elements in the creative process in works both large and small. There was already a foreshadowing of that quality which Beethoven in the middle of his third period was to call 'less lack of fancy'.

Beethoven was not at this time the morose, embittered figure he is often painted. On the contrary, he was as happy and as serenely self-confident as at any time in his life. He was reasonably affluent (most of the time); his health, though never good, seldom gave cause for alarm; he was famous and widely honoured. With the blight of his deafness he had come to terms; and his creative powers had never been more active and fruitful. True, suffering had left its mark on him, and the inner loneliness that is the inevitable portion of all sensitive and greatly inquiring spirits in the midst of this world's society was deeply ingrained in his consciousness. But at no time was he more confident in his own powers or more aware of his mastery over an inescapable destiny. The uncertainty of temper and prickly surface of the man that could so discomfit friends and associates was partly the result of an inborn bias of nature and partly a legacy of the buffeting he had received at the hands of the gods that sport with men. The near despair of the earlier years when Beethoven had been obliged to carve a living out of adversity was gone—he could think now that the battle was over and that he would live on to enjoy the fruits of victory. Because he had come by way of the hardest road to the final (as he thought) acceptance of his destiny, he could, despite continuing personal difficulties and frequent material frustrations, look into the future with cheerfulness and elation. It seemed that his sufferings had served to free him from the misery of the world. He wasn't to know, yet, that the bitterest pill and the sharpest irony were still to come, although there are passages even in his most resplendent compositions which sound ominous warnings that the devils were not entirely overwhelmed—that they could still stir and threaten, quiescent though they were for the time being.

Beethoven has left us a vivid picture of himself as he was during the period that lay roughly between the years 1807 and 1812. In the Eighth Symphony Beethoven the man stands revealed before us in the plenitude of his powers. I believe this small sonata for orchestra to be a self-portrait of Beethoven as deliberate and as accurate as the self-portraits of Rembrandt and Cézanne. I see the essential physiognomy of Beethoven more clearly in the Eighth Symphony than in any other composition. All the basic qualities and ingredients are there—boisterous humour and explosive vitality; robust strength mingled with great tenderness; lissom energy and a matchless assurance of the worthwhileness of living and working. It is Beethoven himself in pure autobiography; or, as Disraeli put it, it is 'life without theory'. Only a man who had arrived at complete self-knowledge could thus have matched the gods in side-splitting laughter, as Beethoven does in the prodigiously impertinent Finale, especially when that laughter was born out of a subjective conflict that had once threatened destruction.

There is too another self-portrait of this period—one from the other side, so to speak—in the String Quartet in F minor, Op. 95. Beethoven himself called this terse and rugged composition 'Quartetto serioso', and a more passionately serious piece of music it would be hard to find. Mendelssohn considered it to be the most characteristic music Beethoven ever wrote, and there is much truth in the assessment. If the Eighth Symphony is from one angle a picture of Beethoven as he appeared to the everyday world in which he lived and worked, a portrait to hang for ever in the gallery of history, the F minor Quartet is a self-portrait from the inside, a depiction of Beethoven's inmost mind and spirit in his private hours. Both are essential to our understanding, and they are to a great extent complementary. They could only have come from the same period of Beethoven's life; they had to be written more or less side by side, and only in relation to each other can they be finally understood. If it is the physiognomy of Beethoven that emerges in the symphony, it is the mind of Beethoven that stands revealed in the quartet—a mind that had endured much and achieved more, and which, because of it, could now contemplate the varied panoply of human life with assurance and enduring comprehension.

The lines of suffering are etched deep into the four movements of the F minor Quartet. But it is not music of anguish or conflict, and it does not strike the note of aggressive assertiveness so familiar in the works of the earlier years of the decade. It is at bottom the music of fulfilment through suffering. Just as the 'Rasoumovsky' Quartets give us insight into the nature and workings of Beethoven's creative processes at a certain period, so the F minor gives us a similar insight at a later date. In both Op. 59 and Op. 95 Beethoven is concerned with the heart and core of his creative activity; in both his genius is revealed working upwards from the formative sources.

There is a compelling unity about all Beethoven's music. Just as the 'Rasoumovsky' Quartets showed direct points of similarity, both spiritual and technical, with the Fifth Symphony, so now the F minor Quartet reveals an equally direct relationship to the Eighth Symphony. The quartet has none of the symphony's bubbling humour; but it tells of the same inner tenderness, the same energy and vitality, a similar order of assured strength and sturdiness. And at the very end of the quartet there suddenly bursts forth what is in effect another aspect of the Olympian laughter of the symphony's Finale—in the spanking coda which so shocked Vincent d'Indy.

The seriousness of the F minor Quartet is entirely characteristic of Beethoven. Despite his natural joviality and inborn cheerfulness, he was at bottom a deeply serious man whose laughter was never a giggle and whose optimism had in it no element of shallowness. He was one who habitually thought and felt with the utmost profundity and who looked so far into the eternal mysteries of this life that he could speak of them in terms often jocular and light-hearted without risk of blasphemy. It is a quality of the highest order of genius that it can, and frequently does, use humour and a sort of divine laughter in a context entirely apart from diversion and entertainment. The good humour and roistering high spirits of the Eighth Symphony could only have arisen from the basis of a profound seriousness. The discomfiting rough-handedness of Beethoven's humorous ejaculations (of which this symphony is the high watermark) is another facet of his inexhaustible vitality and gusto, and in painting his musical portrait it was only to be expected that his most fertile energies should express themselves as ripe and mature comedy.

The Eighth Symphony was a particular favourite of Beethoven's; it was in a very special sense his own living image. He expressed irritation at those who took an indifferent view of it, snapping roughly,

'That is because it is so much better!' One could be rude about the 'Eroica', or the C minor, or the Seventh, almost with impunity, and Beethoven could answer philosophically that no doubt illumination would come one day. But to be rude about the Eighth was to insult Beethoven himself—openly and to his face—and that no man did without risk of summary expulsion from the irate master's presence.

Two large-scale compositions which bear witness to Beethoven's Jovian self-confidence and assurance at this period are the 'Emperor' Concerto and the 'Archduke' Trio. The concerto has been fittingly described as the embodiment of physical and spiritual well-being. The first movement is one of the most masterful creations of Beethoven's second period. It is music of boundless confidence and omnipotent energy—swift, strong, commanding. In the construction of this militantly self-confident Allegro, not less than in its spirit, Beethoven shows his full power. The piano is not merely given the first word— as in the G major Concerto—but immediately integrated with the orchestra in a manner that leaves Beethoven subsequently free to exploit the varied resources of either at will. And by the virtual abolition of the customary cadenza, he announced that no longer had he any interest in, nor would tolerate, the fanfaronades of the virtuosi. The tautness, the masculine strength and assurance of the 'Emperor' left no room for interpolated displays of dexterity, no matter how richly equipped the soloist might be, even though Beethoven gives him plenty to be going on with. The preamble in itself strikes a note of authority not to be mistaken by the most inattentive listener. Schauffler notes an internal affinity of the motive of the principal subject with the germ-motive of the 'Eroica', also in E flat. It might well be that in a straight line of development, the great works promised by the creative vitality of the 'Eroica's' Finale came to fulfilment in terms of second-period activity in the 'Emperor' Concerto.

The ineffable loveliness and radiant calm of the Adagio un poco messo confirms the impression given by the first movement of great creative power employed unassertively; while the final Rondo exults greatly and admirably counterbalances the Allegro by showing that a release of that movement's superbly controlled energy leads not to a sort of blind chaos and destructive violence but to the joyous abandon of a man who knows his own strength and is not afraid to exercise it freely in any and every direction.

These qualities are even more evident in the B flat Trio, Op. 97, the

'Archduke'. The calm, undemonstrative sweep of the first movement shows how far Beethoven had travelled in self-knowledge and awareness of his capabilities. We have previously noted the contrast between the principal subjects of the first 'Rasoumovsky' Quartet and the 'Archduke' Trio. At the time when the latter was composed Beethoven no longer felt it necessary either to ask himself metaphysical questions or to throw the whole of himself violently against his fate.

The process is continued in the Scherzo. There is no need here for the grim, savage grotesqueries of the scherzos of the C minor Symphony and the F major Quartet. The cloud that passes over the Trio is simply another example of the meaningful seriousness so characteristic of Beethoven's humorous movements. For the rest, it is only necessary to observe that once again this Scherzo reveals the scope of Beethoven's emergence from his previous struggles. Its fluent humour, its easy spontaneity, its rhythmic virility and melodic sensitivity is a world away from the spiky, angular rhythms, the grim humour and savage passion of the first 'Rasoumovsky' Scherzo. The fact that the 'cello is principally engaged in both helps to emphasize the contrast.

The slow movement is a set of variations on a theme that is generally, and rightly, thought to be the supreme example of Beethoven's mystical insight in his middle period. I do not, however, agree that it represents a foretaste of the mysticism of the third period. Spiritually it is a recognizable extension of the creative process that began more or less with the 'Eroica' Symphony. It is the ultimate extension of the second period rather than the beginnings of the third. True, as in the F minor Quartet, certain technical and stylistic features point to the coming change; but its spiritual quality grew out of the conflicts and tragedies of the C minor Symphony and the 'Rasoumovsky' Quartets, whereas the spiritual qualities of the third period grew out of the overwhelming tragic conflict represented by the 'Hammerklavier' Sonata. There is a profound and determining difference between the two.

The Rondo Finale of the 'Archduke' is another of Beethoven's sudden and joyous explosions of creative energy. To some listeners it seems like a wilful slap in the face after the exalted serenity of the variations. It is, however, difficult to follow that argument without deliberately calling into question one of Beethoven's most typical qualities—that is, his lifelong ability to see things from two sides. Of all composers none exceeded Beethoven in the capacity for exploring the farthest reaches of the spiritual world while at the same time keeping his feet firmly on the ground. He was the least vaporous and insubstantial of spiritual explorers. His sudden returns to earth after limitless flights of the spirit and the imagination were deliberate and intentional. Thus did he maintain contact with reality on two planes at one and the same time. It is not an easy matter to explain lucidly; but it is fundamental to Beethoven's art. It might be called a conscious intention to render unto Caesar the things which are Caesar's, and unto God the things which are God's.[1] We do well to remember that it is generally recognized that there are things legitimately Caesar's, and that to him they should be freely and properly rendered. We do no sort of service to the creative spirit by pretending that nowhere has it legitimate contact with common earth and the workaday world.

Peace, power, and plenty. At no time in Beethoven's life do these words seem more applicable than between 1807 and 1812. The power that lies behind the 'Archduke' Trio and the 'Emperor' Concerto arises out of a still centre of calm repose—indeed, the two compositions and their smaller companions are based on great strength reposefully deployed, in contradistinction to some earlier works where the power is essentially aggressive, thrown out desperately and for its own sake. The definition might be carried in the direction of an increase in purely artistic maturity, as Beethoven himself intimated when contrasting his earlier with his later music. But that does not go all the way. The situation is as much psychological as musical. At this time Beethoven no longer felt it necessary to assert his power, to challenge the fates openly and with intent to demolish. He had already accomplished that; and having put the forces of destiny, as at the time he himself understood them, to rout, his music gained in serenity what it lost in aggressiveness.

I have used, in discussing the provenance of the Fourth Symphony, the words 'purity' and 'chastity' considered as terms having relevance to Beethoven's music. It is necessary to refer to them again now. All power, according to the celebrated dictum of Lord Acton, corrupts; but Beethoven was one of the very few individuals known to history who possessed great power, and was fully aware that he possessed it, and yet remained uncorrupted by it. It is in this sense that we can legitimately talk of the 'purity' and 'chastity' of his creative faculty. He outgrew the assertiveness of his younger years, and developed a

---

[1] Or, to be less equivocal, to render unto earth the things which are earth's, and unto Heaven the things which are Heaven's.

firm, unruffled sense of self-fulfilment, an ironical humour, and a power that was all the more potent for being held partially in reserve. This is the psychological background of the artistic maturity of the music of the period we are now discussing. T. S. Eliot wrote, in *Little Gidding*:

> And all shall be well and
> All manner of thing shall be well
> By the purification of the motive
> In the ground of our beseeching.

'The purification of the motive'—the robust strength and sense of well-being that characterize much of the music of the last years of Beethoven's second period were arrived at through a process of self-conquest through purification. By purifying the motive of his creative living; by expurgating enmity, aggressiveness, and hostility to the demands of fate, Beethoven had, in fact, achieved a state in which 'all manner of thing' was well, according to the dimension and the terms of reference in which he, for the time being, lived and worked.

The peace of mind expressed in the 'Archduke' Trio, above all in the Andante, is the direct outcome of a sure knowledge of great vital power and the plenitude of its application. All the same it would be dangerous to assume out of hand that this peace of mind and serenity of spirit were of the same order as those which Goethe derived from Spinoza, or which Milton indicated as 'calm of mind, all passion spent'. With Beethoven passion never was 'spent', not even in the third period, where it was transfigured but in no way banished or burnt out. The quotation which may be taken as summing up the heart of the Miltonic attitude, 'They also serve who only stand and wait', could never have been sought and desired as self-illuminating by the deaf Beethoven as they spiritually were by blind Milton. With Beethoven, passion, like strength, could often lie in a state of repose; but never was it brought to an end and no longer operative in the creative life.

Goethe rose to a noble and wise serenity in old age. But Goethe's latter-life wisdom was based on a passive and determinist nature-philosophy derived from Spinoza; and Spinoza, great philosopher that he was, lies outside the direct line that led to Beethoven's active and positive ethic and metaphysic. In music the philosophic spirit of Spinoza runs directly to Bach.

'The wise man,' wrote Spinoza at the conclusion of his greatest work, *Ethics*, 'in so far as he is regarded as such, is scarcely at all disturbed in spirit, but being conscious of himself, and of God, and of things, by a certain eternal necessity, never ceases to be, but always possesses true acquiescence of his spirit.'

It seems to me that such an ethical attitude might be applied very accurately to Bach but hardly at all to Beethoven. There are of course many who admire and prefer that outlook to the more vehement and challenging spirit of Beethoven. Even in the great period of his achievement and sure self-confidence the spirit of Beethoven never ceased to seek and explore, or to challenge the powers of determinism and objectivization. The difference is that between passivism and activism. Spinoza, and by implication those who come into what may loosely be called the Spinozian orbit, deny that the purpose of human life lies in action, but hold that it is rather to be found in the seeking of an ever clearer comprehension of man's place in the universe and in his eventual sinking of himself spiritually in it. It is thus that the wise man of Spinoza's philosophy comes to possess the 'true acquiescence of his spirit' in a 'certain eternal necessity'.

I do not think it will be denied that this ethic of acquiescence in the universal spirit lies directly at the heart of the consciousness of Bach, who attained to great intellectual and spiritual serenity through a voluntary self-abnegation and a profound awareness of the immanence of God. One feels in Bach's most characteristic music, notably in the Cantatas and Chorale Preludes, a sense of fulfilment by way of acquiescence in the will of God. The same is true of Goethe in his old age. After the romantic *Sturm und Drang* of his early life, Goethe found, through the philosophy of Spinoza, great calmness of mind and spirit. Both Spinoza and Goethe sought, and found, wisdom and the higher understanding through a philosophy of pantheistic monism— a philosophy which leads inevitably to passivism and a denial of a self-determined will to activity.

It is clear, however, that such an attitude and such a philosophy throws very little light on Beethoven. Although there is in Beethoven during the middle years of his second period an almost pantheistic reverence for Nature, and no small evidence that he believed passionately in the immanence of God, his life and work were based throughout on the power of positive activity. The note of resignation and acquiescence which appears from time to time in Beethoven's music was the outcome not of an abandonment of self-determined activity but of the acceptance of it through the voluntary taking up of the burden of freedom. The references to 'submission' in his notebooks are indications not of an acquiescence in the demands of an external omnipotent force, but in the tragic demands of creativity. Goethe himself understood this clearly when he called Beethoven, regretfully, 'an utterly untamed personality'. Beethoven was essentially a daemonic nature, as Goethe clearly perceived, although he knew that that quality was not present in himself in later life. Goethe actually refers, in a letter to Bettina Brentano,[1] to Beethoven as 'one possessed of such a daemon, and it is all the same whether he speaks from feeling or from knowledge, for here the gods are at work and scatter the seeds for future discernment, and we must wish that they may proceed to an undisturbed development'. And again, from the same letter, 'his genius lights the way for him and often illumines him with a lightning stroke, while we sit in darkness and scarcely suspect from which side day will break'.

No one familiar with Beethoven's music will misunderstand Goethe's reference to the lightning strokes of his genius. Like Prometheus himself, Beethoven had wrested fire from the gods and would not return it, but used it with ever more powerful effect and purity of motive. 'The Daemonic', Goethe said to Eckermann, 'manifests itself in a thoroughly active power.' Here is not only the contrast between the two outstanding, and in a sense complementary, men of the age, but also the essential insight into the nature of Beethoven's creative processes.

We can legitimately speak of 'serenity' as a quality typical of the Beethoven of the 'Archduke' Trio, of Spinoza and the ageing Goethe, and of Bach, at one and the same time. Serenity is not necessarily of one kind only, stemming from the same spiritual standpoint. Nor need we assume, when we say that both Beethoven and Goethe attained to the highest wisdom through an unusual capacity for experiencing the fundamental life forces, that we mean something identical in each case. To recapitulate the substance of the argument in a few words, we may say that the serenity of Beethoven at the end of his second period arose out of a fierce and finally triumphant challenge to and struggle with the fates, whereas Goethe's was the result of a wise and greatly comprehending acquiescence in them. Both lived and experienced greatly and to the full; but it is obvious that Goethe's acquiescence was likely to

[1] *See* Appendix.

prove more enduring, if less arduous, than Beethoven's positive activity, as in fact proved to be the case. 'My good friend,' said Goethe, once more to Eckermann, 'what do we know of the idea of the Divine? and what can our narrow ideas tell of the Highest Being?' It was, in the end, the fate of Beethoven, driven ever onwards by the daemonic force of his genius, that he was compelled to accept the burden of finding a positive answer to those questions, whereas Goethe was content to leave them in the realm of speculation.

We can most readily throw light on the problem by going back to the myths and rituals of the ancient world—to the opposing principles of Dionysus and Apollo. These two principles have continued right down the centuries of the life of man, and in various transformations remain operative today. Broadly speaking, the spirit of Dionysus is the informing spirit of the romantic, the wild, the daemonic; while the spirit of Apollo is that of the calm, ordered poise and restraint of classicism. The division is not of course rigid; the two are in a constant state of interaction. Just as there is no such thing as pure male or pure female, biologically, psychologically, and emotionally speaking; just as the male with no counteraction of the female is a monster (or would be did it or could it exist), and female without the element of masculinity would be equally monstrous, though in the opposite direction, so the spirit of Dionysus uninformed and unredeemed by the spirit of Apollo is simply bestiality, and the spirit of Apollo with no contrary opposition of Dionysus, devitalized and effeminate. But the distinction remains valid, and it may be taken as symbolic of the dualism, out of the opposition of which springs vital life and activity. Like the positive and negative poles of electricity, the complementary forces of Dionysus and Apollo combine to release new creative energies.

Beethoven, at least in his first and second periods, was strongly possessed by the spirit of Dionysus as it had been transmitted through centuries of European civilization. There was also a strong Apollonian side to his nature; but it is the Dionysian which seems predominant, as with all daemonic natures. When people spoke of Beethoven as drunk, or mad, or 'possessed', they were, if unconsciously, aware of the old Dionysian spirit manifesting itself in the music of their uncompromising and untamable contemporary. There is a strong orgiastic element in much of Beethoven's early and mid-period music; and orgiasm has played a potent role in the development of the human consciousness.

We have seen, while considering the mental and spiritual background of the 'Eroica' Symphony, how the myths and culture of the Hellenic world had some part to play in shaping Beethoven's creative process. In that instance it was the myth of Prometheus that had permeated the thought and consciousness of mankind, and in its new form had exerted its influence over the mind of Beethoven, who was not unfamiliar with Greek and ancient thought and ideals in general. If therefore the inferences and deductions outlined in that chapter were more or less correct, there is good reason to assume that, just as the Promethean principle worked its way through the heroic idealism of the E flat Symphony, another Greek mythological or legendary principle—namely, that of Dionysus or Bacchus, the Thracian god of wine—worked similarly in the mind of Beethoven and emerged as an artistic impulse in another and no less commanding composition.

It is in the Seventh Symphony that the Dionysian or Bacchic principle comes most prominently to the fore. We need not be afraid of using such terms and references as starting points for our understanding of this most exultant and orgiastic of symphonies, any more than we need hesitate to grasp boldly the hint given in the Finale of the 'Eroica' to deduce more general and deep-seated Hellenic connotations informing that masterpiece. Did not Beethoven describe himself as a Bacchus, and is there not in the Seventh Symphony the clearest evidence of the wine which intoxicates men's souls? Although he made no direct reference to a particular composition in that illuminating conversation with Bettina Brentano, Beethoven clearly had in mind some individual quality in his music, if not a specific work, and the evidence leads as unmistakably to Bacchus and the Seventh as it leads to Prometheus in the 'Eroica'. Also, if ever there was a symphony that sounds as though it were composed in a 'raptus', it is unquestionably the Beethoven in A major.

There is no warrant for supposing that Beethoven had the god Bacchus consciously in mind when composing the Seventh Symphony. To assume as much is to perpetrate the insufferable errors and impertinences of the worst programme spinners. Beethoven himself once said, when confronted with one such, that all verbal expositions ought to be confined solely to characterizing the music in general terms. That it is still necessary to refer back to Beethoven's own trials with the evil tribe of literary 'interpreters' is a sad commentary on the as yet unregenerate standards of popular criticism. Despite protest and ridicule it cannot truthfully be said that we have yet done with visions of political revolution, rustic ceremony, processions, masquerades, and the like discovered in the Seventh by a too purple faculty of imagination.

The Seventh Symphony is pure exultation. In it Beethoven exults as nowhere else in the vitality and richness of his creative powers. It is the complementary side of the serenity of the 'Archduke' Trio. Fully to understand the reposeful strength of the Trio and the sense of well-being in the 'Emperor' Concerto, it is necessary to comprehend the scope and passion of the Seventh Symphony's exultation. The one aspect of Beethoven's creative personality is revealed and illuminated only in terms of the others. And in order to put the continual action and interaction in clear perspective, some exploration back into the primary consciousness of the human mind is again required.

In invoking the spirit of Dionysus, or Bacchus, in relation to certain aspects of Beethoven's music in general, and of the Seventh Symphony in particular, it is as well to define the meaning of that term in a manner more detailed and more elucidating than that indicated by the use of such generalized words and expressions as 'exultation', 'exuberance', 'intoxication', and their like. What precisely is the spirit of Dionysus, and whence does it as a driving force in the human mind derive? We can, to be blunt, only apply it meaningfully to the products of the modern European mind if we can first trace it back to its source and then demonstrate it to be a permanent factor in the spiritual and psychological development of mankind—if, that is to say, we can show that it permeates thought and feeling without a conscious, not to say learned, invocation of the ancient Dionysian mysteries and rituals. Those mysteries and those rituals have to become symbolic of the inner life of mankind before they inform particular works or activities.

Originally Dionysus was not a Greek but a Thracian god. The Thracians were a semi-barbarous, primitive people held in small regard by the more civilized Greeks. The Dionysian or Bacchic rites originated in wild fertility cults. Bacchus was in fact the name of the fertility god who, through his connection with the grape harvest and the drinking of wine, became associated with what was thought to be a form of divine madness. At a later date the worship of Bacchus passed into Greece, where it took the form of ecstatic, dangerous and, to the orthodox, quite unwholesome dance rituals. In many respects the spread of Bacchic mysteries and observances in civilized Greece resembled the nineteenth-century spread of Romanticism into the civilization of Europe, which had reached an apex in the eighteenth century. In both cases the motive forces were much the same and accounted for the irresistible spread of the new ideas and feelings—namely, a desire to return to a more 'natural' and instinctive way of living. The cult of the primitive is always a likely outcome of an age of formalism and a certain rigidity. One of the major problems inherent in the historical search for a comprehensive world-view is that of maintaining dynamic contact with the fundamental life forces alongside the ideals of culture and civilization. 'Civic' man and 'natural' man tend always to stand in opposition to each other; which is really only another way of stating the essential duality of the principles of Dionysus and Apollo, the gods, respectively, of wildness and passion, and of formality and restraint.

The cult of Dionysus in Greece was a form of protest against the formalism of civilized life. Bertrand Russell has described its characteristics:

> The worshipper of Dionysus reacts against prudence. In intoxication, physical or spiritual, he recovers an intensity of feeling which prudence had destroyed; he finds the world full of delight and beauty, and his imagination is suddenly liberated from the prison of everyday preoccupations. The Bacchic ritual produced what was called 'enthusiasm', which means, etymologically, having the god enter into the worshipper, who believed that he became one with the god. Much of what is greatest in human achievement involves some element of [mental] intoxication, some sweeping away of prudence by passion.[1]

This description of the Dionysian or Bacchic principle could be applied in broad general outline to the spirit of Romanticism, especially German Romanticism that swept across Europe on the heels of the French Revolution. Thus at the outset we can see that a transformed and modernized equivalent of the Dionysian invasion of Greece was characteristic of the age in which Beethoven lived. In over-simplified but convenient language, it could be said that Beethoven emerged from the predominantly Apollonian eighteenth century into the predominantly Dionysian nineteenth. The eruption of romanticism was in a very real sense Dionysian or Bacchic in its psychological and emotional

---

[1] *A History of Western Philosophy.*

origins. It is of course by no means the only example of an upsurge of the latent spirit of Dionysus or Bacchus known to the western world during the more than two thousand years that separate the first capitulation of Greece to the Bacchic revelries and the beginnings of the age of Romanticism, loosely so called. But what emerges is the existence in one form or another of the Dionysian principle as a constant element in the human conscious and unconscious.

It is not, however, sensible to infer that the spirit of Dionysus came down into modern Europe in its pure form. There was in the original Bacchism a strong element of bestiality, a surrender of moral and intellectual control that was entirely repulsive. After the first ecstatic orgies, the Greeks themselves found it necessary to counter the Bacchic outbursts with more temperate forces. It was thus that the rituals and beliefs surrounding the figure of Orpheus came into prominence. The important feature of the Orphean cult was that it substituted mental for physical intoxication, and it was in its Orphic forms that the spirit of Dionysus became a potent factor in later philosophical and theological thought. The savage, bestial elementalism of Dionysus was transformed and reorientated, with the result that the human image was recovered from the obliteration it had suffered in the unadulterated orgiasm of Dionysian ritual. Through Orphism, the Greeks mingled the Apollonian with the Dionysian principle and so did much to contain the one and energize the other without losing the vital elements in either.

In its transmigration through historical time the Orphic substitution of mental for physical intoxication became again associated with the name of Dionysus or Bacchus. It is thus that Beethoven referred to himself as 'the Bacchus'; and it is thus that we can speak of the Dionysian or Bacchic element in much of his music, and especially the Seventh Symphony.

The pastoral or 'natural' elements that have frequently been discerned in the Seventh Symphony confirm its Bacchic or Dionysian quality; for the original Dionysian rites were especially concerned with pastoral and fertility mysteries. Beethoven's own sensibilities were profoundly and ecstatically stirred in the presence of Nature.

Beethoven's attitude to Nature is not easy to sum up in a word. It was, despite appearances, basically neither pantheistic (which means that God is everything) nor theo-pantheistic (which means that everything is God). He drew constant inspiration from Nature. He felt himself in immediate contact with the underlying creative impulse of the universe when he walked in the woods and fields outside Vienna. But he was as little subjective wallower as objective observer and analyst. His responses to Nature, as to everything else, were essentially creative. He did not strike a romantic attitude; yet there was a strong element of Romanticism woven into the texture of his personality.

Beethoven's personal feelings in the presence of the natural world are most purposefully expressed in the 'Pastoral' Symphony. This is his most authoritative speaking on the subject. The 'Pastoral' is essentially a record of subjective feelings and impressions. There is a sense in which it stands to the Seventh in a form of subject-object relationship. In the one it is the immediate reaction of the subject that provokes a warm and inward-oriented creative passion: in the other it is the creative passion itself, expressing itself outwardly, and in doing so passing over from individuality to universality. The Seventh Symphony represents Beethoven exulting in his creative powers; but not from a solely egocentric angle. The exultation does not pass from subject to object in a simple relationship: it follows a complex pattern whereby the object becomes reinvested with its own creative impulse through the activity of the creative subject. It is for this reason that the musical form and texture of the 'Pastoral' Symphony are considerably more simple and straightforward than those of the Seventh. But the inner relationship to Nature in each remains.

It is clear that Beethoven's attitude to Nature was conditioned both from within and from without. He possessed many of the natural responses of his age. His private feelings were intense and personal; but they stemmed from the more generalized aspects of the nature-feeling of the late eighteenth and early nineteenth centuries. This, again, is in keeping with the nature of the initial responses and impulses that inspired his creativity. From the 'Pastoral' Symphony we can deduce, clearly and accurately, the exact type of Beethoven's nature love. It is immediately plain that it was not pantheism. If we compare it, as a document, with various pieces of pantheistic writing, or music, we can tell at once that here is something substantially different. This in fact is a record of pleasure in Nature; of a warm and spontaneous affection. It is not a composition with weighty philosophic implications. But that does not make it less important as a reflection of Beethoven's innermost experience. Indeed, without the particular orientations of the 'Pastoral' Symphony several other aspects of that experience, and especially those centred in the later years of his second period, would be imperfectly in focus.

The progression of the 'Pastoral' Symphony, as a record of personal and immediate Nature reactions, tells us plainly where Beethoven stood in this matter. It is almost as though he surrendered himself to the romantic 'consolations of Nature'. But there is a significant difference. There is no part of the 'Pastoral' in which Beethoven invests Nature with a human emotionalism, or superimposes upon it his subjective personality. To have done so would have been a purely Romantic attitude. But Beethoven again shows the superiority of his perceptions. He shows that he could have romantic feelings without indulging in Romantic excesses and exaggerations. This is yet another case in which it is necessary to speak of the 'purity' of Beethoven's experience and its projection in and through his music. There is no ethical impulse behind the 'Pastoral', because there is no ethical impulse in Nature; and there is no more emotional significance than the personal reaction it stimulates in Beethoven, and through him, in the listener.

Apart from the thunderstorm, the 'Pastoral' Symphony is a genial and undramatic work. But it is not simply decorative. It is often misunderstood on this point. A dramatic interpretation of the 'Pastoral' usually sounds forced. The secret of it may be discovered by thinking once again of Kant's dictum that 'perceptions without conceptions are blind'. An approach to Nature which merely perceives cannot be more than decorative and superficial. On the other hand, perceptions informed by false conceptions lead to a different but not less dangerous falsification. It is clear from the 'Pastoral' Symphony that Beethoven's conceptions were positive but not egocentrically distorted.

The hostility of Nature, which a later age has been obliged to discover and affirm, plays small part in Beethoven's conceptions. This is simply a part of his psychological and perceptive truthfulness. In his day the hostility of Nature had not been revealed—or rather, it appeared to have been substantially tamed. In the eighteenth century civilization had achieved ascendency. But it did not last. The Romantic generation felt it to be a false position; and the scientific age which succeeded completely altered the balance. In the 'Pastoral' Symphony the worst that happens is the thunderstorm which interrupts the pleasant activities and sensations. But it passes without a real threat, and Hymn of Thanksgiving restores peace and equanimity. There is

H

nothing in the 'Pastoral' analogous to the inherent hostility of Nature that one finds in much of the music of Sibelius. This belonged to a later age when that hostility had been released and revealed by scientific development. In the later symphonies of Sibelius the balance appears once again to have been redressed; a new equipoise has been achieved. In Sibelius's Sixth and Seventh symphonies Nature and the human mind confront one another in a new relationship. The creative energies of each have been brought into a fresh state of action and inter-action. But such an attitude was not possible to Beethoven, who lived in an age when the endemic destructive powers of Nature had not been revealed in their essentially modern aspects. Had Beethoven lived a hundred years later it is certain that his attitude to Nature would have been different. In this respect his subjective responses and perceptions were conditioned by the age in which he lived. The 'Pastoral' Symphony is thus the most externally determined of all Beethoven's major works. But its significance as an expression of his subjective experience must not on that account be minimized. It stands outside all his symphonies, from the 'Eroica' to the Ninth; but it still manages to tell us much that we urgently wish to know about him as an experiencing and responsive active subject. In an important sense, it forms a link between the subjective conflicts of the C minor Symphony and the 'Rasoumovsky' Quartets on the one hand, and the exultation in creative omnipotence, both personal and universal, of the Seventh.

In relating the genesis of the Seventh Symphony, psychologically and spiritually, to the Bacchic rites of ancient Greece, we are in fact following a similar process to that which we pursued when tracing the Promethean connotations of the 'Eroica' Symphony. It is just as necessary in the present context, therefore, to insist that in speaking of the Bacchic or Dionysian elements in the Seventh, it is the Dionysian spirit as it has been transmuted through centuries of Christian civilization alone that has relevance. As a matter of fact, apart from the quality of the music itself, we do not have to rely solely on Beethoven's words as reported by Bettina Brentano in order to establish the consciousness of Bacchus as a fertilizing element in his mind. Many years later, at the height of his third period, Beethoven had plans in his head for the composition of two symphonies, one of them to incorporate a sort of festival of Bacchus in which the god of wine and immortal intoxication was probably to appear in person. In the event, the ideas which Beethoven carried around with him in immature form for half a lifetime, were put into the white-hot crucible of his creative imagination and finally emerged as something very different. Only one symphony was completed, the Ninth, and that in a sense did include something directly related to the Dionysian principle transubstantiated. Perhaps the Bacchanale would have been given even greater force in the Tenth Symphony which was projected, partially sketched, but never brought to completion. We shall never know.

For a musical parallel of the exultation of the Seventh Symphony we have to go to an unexpected source—to the Delius of *A Mass of Life* and *A Song of the High Hills*. There is little inherent connection between the ethical positive activity of Beethoven and the pantheistic nature mysticism of Delius. But through Nietzsche Delius discovered in himself the essentially Dionysian bent of his nature. The Dionysian element in Delius, as in Beethoven, was not contrived but innate. Nietzsche's writings did not convert Delius; they served to focus the nature and inherent capabilities of a man who was not disciple but fellow spirit. The Dionysian spirit in Delius manifests itself in exultation and life-affirmation in Nature, even more in *A Song of the High Hills*, because less forced and consciously assumed, than in *A Mass of Life*. But Delius was at heart a pantheistic nature worshipper: his greatest outbursts of exultation, though genuine enough, could never escape from the conditioned determinism of the natural world. The art of Delius is not transcendent: it has in it a fundamental element of the negative. Side by side with the spirit of passionate affirmation in Delius there is a quality which Tovey described as an almost oriental 'depth of meditation.' The word 'oriental' is significant, for oriental meditation is passive, and the passivism of Delius the dreamer is in strong contrast to the activism of Beethoven. But Delius was visionary as well as dreamer, and in his artistic being he was one who perpetually sought unification and the submergence of an alienated self in the super-being of Nature. This side of Delius is allied to Hindu mysticism, in which mystical contemplation is identified with the object contemplated. But Delius was tragically conscious of the brevity of earthly beauty and of the bloom which passes from the hour.

The spirit of affirmation which stands at the opposite pole to the passive meditation of the native idylls is something that Delius derived from Nietzsche—or, to be more accurate, discovered in himself via Nietzsche—and at times touches the note of authentic exultation that characterizes the Beethoven Seventh. In the end it is probably true to say that Beethoven anticipated Nietzsche in rediscovering the Dionysian spirit. Nietzsche formulated it philosophically; Beethoven felt it instinctively and finally integrated it in a comprehensive life-view.

It was Nietzsche's valuable contribution that he focused attention on the dynamism and vigour of sixth-century Greece. Hitherto critical and philosophical inquiry had been directed largely to the achievements of the Athenean civilization of the fifth and fourth centuries. This was particularly so in the eighteenth century, whose Hellenic ideals derived from the Socratic age of the 'theoretical man', of the later times when order, reason, moderation, and scientific inquiry were thought to be the predominant characteristics.

Ancient Greece was not, however, the well-ordered and equable paradise it is often imagined to be. There was another side to it—the existence of daemonic pessimism and disquiet. And it was this pessimism and this disquiet that manifested themselves in passionate rituals and observances, fierce religious cults, and tragic dramatic conceptions.

The Dionysian elements in the Seventh Symphony are purified and reorientated. The affirmation of the power of creativity and the exultation in positive action are purged of their savage elementalism in which the human image was originally sunk and made unrecognizable. The orgiastic passions are free of natural determinism and psychic objectivism. To see the Seventh as mere animal exuberance, as blithe unclouded happiness, is to misunderstand the tragic element in freedom. The Seventh is not tragedy; neither is it an escape from tragedy nor an attempt to break through tragedy. It is post-tragic; not tragedy itself, its existence is based on a tragic consciousness. Like all Beethoven's major works, it is an emanation of tragedy. Without a tragic background the Seventh Symphony could never have been written. It is in a very real sense the justification of tragedy through the achievement of creative freedom.

Wagner called the Seventh the 'apotheosis of the dance', a remark which has frequently been misunderstood. The dance considered as social diversion has nothing whatsoever to do with this tremendous outburst of vital power. But in the symbolic sense, Wagner's phrase has considerable truth and insight. The Greek tragic chorus danced; and it is the element of joy in tragic drama that differentiates it from mere sadness or self-pity. We remember the Scherzo of the 'Eroica', following directly on the Funeral March. 'Divine Grace is dancing', affirmed Gustav Holst in the *Hymn of Jesus*; and it is in the sense of Divine Grace that the Beethoven's Seventh may justly be called the 'apotheosis of the dance'. Tragedy fertilizes imagination and tempers the spirit. It is in the joyful acceptance of suffering and tragedy that the creative spirit expresses itself through symbolic measures of the dance.

Although Beethoven was predominantly a daemonic or Dionysian nature, there was also a strong Apollonian element in him. The daemon was controlled and harmonized by the more reposeful spirit of Apollo. Even his most violent, passionate, daemonical or 'possessed' music has in it an element of Apollonian calm and lyric beauty. But there are certain specific compositions running through his first and second periods which seem overtly devoted to the spirit of Apollo. The florid beauty and lyric calm of the Violin Concerto is far removed from Dionysian passions. In the music of the second period the Violin Concerto is as representative of the Apollonian Beethoven as the Seventh Symphony is of the Bacchic or Dionysian.

The Apollonian principle in Beethoven is a balancing force throughout the second period. It lies alongside the Dionysian passions, co-existent and counter-balancing. It should not, however, be confused with that lofty serenity which characterizes the 'Archduke' Trio. It is present in that serenity and may be counted as a constituent part of it. But, if we are to continue with the analogy from the Grecian world, the quality which emerges from those compositions of the late second period, of which the 'Archduke' is the crown, must be called Olympian. Again it is in its modern rather than in its ancient or purely Homeric form that the word Olympian is applicable. The gods of Mount Olympus were dictatorial, arbitrary, capricious. They had to pass through many centuries before they became invested with the later attainments of nobility and sagacious austerity. Like Prometheus, and to some extent Dionysus, the Olympians as a permanent idea in the human consciousness passed through many changes and modifications with the evolution of western thought, theology, and philosophy. Again, therefore, it is in the extension of the Greek ideals into Christian eighteenth- and nineteenth-century Europe that we can speak of the Olympian quality in the 'Archduke' Trio and the 'Emperor' Concerto.

If the Apollonian principle manifests itself most clearly in the Violin Concerto, it is hardly less apparent, though in a different form, in the G major Piano Concerto, which is a work of the warmest and most affectionate poetic lyricism. The characterization of the unique Andante as a dialogue between Orpheus and the savage beasts, though fanciful, has the mark of imaginative truth. It was through the figure of Orpheus that the Greek world transformed the barbaric mysteries associated with Dionysus. In this sense the Andante of the G major Concerto could be seen symbolically as the spirit of Orpheus taming the orgiastic spirit of Dionysus.

If we accept the opposing principles of Dionysus and Apollo as the archetypes of the creative spirit, we can see that certain artists appear to be clearly Dionysian, or 'possessed', and others to be predominantly Apollonian, or 'controlled'. I am speaking of course of the major geniuses. Beethoven appears as the typical Dionysian nature, albeit one tempered by Apollonian restraint. The Dionysian element is strong in Shakespeare, but also firmly counterbalanced. It is in fact a concomitant of supreme creative power that the two principles must exist side by side and hold at least a recognizable balance. On the other hand, balance cannot be maintained by any form of denial, a wilful holding back on either side. The freedom of creativity demands a twin release of a composite Dionysian-Apollonian principle or impulse.

At first sight Mozart appears to be the outstanding musical example of an Apollonian nature. The inevitable poise, the formal perfection and absolute beauty, of Mozart's music seem the ultimate expression of the spirit of Apollo. But beneath the surface there is, in all Mozart's greatest music, a strong daemonic element. Mozart is in fact one of the most vital and passionate of all composers, although his innate passion and vitality goes often unobserved simply because of the matchless formal and aesthetic perfection of his music. As Edward FitzGerald remarked, 'People will not believe that Mozart can be powerful, because he is so beautiful.' That is the reason why Mozart was out of favour during the years of the daemonic nineteenth century. Misled by a superficial impression the nineteenth century was lured into the error of seeing Mozart's music as merely decorative and ornamental. We have only just escaped from that fallacy today.[1]

The Dionysian and the Apollonian principles in Beethoven were always present and always active. But during his second period he tended to keep them apart. Although there is an effective counterbalance in all Beethoven's compositions, it is usually possible to characterize them as either predominantly the one or the other: the Apollonian Violin Concerto, the Dionysian Seventh Symphony. What

---

[1] Mendelssohn is the truer example of the Apollonian composer.

this means is that the matching of the two is not yet complete. Although at the end of the second period there is evidence of a riper, more mature mastery of sheer composition, a less obvious and less aggressive antagonism, it is not until the third period that Beethoven appears to have achieved the final resolution. In the music of the third period one is no longer conscious of the individual works as either 'Dionysian' or 'Apollonian': there has taken place a process of spiritual and artistic integration which has resulted in a diminution of neither the one nor the other, but of a fusion or combination which has released a new creative capability. It would in fact be true to say that in the third period Beethoven had transcended both spiritually and aesthetically the ancient oppositions and arrived at complete freedom. When in 1817 Beethoven astonishingly said to Cipriani Potter, 'Now I know how to compose!' did he perhaps, instinctively, mean precisely that?

6

The Place of a Skull

IF BEETHOVEN had died in 1813 (or in any year between 1812 and 1817) he would have been regarded by posterity as a man whose life had reached fulfilment. The great works of the preceding years would have stood as enduring monuments to the creative life and spirit of one who had lived greatly and suffered greatly, and had won through to lasting peace and to a ripe wisdom. The second period came to its conclusion around 1812. By that time Beethoven had reached a spiritual and artistic maturity which would have seemed to justify him as man and artist. The 'Archduke' Trio, the 'Emperor' Concerto, the Seventh and Eighth symphonies, the F minor Quartet—these variously resplendent compositions would, had they in fact represented the culmination of his career, have marked a completely satisfying outcome of the tragic conflicts of the C minor Symphony and the 'Rasoumov-sky' Quartets, and the metaphysical propositions of the Third and Fourth symphonies.

It is as well to consider this for a moment. Ernest Newman, arguing in support of Hugo Wolf's contention that every man is allowed sufficient time on this earth in which to do his appointed work, cites Beethoven as the outstanding example:

> Beethoven seems to me the supreme instance of this. Was not his work really finished with the last quartets and sonatas? It is difficult to imagine him reverting, after achieving these, to any earlier practice of his, while any further development seems a pure impossibility. Beethoven, when he died, was only fifty-six, yet his task, I believe—a task which only he among all the musicians who have ever lived was capable of merely attempting, let alone accomplishing—was completed.[1]

There is considerable truth in these words. It is difficult, to say the least, to imagine Beethoven reverting to any previous practice (indeed,

[1] *The Sunday Times*, 2 December 1956.

his violent treatment of the English General Kyd, who asked him to compose a symphony in his 'earlier manner', is clear indication of Beethoven's own attitude, and sufficient evidence that any such return can be discounted). It is also true that any further development from the heights attained in the last quartets and sonatas seems 'a pure impossibility'. The third-period music is, in the end, only credible because it exists. The last quartets and sonatas of Beethoven are unique. If, therefore, they find no parallel elsewhere, is it reasonable to assume that had Beethoven not lived to complete them, we in our turn could have any reason to anticipate them?

It is impossible now to imagine the life and work of Beethoven without the third period. All the same, if the imaginative effort can be made only as far as 1813 and no further, is it unreasonable to discern the workings of a single process brought to completion? It is true that in the last works of the second period, notably the F minor Quartet and the 'Archduke' Trio, there are indications of the stylistic elements of the third period. Even so, there is small warrant for anticipating the cataclysmic transformation that the third period in fact represents.

If, therefore, it is possible to assert that the music of Beethoven's third period is to be believed only because it exists, is it reasonable to assume out of hand that any further development is in the nature of 'a pure impossibility'? The normal human mind, contemplating the mystical illumination of the last quartets, cannot conceive of a further extension or development. But, having been vouchsafed one series of miracles, is there sound reason to deny the possibility of further and even more incredible ones?

I ask these questions not because I necessarily wish to dispute the contention of Wolf and Newman, but simply because the posing of them seems to throw valuable light on the astonishing transformation in Beethoven's creative life with which we are faced in the long years of virtual silence that lies between the conclusion of the second period and the inauguration of the third. The position would be simplified if Beethoven at the time of his death had shown signs of having exhausted his creative potentiality. But we know that he died when his powers were at their height. He was full of new projects for composition. Great new works were already past the embryonic stage. Exactly what form these fresh works would have assumed we cannot even begin to imagine; but we have to accept one of two things—either he would in fact have achieved some further development, impossible though it must seem to the ordinary human mind, or his creative life would have ended in an anticlimax from which he was delivered by the merciful hand of death. That Beethoven should have relapsed at the end into a form of artistic stagnation is as unthinkable as that he should have fallen back on to some earlier practice of his; the whole being of the man cries out to us across the years in protest against such an assumption.

The truth seems to lie in the conclusion that the ultimate freedom attained by Beethoven in the last quartets left the way open for a development which was in the fullest sense boundless. We ourselves cannot hope to comprehend the nature of such a development; but if we could rise to the spiritual eminence of Beethoven at the end of his earthly life we should find comprehension at least not impossible. The mystical ways of the spirit are only to be understood by those who have partaken directly of them—transcendental experience must be personally entered into if it is not, to all intents and purposes, to seem incomprehensible. It is for this reason that the substantially non-productive years between Beethoven's second and third periods are so difficult to understand, and even more difficult to analyse. Through a form of comparative inference their significance can be deduced; but they themselves must remain for ever shrouded in mystery.

The phases of Beethoven's combined spiritual and artistic development are more accurately termed 'cycles' than 'periods'. This is particularly true of the so-called 'second period'. The transition between the first and second periods is to some extent logical and definable—that is to say, far-reaching and fundamental though it was, it was not cataclysmic in the sense that the transition between the second and third periods was cataclysmic. But even here one has the sense of a completed cycle, of the wheel coming full circle on its given axis.

The first period reveals Beethoven as the young lion, slowly feeling his strength and accustoming himself to the exercise of it. Thus he is principally concerned with music as such, with forms and styles more than with content. There is plenty of feeling and depth of emotion in Beethoven's first-period music, but it is subordinate. Beethoven began his career as a composer from the social standpoint. He not only achieved, but consciously desired, widespread fame as a piano virtuoso; and although he was probably aware from the beginning that such was not to be his permanent position, it remained his starting point. As Sullivan observes, Beethoven's first-period music is chiefly a music that expresses *qualities*. Then came the crisis that led to the Heiligen-stadt Testament, the outer and visible symbol of an inner and spirit-ual conflict only in part related to the growing encroachment of his deafness.

The import of the crisis that became expressed in the words of the Testament to all intents and purposes brought the first period to an end. Even so, there are still to be discerned the outlines of cyclic completion. Beethoven had gone as far as he, being true to himself, could go in that particular direction. He had to make a new beginning, the fresh start that came with the conception of the 'Eroica' Symphony. And he never went back; nor could he, either as developing human being or creative artist, return on himself. The criticism, therefore, which intimates that in certain of his later compositions Beethoven 'reverted' to the forms of Haydn and Mozart, as is sometimes said of the Fourth Symphony, is myopic. Neither Haydn nor Mozart could have conceived and composed anything like the Fourth Symphony— which is a stylistic and not a qualitative judgment. The Fourth belongs to the same world as the 'Eroica'; and while there are technical resemblances of both to the lineage of the Viennese classical symphony, they are stylistically worlds apart from it.

The second period reveals considerably more of a full cycle than the first. From the creation of the 'Eroica' Symphony to the great works of 1811 and 1812 a complete process is evolved. This process, it is true, comprehends in itself the durable aspects of the first period, for to say that Beethoven could never return to the premises of the first period is not to say that there was nothing in that period of lasting value—only that what was carried over was, and had to be, essentially transformed. Thus Beethoven's career up till the end of the second period reveals a basic continuity, but with a major change of direction about half way through. This combined yet differentiated period might best be seen as a circle within a circle, the larger and outer circle of the second period encompassing the inner one, which is yet substantially complete in itself.

Marion Scott described the essences of Beethoven's three 'periods' as:

> In the first, Beethoven saw the *material world* from the *material stand-point*; in the second he saw the *material world* from the *spiritual standpoint*; in the third he saw the *spiritual world* from the *spiritual standpoint*.[1]

[1] *Beethoven.*

These distinctions are fundamental. The differentiations between the first and the second are not difficult to follow and understand—a change from a material to a spiritual view of the world is within the experience of most active human minds. That few individuals attain to it with anything like Beethoven's force and clarity of vision is largely because the majority of humankind remain all their lives in a state of non-activity and non-perception. The direct ethical idealism of the 'Eroica' and the B flat symphonies, the dramatic conflicts of the C minor, the profound searchings of the mind's sufferings and motivations of the 'Rasoumovsky' Quartets, are all the productions of a creative faculty that moves in normal and familiar, though enormously extended, dimensions; that is the reason why Beethoven's second-period music exerts such a hold over the public mind. Beethoven's experiences here are the universal, though frequently but dimly apprehended, experiences of the human mind and spirit—at least of the western or European mind and spirit. And the experiences that lie behind the later works of the second period, the works that fall between the years 1807 and 1812, have also this universal and readily identifiable quality. The intelligent and perceptive listener, confronted with the burgeoning spirit of Beethoven as revealed in the second-period music, can say, sincerely and without affectation, 'There, with the grace of God, go I.'

The transition to the third period, however, presents a fundamentally different process. It is hard for any man to look penetratingly and steadfastly on the material world from a spiritual standpoint. But to look on the spiritual world from the spiritual standpoint is harder by far, for it requires a transformation of consciousness to which few men in the world's history have aspired or have even been able to aspire. To have such vision is to come into direct contact with the ultimate reality, to break free from the natural world and, as it were, to enter into direct communication with the Godhead. For man, born into the natural world and existing as a part of it, the final 'break through' into the world of the spirit is the hardest, most terrifying experience of all, which summons the last resources of tragic fortitude and endurance, even though it leads in the end to eternal blessedness and to the most perdurable liberation from the misery of the world.

That blessedness and that liberation are made manifest in page after page in the last quartets and sonatas, the Mass in D and the Ninth

Symphony. But the process by which they were achieved led Beethoven along one of the most tragic and bitter paths a man can be asked to travel—a path of intense loneliness and almost unendurable inner conflict, in which the strength and integrity of personality must stand alone and in isolation, without hope and with an endurance unfortified by the expectation of reward. Voluntarily to relinquish everything that means life to the intelligent and sentient human being without at the same time being aware of fresh benedictions at the end of it is to face a tragic destiny which requires for its acceptance a courage that is, in the most real and awe-inspiring sense, superhuman.

During the more or less non-productive years between 1812 and 1818 Beethoven was beset by material trouble and worries. The endless lawsuits over Karl, almost continuous poor health, lack of money, plus an increasing deafness that isolated him more and more from the world of his fellow men—such trials and tribulations combined to make these years particularly miserable for Beethoven. But to attribute either the creative silence or the transformation that was revealed when Beethoven again plunged whole-heartedly into composition to any or all of them, especially, as is often done, to the litigation over and tragic personal relations with the nephew Karl, is to perpetrate the most far-reaching of errors. Personal difficulties, awkward relationships, poor health and poverty were Beethoven's portion to a greater or lesser extent for the best part of his life. That they happened at this time to be particularly pressing, both individually and collectively, is in no way fundamental to his spiritual life at this most critical period.

I do not wish to minimize the magnitude of Beethoven's personal difficulties. But it is necessary to protest vigorously against the idea that they were in any sense the direct cause of the transformation of consciousness that divides his second from his third periods, or that they were responsible for his years of silence.

As a matter of fact, these years were not entirely barren, even if no major works were composed or conceived during them. To them belong the piano sonatas in E minor (1814) and A major (1816), the two 'cello sonatas of Op. 102 (1815), the song-cycle *An die ferne Geliebte* (1816), and the concert overture *Namensfeier* (1814), in which Tovey discerned, not unreasonably, some kinship with the great *Weihe des Hauses* overture of 1822. There were also sketches for a piano concerto (in D major) and a symphony (in B minor); but these came to nothing and must be classed among those passing ideas which often engaged Beethoven's attention without depositing the seed of creativity.

The most important works of this period—the two sonatas for pianoforte, the two for 'cello and the song-cycle—although strong and original compositions, seem to be the result of the creative vitality of the second period carried over by its own momentum. While there are stylistic developments indicative of the coming third period proper, the creative process behind them shows that the transformation was not yet complete, and that as an artist, no less than as a man, Beethoven was living in a sort of in-between-time. The ineffable loveliness of the A major Piano Sonata looks forward to a similar quality in the E major, Op. 109; while the gritty fugue of the D major 'Cello Sonata, and the extended 'adagio con molto sentimento d'affetto' in the same work, look forward to the essentials of Beethoven's third-period style without fully assuming it. It seems as though the creative energies of the second period could not be stilled, and so threw up the furtive outriders of the forthcoming transfiguration.

The song-cycle *An die ferne Geliebte* occupies a unique position, not only in Beethoven's own creative catalogue, but also in the history of the art of music itself. Beethoven felt intuitively, though he did not live to see it, the dawning of the German *Lied*. Beethoven was not a born writer of romantic song; but he composed the first true song-cycle, and in some of his individual songs there are tentative feelings towards the *Lied* as it grew to splendour and fulfilment in the hands of Schubert, Schumann, Brahms, and Hugo Wolf. *An die ferne Geliebte* ('To the Distant Beloved') has the same quality of tender lyricism as the G major Violin Sonata, Op. 96. It is music of great warmth and a luminous though undemonstrative passion. Its emotional reticence is perfectly poised, and its understanding of the human heart reveals the innocence and clear insight of Beethoven's mind—the same that had made possible the composition of the 'Eroica' and the Fourth symphonies, and the best parts of *Fidelio*.

We do not know, nor ever shall, who was Beethoven's 'distant beloved', if indeed she existed at all, just as we shall never know for sure the identity of the 'Immortal Beloved'. And yet it is perhaps not too fanciful to see Beethoven now, when his spirit was withdrawing farther and farther away from the material world, looking back with a calm, poignant resignation over the blue hills of a decade, his mind full of an emotion 'recollected in tranquillity' of some earlier beloved (possibly Therese von Brunswick) whose memory stirred in him this vein of tender lyricism.

Remembering all the variety, power, and vitality of the second-period music, it is impossible to regard Beethoven's remark to Cipriani Potter in 1817, '*Now* I know how to compose', without astonishment and plain incredulity. In any other man such words would have smacked of affectation and pretension. But in Beethoven's case they were, simply and unequivocally, true.

The first fruits of this new knowledge were revealed in the Piano-forte Sonata in B flat major, Op. 106, known as the 'Hammerklavier'. This enormous and overwhelming composition, written in 1817–18, is the record of Beethoven's personal destiny during the non-productive years. In it, and in it alone, is revealed all we can ever know of the spiritual crisis through which Beethoven was obliged to pass before he could come to the understanding of the spiritual world from the spiritual standpoint. There is no more terrible piece of music in existence than the 'Hammerklavier' Sonata. Those who shun its implications and who will not submit themselves to the tragic experience that lies behind it can never enter into the kingdom of blessedness revealed in the C sharp minor Quartet and the Arietta of the C minor Piano Sonata.

That the transformation which took place in Beethoven's consciousness in the years preceding the flowering of the third period should have been accompanied also by a transformation no less far-reaching in his art is but one more illustration of the way in which he lived entirely in and through his music. It was impossible for Beethoven to make a spiritual advance without a corresponding development in his creative capability. His life and his art are indivisible—the one is a continuous revelation of the other. Outside his art Beethoven hardly lived at all; and when he said that he had learnt to compose he meant also that he had learnt to live. Again an astonishing assumption; but no other explanation is conceivable.

A work of art is seldom a direct transcript of experience at the moment it is lived through. More often it is what may be termed the 'end-product' of experience. By the time the experience is sufficiently assimilated to be realized in terms of art the experiencing personality has already passed beyond it. The fever, or 'raptus', that overtook Beethoven in his hours of creativity was the result not of a contemporary living out of the experience, but of the supercharged necessity of organizing it in recognizable forms and concepts. As Ernest Newman said of Beethoven's creative processes, 'We have the conviction that his mind did not proceed from the particular to the whole, but began, in some curious way, with the whole and then worked back to the particular'.[1]

Nowhere does this hypothesis seem more valid than in the case of the 'Hammerklavier' Sonata. It is clear that by 1817, when this tremendous composition was begun, Beethoven had lived through and thoroughly assimilated an overwhelming inner experience, and that this experience had transformed him entirely, both as man and musician. The inmost nature of that experience can only be deduced from the music of the sonata itself; and its full import can only be grasped by those who are ready and able to surrender themselves to it without stint or condition.

The opening chords strike a note of heroic resolution unlike anything that Beethoven himself had hitherto conceived. I believe Sullivan to be fundamentally wrong when he says, 'The old experience is once again to be lived through, but the spirit in which it is approached is very different.' It is not only the spirit which is different; the whole of this movement, indeed the whole sonata, indicates that the experience itself is fundamentally different. There is nothing here of that personal assertiveness—the aggressive will to live and create—which characterizes much of Beethoven's earlier music, and which led to the unclouded self-confidence of the later works of the second period. The heroism is no longer that of a man of infinite courage matching himself consciously against fate, but the sheer selfless fortitude of one who has come tragically to know that only by losing his life can he save it. Aesthetically this is one of the most richly varied movements ever composed by Beethoven. To understand the magnitude of the transformation that had overtaken Beethoven's art between the end of the second period and the beginning of the third, it is only necessary to place the opening Allegro of the 'Hammerklavier' Sonata side by side with the first movement of the 'Eroica' Symphony. No one could say that the 'Eroica's' exposition lacks variety or imaginative plenitude; but how much richer is the 'Hammerklavier'; how much more melodically potent and more subtly interrelated is this, the first completely realized example of Beethoven's new knowledge of composition!

[1] *The Unconscious Beethoven.*

The single-minded heroic idealism of the 'Eroica' is now replaced by a creative process which seems to comprehend the stark omnipotence of Being itself. The melodic fertility alone far surpasses the simple thematic opposition of the 'Eroica' and C minor symphonies, the 'Rasoumovsky' Quartets, and the 'Appassionata' Sonata. This is neither the music of plain dramatic conflict nor of passionate life-affirmation. The thematic juxtaposition no longer contains the germ of straightforward psychological drama. To Beethoven the ideas of single combat with Fate and a self-confident affirmation were now not so much insufficient as meaningless. He had passed beyond conflict leading to triumph through positive activity, and the exultation in a personal capability, to some exalted spiritual region where only through the total abandonment of self could the ultimate life-force be engaged and revealed. The alternation of passages of heroic resolution with *cantabile* themes of a celestial beauty and expressiveness result not in conflict but in a suprahuman richness and abundance. Beethoven had come by the hardest of all roads to the knowledge that only by working with his destiny, instead of, as before, by opposing it, could the Kingdom of Heaven be revealed.

The Scherzo is brief, capricious, and infinitely fanciful. Gone is the giant grotesque, the savage, grimly protesting humour of the typical second-period scherzos. Instead there is a superabundant quality of the fantastic, although something quite unrelated to the sense in which the *Queen Mab* Scherzo of Berlioz is fantastic. As in the first movement there is a richness and variety of thematic invention related in the most subtle manner to the whole sonata. The 'Hammerklavier' Sonata is absolutely of a piece—an incredible example of unity in diversity. It is inconceivable that a single bar should be altered: it has on every page a miraculous inevitability, even though Beethoven himself, despairing of contemporary comprehension and in dire need of money, at one time countenanced the interchanging of the movements, and even the omission of parts that did not please!

The slow movement is perhaps the most heart-rending music ever composed. If the Arietta of the C minor Sonata evokes the stillness of eternal peace, the Adagio sostenuto of the 'Hammerklavier' seems to evoke the stillness of eternal pain. A terrible ache of loneliness, an unbearable sense of isolation from the world of human emotion and human happiness informs the whole of this movement. Beethoven had come to the point where he knew he must relinquish everything that

I

to the ordinary intelligent man spells happiness and community in this world; but he had not yet entered directly into the kingdom of blessedness and partaken of eternal life. Here is the key to the 'Hammerklavier' Sonata. Only the necessity of renunciation and abandonment of the life of this world had been revealed to Beethoven. He was obliged to endure the virtual collapse of his earthly life and hopes as symbolized by the triumphant music of his second period; but not yet was he vouchsafed the final understanding, the ultimate freedom. Beethoven believed profoundly in the immanence of God and the reality of salvation. But now the optimism of personal faith was not enough. He had actually to pass through the Valley of the Shadow of Death. And it is that shadow which falls across this long, resigned, and infinitely suffering Adagio.

The effort of will and the extent of the fortitude that were demanded of Beethoven to keep to his voluntarily accepted path is revealed in the huge three-voiced Fugue with which the 'Hammerklavier' concludes. A Largo introduction leads from the resignation that is the Adagio to the eruptive energy of the Fugue. The ghostly chords of the Largo emerge from such depths as few human minds have plumbed, and lead to a figure wildly rushing as though all the hounds of hell were let loose. Then sounds the first of those thematic trills which play such an overwhelming part in this movement; and almost before we can grasp the significance of them, the Fugue is upon us. The cold fury of the Fugue and the terrifying insistence of the trills which continually stab to the heart of the listener threaten to engulf mind and spirit entirely. It is frankly inconceivable that the human mind can encompass such blind, passionless energy without disintegrating under the impact. For this Fugue is a supreme test of endurance for performer and listener as it was for Beethoven himself. There is nothing, absolutely nothing, of the triumph of the Fugue which ends the 'Rasoumovsky' Quartets. There is neither hope, nor victory, nor even the stimulus of defeat with honour after the best of fights. There is only endurance, only such tenacity as brings into open question, not simply the individual will and creativity, but the creative spirit itself. At the climax there comes a glimpse, brief and heavenly, of that eternal blessedness that lies beyond the annihilation of human hope and human aspiration. If it were not for that one brief glimpse one feels that this Fugue would be quite unendurable. As it rages to its inhuman end it is possible to know that because of that one look into the eternal peace of the future all this energy is not finally blind, hopeless, and beyond the mind's fortitude to support.

If the 'Hammerklavier' Sonata is in effect the record of Beethoven's spiritual journey that led from his second to his third periods, via some five years of comparative silence, it is necessary to ask what precisely was the nature of the crisis that led to the composition of such music. It is, as I have said before, impossible to indicate precisely and in detail the nature of the change which brought about the catastrophic trans-formation of his consciousness, for that is shrouded in the deepest mystery of the spiritual life. All the same, without some attempt to understand it, anything like an adequate comprehension of the third-period music is impossible.

When Beethoven to all intents and purposes broke off active com-position in 1812, when he was in the plenitude of his creative powers, it seems that the overwhelming truth had come to him that the great victory of his life as it was up till then was inadequate. He had suffered much and fought valiantly on behalf of his genius; he had emerged triumphant from his darkest hour. But it was not enough; he had to understand that the victory itself was turning hollow. I do not believe that it was simply that Beethoven in 1812 had reached an apparent solution to his problems that was found wanting only because it was premature. The self-confidence, the assurance in the fruits of victory made manifest in the last works of the second period was in fact full and comprehensive. There was no further progress to be made along that particular road. The cycle was complete.

But Beethoven was essentially a developing personality. It was as impossible for him to deceive himself as it was for him to stagnate. Therefore, at the height of his contemporary triumph, he was obliged by inner necessity to admit the emptiness of it. The tragic implication cannot be ignored—in the very creative process that had led him through the conflict and victory of the C minor Symphony and the 'Rasoumovsky' Quartets there was already the latent seed of inade-quacy. Beethoven himself couldn't know it at the time; he had every reason to exult in his triumph, in his creative powers, and in a personal courage and endurance in the face of adversity. But in that very self-knowledge lay the germ of its barrenness.

To explain adequately the cause of that barrenness and the hollow-ness in the second-period triumph is probably a task beyond the scope of language to accomplish. But it may be possible to indicate the nature of it by saying that even in the crowning works of the second period the psychological Ego of Beethoven still obtrudes, and he had to come to the knowledge that only through the complete transcendence of self can the personality achieve ultimate liberation and enter into the free-dom of the spiritual world. It is necessary to mark the difference between the self and the personality. Personality belongs to the world of the spirit; the self is determined by and related to the natural and the objective world. The dramatic conflicts and victories of Beethoven's second period arose largely from the opposition of spirit and nature. To say that during this period Beethoven saw the material world from the spiritual standpoint is essentially to postulate that opposition. But when, following the transformation of his consciousness that preceded, and had to precede, the third period, he came to see the spiritual world from the spiritual standpoint, that opposition ceased to have ontologi-cal meaning. The old experience, the conflict between spirit and nature, is no longer operative—that had been successfully accomplished in the second period, and is the inner meaning of the music of that period. The C minor Symphony opposes spiritual freedom to material necessity; but in the third period material necessity no longer exists, and consequently the old opposition and the old dramatic conflicts find no place. Therein lies the reason for the unique spiritual quality of the third-period music.

Beethoven had literally to surrender his life as a man in order to find it as a spiritualized being standing face to face with God. To a man of Beethoven's warmth of nature and very human and natural aspira-tions and hopes it was the hardest road of all. He had already attained to spiritual freedom vis-à-vis material determinism, and he had freely and willingly accepted the tragedy of that freedom; but he had now to accept the infinitely heavier, and hitherto unsuspected, burden of freedom vis-à-vis spirituality itself.

The note of hopelessness and isolation that characterizes the 'Hammerklavier' arises out of the sacrifice Beethoven was called on to make combined with the lack of any foreknowledge of reward. As the Finale storms forward to its appalling climax we understand the mean-ing of those heart-rending words written in his diary around 1816, 'God have mercy on me; I regard myself as good as lost.' There are moments in this portentous Fugue which seem to echo Christ's words from the Cross, 'My God, My God, why hast Thou forsaken me!' In very truth, the 'Hammerklavier' Sonata is Beethoven's spiritual Calvary.

7

'God above All'

EARLY IN 1819 Beethoven heard that his friend, patron, and pupil, the Archduke Rudolf, was to be enthroned as Archbishop of Olmütz on 20 March 1820. At this time he appears to have been much occupied with liturgical music, and the news of the forthcoming enthronement provided a focal point. He conceived the idea of composing a great Solemn Mass in honour of his royal friend; and, although by the time of the event itself only a small portion was completed, it was the ceremonies surrounding the enthronement which led to the composition of the Mass in D.

Just how far the archducal activities actually impinged on the conception of the Mass is both open to question and not very important. It is probably safe to say that the idea of paying tribute to the Archduke is to some extent responsible for the external splendour and magnificence of the composition which finally emerged, but that the internal power and creative passion owed nothing whatsoever to it. The impending ceremonials surrounding the enthronement are, in fact, only one more example of an igniting spark—an external circumstance that served to channelize an internal creative force already latent and only awaiting some impulse to set it into motion. The pattern is a familiar one. The Archduke Rudolf stands in the same relation to the Mass in D as General Bernadotte had stood to the 'Eroica' Symphony, Therese von Brunswick (probably) to the Fourth, Count Rasoumovsky to the Op. 59 quartets, and as Prince Galitzin was in a year or two to stand in relation to the last quartets. Beethoven did not always need these igniting sparks; but often they helped to direct his creative energies and to release forces gathering just below the surface. He admitted that, especially late in his life, he had difficulty in beginning big new works. Once into them, all went well. But often some objective impetus—a passing suggestion, a commission, a sudden personal turn of circumstance—even a trivial one, served to overcome his subjective inertia.

It was characteristic of Beethoven that having launched into the composition of a Grand Mass he should have spared himself no preliminary labour to get to the heart of the matter. Because his Latin was shaky and, despite his religious nature, his attendances at church more or less non-existent, he went to some pains to have the text of the Mass translated for him into German. I do not follow Schauffler's argument that because he found this process of translation necessary Beethoven was not close to or in sympathy with the text. The evidence seems to point to a contrary conclusion. Beethoven was brought up a Roman Catholic, and all his life he thought deeply and passionately on the innermost mysteries of the spiritual life. But he was no more orthodox in religion than he was in art or social behaviour. Schindler records that religious topics and the dogmas of the churches were subjects on which he never spoke or delivered an opinion. He was familiar from childhood with the broad general meaning of the words of the Mass, and those words carried some profound, though probably unconventional, meaning for him. But with his present task before him that was not enough. He needed now to have the words in a form and a language where they yielded up not simply their overall meaning, but where he could examine and absorb into his own mind every detail and every inflexion.

The *Missa Solemnis* was not Beethoven's first setting of the Mass. The Mass in C of 1807, composed for Prince Esterházy, anticipates it by more than a decade. It is therefore more than ever likely that Beethoven's concentrated study of the text in 1819 was in no way the result of unfamiliarity or lack of sympathy. The earlier work, even though it does contain arresting and original features, and even though the treatment of the text is frequently individual and obviously deeply felt, does not strike home with the immediacy and authenticity of Beethoven's instrumental music of the same period. It is reasonable to assume that in many respects the Mass in C is in the nature of an experiment. One thing, however, is clear—Beethoven must have understood and felt some import in the words of the text because he could not otherwise have frequently illustrated and illumined them musically with such insight and imaginative perception as he did. The previous Mass shows that Beethoven had thought profoundly and, according to his own conception, devoutly on the inmost meaning of the liturgy as at that time he saw and comprehended it.

With a fresh, and a far larger and more personal, setting of the Mass before him, Beethoven felt an imperative need to restudy and reabsorb the text, from the outside inwards. It was not a case of unfamiliarity, but more likely of a too great familiarity having blunted the sharp edge of meaning and significance. Only by returning, not to the Latin forms of words, but to the detail and smallest innuendo rendered into his own language, could Beethoven be satisfied that final understanding would be his. Only from that standpoint could he be certain beyond all possible doubt that he could emphasize just what he wished to emphasize and so shape the spiritual and dramatic pattern according to his own faith and purpose. Despite his Catholic upbringing, and his inherent religious feelings, he was not prepared to swallow the words of the Mass wholesale: he would not accept the substitution of forms and symbols for personal thought and feeling. The Mass, for Beethoven, was not a form only, an objectivization of faith—it was a means of personal communication with God, or it was nothing. Hence the need to seek again the living heart of the traditional words.

More important and far-reaching than this personal absorption in the text, however, was the musical study to which the composition of the Mass led Beethoven, for this study exercised the profoundest influence over the style of his latest compositions. The clue is to be found in an entry in his journal in 1819:

In order to write church music look through all the monastic church chorals, and see also the Strophes in the most correct translations and perfect prosody in Christian catholic psalms and hymns generally.

The immersion in modal music and sixteenth-century polyphony was of the utmost importance to Beethoven's third-period style. To it we owe, not only the modal sections of the Mass itself and the *Heiliger Dankgesang* of the A minor Quartet, but also that freedom of voice-leading, subtlety of melodic line and plasticity of form which are such outstanding features of the last quartets and sonatas.

For Beethoven the study of the modes and polyphony in the old church music constituted a discovery of the first importance. For the art of music in general it was a species of rediscovery hardly less significant. As Tovey reminds us in his analysis of the Mass in D:

> Such harmony had not been heard since the time of Palestrina, except in a modernized form in certain works of Bach which Beethoven did not know, and in academic exercises by persons who themselves regarded such modes as archaic.   Beethoven was enormously in advance of his time in recognizing that they are nothing of the sort; and until we begin to share his culture in this matter, we have no more qualifications for appreciating the aesthetics of choral music than an eighteenth-century dandy, fresh from his Grand Tour, would have had for appreciating the Elgin Marbles.[1]

We need to remember that in Beethoven's lifetime the works of Bach had not yet achieved rediscovery by the musical world at large. Certain compositions of Bach were familiar to cultured musicians; but it required some years yet before the whole corpus of his work was to be rescued from the limbo of obscurity where it lay for so long after his death. Thus, even the modernized forms of modal harmony occasionally resorted to by Bach were not common currency of the musical language when Beethoven set himself to the composition of his second Mass. It is all the more tribute to his exceptional insight into and innate perception of the essentials of the art of music that he should not only have gone right to the heart of the matter, but even more that he should have made such outstanding and original use of his discoveries.

The influence of the modes and sixteenth-century polyphony on Beethoven's third-period style is an intricate question. Its full scope and potency only emerges fully when we inquire into the nature of his last piano and chamber music. But what concerns us here is that the impetus towards its discovery came from the preparatory studies for the Mass in D.

In considering the *Missa Solemnis* it is well to reiterate that it was originally designed as a part of royal celebrations of great pomp and ceremony. That Beethoven soon became entirely absorbed into it as into a fierce spiritual testament which left all pomps and ceremonials far behind is only in keeping with the course followed by all his major works inspired in the first place by some event, suggestion, or commission. The Mass as it finally emerged, after some five years of Herculean labour, had about as much to do with the enthronement of

---

[1] *Essays in Musical Analysis*, vol. v.

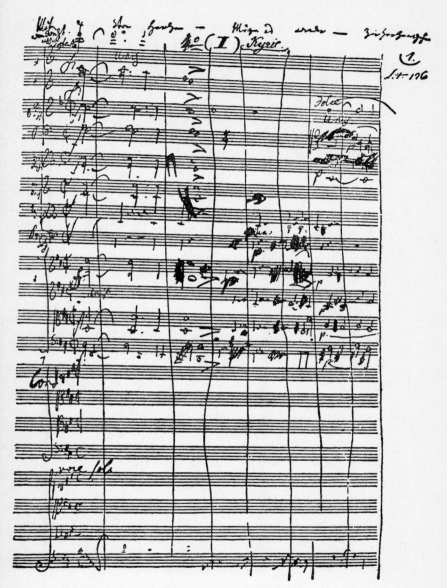

Beethoven autograph: introduction to Kyrie of Mass in D

the Archduke Rudolf as the 'Eroica' Symphony had to do with Napoleon Bonaparte. Yet some clue to its exalted dimensions and magnificence may be found in an idealized vision in Beethoven's mind of a great royal ceremony. Although Beethoven seems on the whole to have despised Rudolf as a man, and probably with justification, he appears also to have had a genuine affection for him, and there is little doubt that his original intention of honouring a royal patron and pupil on the auspicious occasion of his enthronement was entirely sincere. Thus, having set his mind to a particular task, it is only to be expected that Beethoven would do the royal occasion royal honour.

That the sheer size and splendour of the Mass in D was to some extent the result of the use for which it was originally intended is not, however, the only significant aspect of that accidental circumstance. More important is the fact that it was conceived in the first place as a liturgical work. Even in its final form Beethoven considered it to be a piece of music for the liturgy, and despite the strain it inevitably puts on ecclesiastical usage, only as such does it fulfil itself. It differs in this respect from the Mass in B minor of Bach, which was a musical setting of the text of the Roman Mass, more or less unrelated to church practice and public worship. It is ironical that Beethoven, the man of deep religious feeling but little or no practical church-going, should have composed the greatest of all liturgical masses since the sixteenth century, while Bach, the pious Protestant whose whole life was pivoted on the observances of the church, should have written one of the greatest of all his sacred works outside the liturgy.[1]

A more important distinction is that between the religous mind of Bach, considered as a whole and not as revealed only in the B minor Mass, and the religious mind of Beethoven. It is here more than anywhere that we can account for the proper difference between the church music of Bach and the church music of Beethoven. This is far more than the difference between a Catholic mind, even a highly unorthodox one, and a Lutheran mind. Beethoven had as little opinion of ecclesiastical courts and offices as he had of secular courts and offices (he would probably have agreed with Kierkegaard that 'officialdom is incommensurable with Christianity'); while Bach, though in no sense a

[1] Except for the directly Catholic offertorium Luther did not banish the Mass from the public service. Bach's smaller Masses were clearly intended for liturgical usage. But the B minor Mass stretches out beyond the liturgy of the Lutheran Church to embrace the Church Universal. *See* Schweitzer, Terry, and Tovey.

lackey of prince or pontiff, was essentially one whose being found its fulfilment in communal worship and the organized religion of the Church. All the same, the Catholic in Beethoven was stronger than is usually admitted, or even suspected—not the catholicism of the Roman Church in its external manifestations, but a passionate view of God and the Christian mysteries from a basically Catholic viewpoint. Beethoven's religious thinking and feeling must have been in many ways of the same order as Kierkegaard's (who was not, however, a Catholic)—a 'true inwardness' which, in the words of Sir Herbert Read, is a passion that pierces through all collective forms of religion to 'the contemplation of God face to face'. The contemplation of God face to face—language could hardly sum up more accurately or more succinctly Beethoven's spiritual quest and ultimate achievement.

There is a sense in which the religious minds of Bach and Beethoven can be seen most clearly by referring back to the great upheaval in the spiritual life of Europe represented by the Reformation and the Counter-Reformation, and individually centred on the persons of Luther and Loyola. Bach was the greatest single product, at more than a century and a half's distance, of the Reformation—not of the bitter spirit of dispute and political and theological challenge to the authority of the Pope, but of the innermost meaning and spirituality of the Lutheran faith. And one of the pivot-points of Lutheranism was the doctrine of predestination, the insistence on which played a leading part in breaking, or at least in seriously weakening, the power of the priests.

It is the doctrine of predestination which lies at the heart of Bach's religious life, and therefore of his music. By accepting this doctrine the followers of Luther freed themselves from dependence on priests and the authority of the Church for salvation. That was its initial purpose. But spiritually it went much deeper. In the music of Bach the belief in predestination is all-pervading. In the Chorale Preludes, the Passions, the Cantatas, and the Masses Bach gives the fullest expression of that central tenet of the Lutheran faith. The exalted calm, the supreme feeling of certainty and spiritual acceptance of the Divine Will, the profound *wisdom* of Bach's music arise directly from the belief that the destiny of man is in fact predestined. The dramatic element, too, is centred around this same belief. Destiny for Bach is predetermined, and the task of the human mind and spirit is to prepare and fit itself for the ultimate fulfilment of that destiny. Passage after passage in

Bach bears eloquent witness to the sense of life and ultimate fulfilment from the beginnings of time predestined.

The most formidable challenge to the Reformation came from the Counter-Reformation in the emergence of Loyola's Society of Jesus. The Jesuits rejected the doctrine of predestination: they believed that salvation was not dependent on faith alone, but on faith coupled to works. The difference is fundamental. The Jesuits believed in free will, in the necessity for positive activity as a condition of salvation. Since salvation was not predestined man is free to find or to reject it; and in this belief in freedom of will lay the cause of the Jesuits' persecution of heresy.[1] Once the principle of individual freedom is conceded it is easy to understand a complementary belief in the necessity for stern guidance and fierce punishment for 'heretical' use of that freedom. If a man is equally free to love God or follow the Devil it can readily be seen how the idea arose that the task of saving him from the latter for the former is onerous and compelling beyond the mere dictates of humanism and liberality. Eternal vigilance backed by the sternest impositions is far more necessary within the framework of a belief in freedom than within the framework of a belief in predestination. That, fundamentally, is why the warfare against heresy has throughout history been pushed to its fullest extremes from the Catholic side, and much less so, and then largely for political reasons, by the Protestants. It is not, and never has been, simply that Protestants are more liberal-minded, or more indifferent, than Catholics: it is simply that the fundamental tenets lead naturally and logically to a difference in activity and approach.

Although, from the spiritual standpoint, Beethoven would certainly have rejected the military organization, the rigorous orthodoxy, and inherent authoritarianism of the Society of Jesus, he stands close to them in spirit and was a living example of the potency of freedom, whereas Bach stands at the opposite pole, as the supreme musical example of an exalted faith in the doctrine of predestination. It is of no consequence whatsoever on which side we ourselves may chance to be found. But it is of importance to understand the essence of the religious minds of Beethoven and Bach if we are fully to comprehend and enter into communion with them in their religious music.

In a celebrated comparison between Beethoven's Mass in D and Bach's Mass in B minor W. J. Turner sought to make out a case for

[1] In other respects they were notable for leniency and broadmindedness.

the superiority of the former. But Turner missed the point of the different spiritual standpoints of Bach and Beethoven. He did not see that Bach had to compose the Mass as he did—not only because he was the musician Johann Sebastian Bach, but also because he was a profound Lutheran. Freedom, as Beethoven understood it, was not an element in Bach's spiritual make-up: his music moves with a sense of inexorable inevitability—of, in fact, predestination. Beethoven's, on the other hand, is full of the dramatic struggle and conflict of one for whom salvation has to be achieved through personal effort, aided by Divine dispensation.

To say that Bach wrote the music of public worship whereas Beethoven composed the spiritual odyssey of a single human being is to adopt more than a form of words. Bach formed and embraced his ideal of the relationship of music to public worship during a visit to Lübeck in 1705, even though he did not contrive to realize it until late in his life, at Leipzig, and then only in part. With Beethoven the case is very different. Not in the communal spirit; not as one moving forward to a predestined life everlasting and eternally blessed in the certain companionship of a believing humankind did Beethoven set his mind to liturgical composition; but as a great solitary, a seeker and explorer who might lead and inspire and in the truest sense be himself the power of revelation, but for whom the ultimate burden had to be accepted personally and individually.

Only by a conscious effort at understanding the spiritual premises of Bach and Beethoven can the nature of their sacred compositions be discerned, even though that understanding and that discernment are not confined only to their specifically religious thought and their specifically sacred music. The whole of the two men is comprehended, comparatively speaking, by that study. Perhaps the best summary is in the end to be found by recalling that whereas Bach was accustomed to attributing his creative power and the successful completion of his compositions to the direct agency of the Almighty, Beethoven, on a famous occasion when Ignaz Moscheles wrote at the foot of the laboriously accomplished piano score of *Fidelio*, 'Finished with God's help!' immediately added a characteristic comment: 'Man, help thyself!' That was in 1814, during the period of crisis between the end of the second and the flowering of the third periods. The words have much relevance to the whole of Beethoven's creative life, but they are especially pertinent at this time, when Beethoven was engaged in a spiritual struggle that was, if the music it led to is to be believed, of a quite unparalleled magnitude and intensity.

The Mass in D is in every sense a third-period work. That it is too powerful, too dramatic, too subjectively afire for any liturgy is a point that criticism has not overlooked. Sheer physical dimensions apart—and in this respect the Mass of Bach is even less amenable—the *Missa Solemnis* is so surcharged with a personal inwardness, a single and individual assumption of spirituality, an overwhelming aspiration towards 'the contemplation of God face to face' that it stands, and must stand, outside and apart from collective religion and public worship as we so far know and understand it.

Musically the Mass in D is so remarkable a composition that a whole volume might be devoted to it alone.   The influence of Palestrina and modal church music is only one of the ingredients which give it its unique stature. It is not only the direct use of the modes as at the words *Et incarnatus est* (Dorian) and *Et resurexit* (Mixolydian) that those studies bear fruit. There is throughout the whole of the Mass, as in the last quartets and sonatas, a freedom and flexibility of melodic line and voice leading previously lost to European music for two centuries. And then there is Beethoven's extraordinarily vivid and powerful use of fugue, also a characteristic of the whole third period. We remember his remark made to Holz: 'To make a fugue requires no great skill—in my student days I made dozens of them. But today imagination asserts its right, and a new and truly poetic element must be introduced into the traditional form.' For the third-period Beethoven the fugue had a far-reaching significance, and the poetic infusion into the traditional form of which he spoke was originated in his imagination by his contact with the old masters of sacred music.

Each section of the Mass has a particular and individual meaning, although one that is integrally related to the whole. Schindler relates how during August 1819 he surprised Beethoven in the act of composing the Credo, and found him 'singing, howling, stamping'—in a proper 'raptus' in fact! In almost every part of the Mass there is a blazing intensity, a passionate absorption and searing force of imagination which tell us plainly that during its composition the raptus must have been continually upon him. The supernal sensitivity and luminosity of the Kyrie; the superhuman exultation and sense of Divine glory in the Gloria, followed by the passionate conviction of the Credo (although conviction is a crude and mundane word for what Beethoven expresses in this most personal and most awe-inspiring affirmation of belief) which reaches its high peak in the sublime fugue in B flat on the words *Et vitam venturi seculi*—it is only necessary to indicate these near miraculous assumptions of the spiritual life. In all art, in all human thought and activity, only the most exalted of the saints and mystics have attained to such a vision and such a penetration of the divine essence at the fountainhead, and few even of them have left a record of that vision and that penetration as intelligible and as coherent as Beethoven somehow contrived to leave.

The Sanctus begins incomparably with the solo quartet leading to another great choral movement; but the Benedictus defies even indication, with its soaring obbligato for violin and the unearthly, almost terrifying calm as the voices enter in hushed reverence. 'Blessed is he that cometh in the name of the Lord.' Could ordinary humankind even but conjure up in the imagination some distant understanding of the nature of the blessedness directly apprehended by Beethoven here it is likely that the end of the world would be at hand.

For the Agnus Dei Beethoven reaches out, not to the old triumphant conclusions of his earlier days, but to a spiritual consummation that ultimately embraces triumph but also passes far beyond it. The *Dona nobis pacem*—a 'prayer for inward and outward peace'—is not only a triumph of creative art; it is also a stumbling block both to the literal-minded and to those whose minds cannot transcend a soulless ortho-doxy. The clamour of trumpets and drums, which have reference to both material warfare and spiritual conflict on the part of one who knew to the full the terrors of both, now mysteriously threatening from afar, now grimly near at hand, are set against the impassioned supplication of human voices, individual and collective. The effect is one of un-paralleled power and mystery. It is probable that the initial idea was derived from Haydn's *Paukenmesse*, or 'Mass in Time of War', in which the corresponding sections are also disturbed by martial-sounding trumpets and drums. Haydn's Mass was inspired by a desire for peace among men in the midst of the Napoleonic wars: Beethoven, starting from a similar basic idea, enlarged and expanded the conception so that it embraced the whole of life, physical and spiritual. In view of the musical correspondence it is impossible not to think that Beethoven was directly inspired by Haydn in the matter of musical procedure and construction.

Beethoven was above all a dramatic composer. His conception of

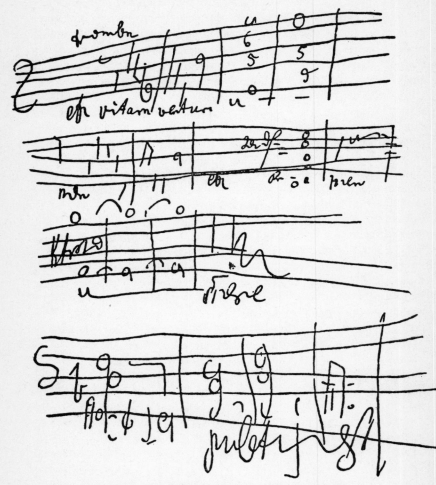

Beethoven notebook: draft score for Mass in D

the text of the Mass was therefore essentially dramatic. It is generally thought that a Mass should not be dramatic—at least not in the sense in which the *Missa Solemnis* is dramatic. But Beethoven, by infusing an intense personal vision and all-penetrating mysticism into the musical setting of the text, transformed and illuminated anew traditional practice. Beethoven really stands nearer to Victoria in spirit than to Palestrina, as a church composer. He has not Victoria's brooding emotional passion and bitter sense of human mortality; but he shares with the great Spaniard a surcharged dramatic sense and a burning vision of the spiritual life and the magnificence of divine glory. If there was a strong strain of Spanish blood in Beethoven, it would possibly account for the kinship one feels in his sacred music with that of Victoria.

Although the Mass in D is a choral composition, the orchestra plays an exceptionally important role. Frequently the clue to Beethoven's meaning is to be found in the orchestra and not in the voices. Beethoven was concerned to illustrate the words of the text and to place emphasis just where he wanted it; and in passages sufficiently numerous to be notable the orchestra rather than the voices is entrusted with that illumination and that emphasis. In a later age Wagner found in the Finale of the Ninth Symphony the inspiration for his own idea of the interrelationship between words and music. The Mass is no less remarkable in this respect—indeed, it is even more remarkable. The orchestral commentary as developed and explored in the mature music dramas of Wagner is more than hinted at in the Mass in D. With Beethoven the orchestra is far more than accompanist, far more than foundation-stone, far more than the repository for varied effects of colour and obbligati —it is at the heart of the whole conception, as often as not the protagonist.

Only a man who had behind him Beethoven's achievement in the realm of orchestral symphony could have attained to such a mastery of the orchestra in a choral composition. How often in the Mass do the voices state the words and the orchestra tell us just what they really meant to Beethoven? Haydn, also a master of orchestral symphony, had a fine sense of orchestral usage in vocal music; but nowhere does he give the orchestra the prominence Beethoven gave it.

The comparisons with Haydn are apt. In his youth Beethoven had studied with Haydn. It turned out that the two men were too far apart in age and too near together in temperament for the association to be

K

particularly fruitful. None the less, it existed for a while, and certain parallels, though not obvious and readily recognized in the history books, can be carried through to the end. After his second London visit Haydn, a man widely famous and sixty-three years old, gave up writing symphonies and concentrated his ripest experience and maturest genius on the composition of choral music. The result was six Masses and the two oratorios, *The Creation* and *The Seasons*. The late string quartets apart, these choral works represent the culmination of Haydn's creative life. Although he had composed for voices all his life, it is in these final masses and oratorios that his genius elected to say its last and not least impressive word. Something of the same is true of Beethoven, or rather, might have been true. Beethoven was not by nature a vocal composer, although he is frequently less appreciated in this respect than he properly deserves. However, at the end of his life he was much concerned with the prospects and possibilities of vocal music. The Mass in D was intended to be one of three; an oratorio was in his mind; and a tenth symphony threatened choral ingredients.

Beethoven had much to contend with as a choral composer. The conventions of the age were all against good choral composition. And Beethoven himself lacked the sheer experience that lay behind him in symphony, string quartet, and pianoforte sonata. The Mass in D caused him appalling labours and tribulations, just as in the earlier years *Fidelio* had done. But it is clearly recorded that Beethoven became engrossed in projects for choral works. That he in the end turned to the string quartet and there remained for the rest of his days is, of course, plain fact; but there is no reason to suppose that had he lived longer than he in fact did he would have confined himself to any one musical form or medium. Indeed, it is not far-fetched to argue that the extension and development of the third period that would have been required of a longer-lived Beethoven might well have come in the direction of choral music. Tovey openly opines that such a development 'should have been distinguished by a body of choral work fully equal in power and perfection to the symphonies and string quartets'. The life of Haydn's untamable and uncontrollable pupil might well have followed the broad pattern of his own, musically speaking, and have also concluded in a dual triumph of choral music and string quartet.

It is idle to pretend that the Mass in D, any more than the Ninth Symphony, is a perfect composition—at least in the sense in which the

C sharp minor Quartet and the last three piano sonatas reach out towards perfection. To argue that it is Beethoven's greatest composition is to push admiration too far. But in one sense it is not an overestimation. For greatness of spirit and splendour of devotion the *Missa Solemnis* stands second to no composition whatsoever, and even though its machinery is at times less than entirely satisfactory, its finest and most characteristic parts go farther than any yet composed for the liturgy to transcend human mortality and fallibility. It cost Beethoven immense pains and labour; but he was again true to himself. He lived out his own words: 'Once more sacrifice all the little things of social life to your art. Oh, God above all!'

8

The Brotherhood of Man

FROM HIS earliest years Beethoven was stimulated by the ideal of human brotherhood. Springing in the first place from the French Revolution, such ideals were rife throughout Europe during Beethoven's young manhood, and he was by no means exceptional in that they went to his head. All through his early and middle years these ideals occupied a leading position in his consciousness and his view of human life. How much they endured, at least in their original form, is perhaps another matter. Ernest Newman has written:

> I do not myself believe that the mystical Beethoven of the last years retained any faith in that naïve doctrine of the brotherhood of man that had been at the very heart of his thinking about life in his early and middle years. The mystic sets no store by commonplace fancies of that sort; and it happens to be in mysticism of one kind or another that many of the greater minds and the greater centuries make their abode towards their end.[1]

There is much food for thought in those words. But it is possible that they do not lead to precisely those conclusions which they appear superficially to invite. It is, of course, true that Beethoven in his later years made his abode in the realms of mysticism. And that mysticism assuredly had no room for the commonplace fancies about human brotherhood as entertained by the politician, the professional philanthropist, or the self-conscious idealist. The operative word in Newman's argument may well be 'naïve'. We may assume that in his last years Beethoven had far surpassed and outlived the ideals of brotherhood let loose by the French Revolution and suchlike phenomena. Never a fundamentally political thinker, Beethoven, even in his

[1] *The Sunday Times*, 2 December 1957.

136

younger days, was animated by ideals beyond those of even the most
elevated and expansive political philosophies and systems. We have
already examined the nature of Beethoven's consciousness during the
years of his mature manhood, and if that examination has been anything like adequate it must be clear that his ideals and his spiritual
awareness were of a very uncommon order. In the third period,
however, Beethoven took an enormous leap forward, a leap across an
abyss, towards the furthest development of spiritual awareness. And
in so doing he entered a world completely removed from ordinary
day-to-day thought and feeling, even the most mature. Therefore, such
ideas and ideals as he took with him underwent their own transformation and reappeared, if at all, only as dimly related to their earlier
and more mundane selves.

Some such process took place with Beethoven's ideals of human
brotherhood. That he retained correlated ideals is clear from the
Finale of the Ninth Symphony, which was no mere capricious sprout-
ing of the moment but a deeply considered and passionately felt
utterance. The choral Finale of the Ninth Symphony was closely
linked in Beethoven's creative mind with the Mass in D; not only
technically, but in spiritual outlook and awareness the one has much
in common with the other. In reaching out towards 'the contemplation
of God face to face' Beethoven also came to a spiritualized view of
mankind and human destiny.

The argument that the Ninth Symphony is concerned only with the
brotherhood of man is too naïve to linger with beyond an idle moment.
None the less, the three orchestral movements do lead naturally and
logically to the choral Finale, however much we may feel disposed to
quarrel over the execution of that complex movement. The setting of
Schiller's *Ode to Joy* was long prepared, and though it cost Beethoven
some misgiving, both during the composition of it and afterwards, it
was what he meant to do and say.

Beethoven's finales are frequently made the excuse for dilating on
his inborn 'optimism'. It is doubtful, however, whether the majority
of those who so readily have recourse to that much abused word have
really taken time off to ponder its meaning. If we are content to accept
at their face value the usual associations of optimism—that is, a sort of
cheerful confidence that everything will come out right in the end—
then we cannot apply it to Beethoven at any stage in his life, least of
all in the Ninth Symphony. Beethoven was never optimistic in the

facile and flabby-minded sense of expecting a happy ending to come along by itself, given patience and a modicum of tenacity. If optimism and pessimism simply mean the taking of either a hopeful or a gloomy view of life and the world, then neither has any meaning from the spiritual point of view. Schweitzer has written on this subject:

> What passes for optimism with the mass of people is the natural or acquired faculty of seeing things in the best possible light, this being the result of lowered ideals for the future no less than for the present.[1]

And,

> True optimism has nothing to do with any sort of lenient judgment. It consists in contemplating and willing the ideal in the light of a deep and self-consistent affirmation of life and the world.[1]

Again, Schweitzer speaks of 'the only legitimate optimism, that of volition inspired by imagination.' [1]

It is from such definitions that optimism emerges as a positive and creative force, and becomes in part at least akin to Nietzsche's 'tragic optimism' which transcends both the commonplace pessimism (which is a sign of incipient decay) and the commonplace optimism (which is the sign of superficiality.)

Beethoven was essentially a man animated by 'tragic optimism' and 'volition inspired by imagination'. Optimism for Beethoven was never a form of cheerful self-confidence, but something which arose out of the vision of ideality to be created through positive activity. The ideal does not exist in and by itself—it has to be positively created and worked towards through the acceptance of the tragedy of freedom. This was true just as much in the second period as in the third; but in the latter there was a fundamental change of spiritual premises.

The Ninth Symphony is not concerned with the creative aspiration of the individual, but with the universal life itself. The spiritual world seen from the spiritual standpoint in the Ninth Symphony, the Mass in D, the last sonatas and quartets passes beyond individual destiny. It does not negate personality—rather does it elevate personality above simple individuality. Only a man who had lived through the complex spiritual experiences of the second-period music—truly lived through them, lived them out to the end, and not merely been aware of them from the outside—could have passed into the third period.

[1] *Civilization and Ethics.*

The term 'catastrophic transformation of consciousness' must be introduced here, for it is especially relevant to the Ninth Symphony. This is, of all Beethoven's works, the most directly catastrophic in its spiritual processes. The ideal of human brotherhood expressed in the choral Finale is dependent upon and the outcome of the catastrophic vision of the three preceding movements. The first movement sounds in very truth the end of the world, bearing in mind that 'the end of the world' is a spiritual eventuality not necessarily, or even possibly, dependent on material destruction from solar accident, cosmic collision or nuclear explosion, man-made or natural. The vastness of the cataclysm through which the opening movement of the Ninth Symphony passes embraces the whole of life, and it is only by passing through this upheaval, which leads at one point to the brink of cosmic chaos, that the spiritual ground can be prepared, not only for the choral Finale, but also for the forces of regeneration and rebirth that are unleashed in the Scherzo.

This latter is the archetype of the third-period Scherzo. It sets the pattern of dynamic impetus and rhythmic groupings coupled with a trans-personal energy and vivacity that were to reappear in the C sharp minor and the F major Quartets. Just as the catastrophic power of the first movement stands outside individual conflicts and individual destinies, though by its very nature it comprehends them, so does the regenerative force of the Scherzo stand above and outside individual emergence from tragedy and tribulation. Its eruptive energy and humour are in no way related to particular problems and particular rebirths. This is nothing less than the resurgence of the inner life of the universe as spiritually apprehended in the mind of a single man. Its impersonal power and vigour are not anti-personal but trans-personal. It is a part of the process by which Beethoven's innermost development grew out of the 'Hammerklavier' Sonata and precedes the spirituality of the late quartets.

The process is not, however, complete as it relates to this particular composition. The regenerative force of the Scherzo does not lead directly into the universal joy and harmony of the Finale. There is interposed the long, slow movement in which the reborn spirit opens out and flowers in all its manifold richness. There is a duality here, in these variations on the twin themes, Adagio and Andante moderato. It is as though an exalted quality of mystical contemplation were mingled with a passionate regret for beauties and felicities from the old world which have had perforce to be abandoned in the attainment of the new spirituality. In the latter aspect there is a connection between this slow movement and the Cavatina of the B flat Quartet, in which is to be found the same passionate regret, the resigned backward glance, the sense that even the most luminous and transcendant of gains is accomplished at some cost and with a loss of things dear to the heart of man's human and mortal nature. I find it impossible not to feel at the entry of the Andante theme, 3/4 in D major, that the human heart is moved most profoundly by the sweet remembrance of what belonged to another world and another life. It is fundamental to Beethoven's spiritual growth at the end of his life that it was not achieved heartlessly.

Beethoven said of the Cavatina of the B flat Quartet that: 'Never did music of mine make so deep an impression on me; even the remembrance of the emotions it aroused always cost me a tear.' One understands these words particularly in the section marked 'Beklemmt' (anguished). This music strikes a note of poignant sadness far removed from the rarefied serenity of, say, the opening fugue of the C sharp minor Quartet; and it is a note not unlike, in its own context, that struck by the Andante sections of the slow movement of the Ninth Symphony. The other side of that movement rises to heights of mystical absorption akin to the opening of the C sharp minor Quartet and the last movements of the E major and the C minor Piano Sonatas.

We have now arrived at the point where Beethoven felt imperatively the need for the new element represented by the human voice. Whether or not he was right in that feeling, or in the manner in which he subsequently carried it into practice, is a question over which there never has been, or ever will be, unanimity of opinion. Its opponents have seized upon and made great capital of Beethoven's own doubts, after the event. That he did express misgivings is not in dispute; but we have to ask from what premises he came to utter them. Tovey, as so often, wrote intelligent and perceptive words on the subject:

> The only way to understand, not only the choral finale, but the other three movements of the symphony, is to attend strictly to the music from its own point of view as Beethoven wrote it; and not to be distracted by what he may have said about it when he was thinking of something else. We have no right to dismiss it as a mistake until we have thoroughly followed its meaning, whether we like it or not.[1]

[1] *Essays in Musical Analysis*, vol. ii.

This, it seems to me, is a more valuable and penetrating piece of reasoning than Tovey's more celebrated words, from the same essay, about there being no part of the Choral Symphony that does not become clearer when we assume that the choral Finale is right. That is true, but it does not take account of the circumstances under which Beethoven expressed his doubts—it doesn't, out of context, make the point that Beethoven's dissatisfaction arose at a point when he had already passed beyond the state of mind which produced it, and was in all probability immersed in some other project.

The problem of making a transition to the Finale caused Beethoven even more trouble than usual. We know that material which eventually appeared in the A minor Quartet was originally intended for the concluding movement of the Ninth Symphony. But the existence of the symphony as Beethoven left it tells us that the instinct of his genius obliged him to work his way through the long transitional passages, with their recalling of the principal themes of the preceding movements and recitatives for the double basses, to the great affirmation of joy and rejuvenated existence that is the choral Finale.

The making of that transition was a task that only Beethoven at the height of his third-period mastery could have attempted. Even so, it is possible to argue that he did not solve the problem absolutely. This was not, of course, the first problem of transition that Beethoven had had to cope with in a symphony, although it was the only time where the transition had to be made not only from one 'mood' to another, but also from one plane of tone to another. In the C minor Symphony occurs the most famous of his middle-period transitions, at the same structural place in the grand design, but without the added burden of the introduction of an entirely new tonal element.

More than one critic has felt that in the Ninth the process, though ingenious, is not entirely convincing. Ernest Newman has laid a finger on the sore spot by pointing out that when the baritone soloist enters with the words (Beethoven's own), 'O friends, not these sad tones!...' he is in fact rejecting not only the three instrumental movements, but also the 'Joy' theme itself, since that supreme melody has already been stated and orchestrally developed. Newman argues, and it is impossible satisfactorily to refute the conjecture, that only a composer of Beethoven's musical alchemy (and Beethoven's enormous reputation) could have 'got away with it' without inviting cries of derision.[1]

[1] *The Sunday Times*, 8 April 1956.

This is perfectly logical and perfectly true. It is impossible to deny that on the face of it there is, even after all the work and sketching that preceded its completion, a flaw in the transition from the end of the slow movement to the beginning of the choral movement proper. Examination of the score suggests that Beethoven himself was here groping towards something which he never achieved in its intended ideality. Of course, it could be argued that this sense of groping and uncertainty was something deliberately created by Beethoven as an integral part of his musical conception. But that argument does not ring true. It is more reasonable to argue that for once Beethoven's sheer skill as a musician had to carry him through what remained to the end an imperfectly realized idea.

Criticism has agitated itself overmuch on the subject of the so-called inanity of Schiller's words chosen by Beethoven for his purpose. He made a judicious selection of stanzas from the complete poem, avoiding certain parts that were frankly ribald. But even what he did choose is frequently thought to be beyond even his powers to transmute into pure gold.

Beethoven cherished ambitions about setting Schiller's verses from his earliest years. No doubt as an ardent young man the sentiments appealed to him, or he thought they appealed to him in the period of his 'naïve' belief in simple human brotherhood. But by the time of the Ninth Symphony I do not believe that the actual sense and meaning of the words were operative with him, except in a generalized and unspecific sense. There were other than literal qualities in the verses which excited his imagination now, when his mind was much concerned with the aesthetic problems of combining the largest vocal and orchestral forces. He wished to give expression to some exalted idea of human brotherhood in the new life which springs from the complex world-view as it emerges from the three preceding movements; but he was not intellectually naïve, not now at any rate, whatever may have been the case in the days of his heady youth. The appeal was no longer in the word-meaning of Schiller's poem: the overwhelming conviction of the Finale of the Choral Symphony arises out of a visionary conception in Beethoven's own mind animated by the *musical* implications of Schiller's poetry. Albert Schweitzer has written a pertinent description of Schiller:

> We reckon Schiller among the poets. He himself held that he was really a musician. On 25th May 1792 he writes to Körner: 'When I sit

down to express an idea, I am more often possessed by the musical essence of it than by a clear conception of its contents, as to which I frequently can hardly make up my mind.' Behind his words, indeed, there is not pure intuition, as with Goethe, but sound and rhythm. His description is sonorous, but pictorially unreal, presenting no living scene to the reader's eye.[1]

It is precisely the musicality of Schiller the poet that appealed to Beethoven. Whether he at first knew it or not, it is likely that even as a young man what really touched his imagination was not the simple concept of human brotherhood and universal joy, imperfectly assimilated intellectually by the poet, more or less on his own admission, but the musical shape and rhythm of the stanzas.[2] In this sense the Finale of the Ninth Symphony is a purely musical conception of a meaning which lies beyond Schiller's or anyone else's words. Indeed, it is often no bad thing if the words of the chorus are imperfectly heard in performance, for the musical meaning lies in the sound of the voices themselves, and in the melody, harmony and, perhaps above all, the rhythm. It was the dithyrambic rhythms of Schiller's verses that fired Beethoven's imagination for the better part of his life and finally flowered into creative utterance as the consummation of his greatest symphony.

To strip the structure of the Ninth Symphony to its elements is to see that in the first three movements Beethoven explored to the utmost the three fundamental ingredients of music. The first movement explores the potentialities of an interval, the second of rhythm, and the third of melody. In these three movements the essence of orchestral music is laid bare with the most commanding power and imagination. Then comes the great 'Joy' theme—a melody which sums up in itself and blends into one single outpouring all that has gone before. The great diatonic tune with its clear outlines and forward moving rhythms is the direct outcome of the entire musical complex of the first three movements. Its claim to that exalted title is further consolidated by the instrumental variations which follow directly on the initial statement,[3] during which the tune burgeons out in all its richness and splendour before it is passed dramatically to the human voice.

The ensuing vocal variations equal, and in some respects surpass,

[1] *J. S. Bach.*
[2] *See* Appendix for Beethoven's view of the musical quality in Goethe's poems.
[3] Not variations so much as expansions.

the Mass in D in the way in which the orchestra is thrust boldly into the foreground and is frequently the protagonist, even though the *raison d'être* of the Finale lies ultimately with the voices.

In considering the musical implications of Schiller's verses in relation to Beethoven's setting we must not forget the mental associations of the sound of words. An example may be found where, after his recitative, the bass soloist utters his great shout of 'Freude', to be answered immediately by the chorus basses. To a German ear the sound of the word 'Freude' has particular evocations which are no doubt lost to non-Germans and which cannot be restored in translation. Much the same is true of the German word 'Tod' (Death) which has a faintly ridiculous look, if not sound, to Anglo-Saxon ears, but which in the hands of Bach produces a profound and ominous impression on German minds. As I say, we cannot usually get over the difficulty by means of translation, because, literal meaning apart, the sound of the words of one language cannot be relied on to retain their associations in another. In the Finale of the Choral Symphony Beethoven frequently makes his most eloquent points by using the sound of words allied to rhythmic accentuation, harmonic support, and skilful placing of vocal and instrumental parts. Too much attention has been focused on the dubious literal sense of the words and too little on the musical ideas inspired by their sound and rhythm in Beethoven's mind.

Growing out of this misplaced emphasis between meaning and sound is the problem of adequate performance of this Finale. It is generally agreed that here, as in the Mass, Beethoven made outrageous demands on the human voice. All the same, he knew what he was doing, even if his consideration of practical possibility was over-ambitious. Some relief, however, might be found if chorus-masters and conductors realized more adequately that the important element here is indeed sound and not sense, and thus went for strength and beauty of tone instead of hopelessly straining after precise articulation of words—often, especially in translations, awkward words—on high notes where all that is wanted is rhythmic precision and freedom of tone. What we have to ask ourselves is not whether Beethoven miscalculated the capacity of the human voice, but what his music would sound like if we were ever to hear a perfect performance of it—if, in fact, we were to hear it as Beethoven himself heard it in the potent solitude of his own deafness. We cannot truthfully claim that Beethoven was wrong and produced ugly effects until we have steeled ourselves to sing what he actually wrote as he intended it should be sung. It is a tall order, no doubt, but it is the only one that will do justice to Beethoven.

Picturesque analysis of the Ninth Symphony has often seen it as either a Christian document or a pagan celebration of beauty and goodness. Neither can be accepted because both are too particular. The Ninth Symphony, like all the third-period music, stands solidly outside classification. It is a gigantic extension of the spiritual awareness. Thinkers and prophets in all ages have known that the ultimate beauty and goodness of human life could only be achieved through a catastrophic transformation of consciousness. It is explicit in Christianity, implicit in Plato and in Buddhism, and central to all significant philosophical systems which seek to restore the human image to its position of uniqueness and primacy. And in the Ninth Symphony of Beethoven the internal process is laid bare with overwhelming imaginative power. The brotherhood of man can, by a stupendous act of 'volition inspired by imagination' be made living reality; but only after the cataclysm of the first movement, the dynamic rejuvenation of the Scherzo, and mysticism plus poignancy of the slow movement have been lived out to the full. Only then will man look upon man truly as brother. One is tempted to think of the words Shelley put into the mouth of Demogorgon at the conclusion of *Prometheus Unbound*:

> To suffer woes which Hope thinks infinite;
> To forgive wrongs darker than death or night;
> To defy Power, which seems omnipotent;
> To love, and bear; to hope till Hope creates
> From its own wreck the thing it contemplates;
>   Neither to change, nor falter, nor repent;
> This, like thy glory, Titan, is to be
> Good, great and joyous, beautiful and free;
> This is alone Life, Joy, Empire, and Victory.

But that really is a second-period attitude, applicable to the 'Eroica' and C minor symphonies and the 'Rasoumovksy' Quartets. It is not a third-period attitude because it is insufficiently expressive of that transcendental objectivity to which Beethoven miraculously attained after the composition of the 'Hammerklavier' Sonata. The words themselves indicate that greatly though Beethoven merited them before 1818 the experience enshrined in them still belongs to the individual and the material aspects of life upon this earth. 'Suffer woes', 'forgive wrongs', 'hope', 'defy', 'falter', 'repent'—these belong not to the spiritual realm of the third period but to the challenging, self-assertive world of the second period. Their very inadequacy to the third period reveals why the music of Beethoven's last years can never be satisfactorily elucidated. All the same, Shelley's words lie staunchly across the path which led to the third period. Without them, and their innermost meaning and truth, there could have been no third period—they represent in respect of Beethoven the stepping-stones from the second-period symphonies, quartets, and sonatas, to the world of the Ninth Symphony, the Mass in D, and the final quartets and sonatas.

All art, said Schiller, is dedicated to joy—a sentiment which Beethoven would have wholeheartedly endorsed, even though he knew more than ever Schiller did what was real joy and the road along which the human mind and spirit were called upon to travel before it could be reached. The Ninth Symphony carries not the individual but the universe itself along that road. It is not a work of perfection in all its parts, especially in so far as the choral Finale and the transition to it are concerned. But the symphony as a whole is transcendent, and the Finale justifies itself when seen in its true perspective. Sections of it are, unquestionably, enigmatical; others seem to the ordinary glance surprisingly imperfect. Taken as a whole there may appear errors of execution—but the conception is magnificently right.

9

The Ultimate Freedom

In tracing the process of Beethoven's development as spiritually active human being and creative artist, we have seen that between the close of the second period or cycle and the flowering of the third there took place a transformation of consciousness, during several years of relative silence, which is revealed in the 'Hammerklavier' Sonata, and which resulted in a similar transformation in the quality and style of his music. And both transformations were symbolized in his words to Cipriani Potter, '*Now* I know how to compose'. It is, of course, possible to argue that this new knowledge was due to a long period of meditation on the problems of the musical art alone; that it was the result of a direction taken inevitably by his innate musical faculty at a certain point of time, and was thus in no special way accountable to a drastic process of transformation in his spiritual consciousness. Such an argument finds some support in the undoubted appearance of elements of the third-period style in certain late second-period compositions—notably in the F minor Quartet and the 'Archduke' Trio. Beethoven's purely musical impulses had at the conclusion of the second period come full cycle; further development along that particular line had become more or less impossible. Therefore, it could be held, his remark to Potter should be taken at its face value—that is to say, as referring solely to the solution after prolonged meditation of a fundamental musical problem that did not in itself postulate a spiritual transformation.

However, such an argument, legitimate though in its own way it is, takes no account of the *content* of the third-period works. If the new knowledge of composition was something that originated and developed in and for itself alone, then how are we to account for the constant impression we receive from the last quartets and sonatas, from the Ninth Symphony and the Mass in D, of a transformed spirituality the like of which is not to be found anywhere in the first- and second-period compositions? It does not, in short, explain the spiritual difference of the latter, a difference fundamentally in *kind* and in no sense only one of degree. The more one surveys the creative life of Beethoven as a whole, the more one listens to his music from first to last, the more one sets the characteristic works of one period beside those of the succeeding one, the more does one become convinced that Beethoven's musical faculties and spiritual faculties, if one can so speak, go continually hand in hand, and are from beginning to end bound firmly and inevitably one to the other. There is no point in Beethoven's life where a marked development or transformation of musical style takes place which is not also the point at which there is evidence that he underwent an equal spiritual development. And furthermore, such evidence clearly suggests that the spiritual transformation or development was the immediate cause of the musical one.

Beethoven's life reveals a process of the most comprehensive spiritual and artistic development—something that has escaped few of his commentators, who see in it, and rightly, one of his most distinguishing characteristics. All the same, it is doubtful if such a development is in the nature of a steady and continuous growth of the sort that might be drawn on a graph as a steadily ascending line. I have already suggested that his three so-called 'periods' would be more accurately described as cycles, each in a sense complete in itself. If we look on the second period in particular as a completed cycle of artistic and spiritual development we see a process which leads along a precise and recognizable path; or, to be perhaps more accurate, which revolves around a particular and recognizable axis. From the 'Eroica' Symphony to the 'Archduke' Trio is a single line of development, and one which richens and ripens as it matures but does not show any fundamental change of direction. When we speak of 'development' within the second period we do not mean the same thing as when we use that term as generally applicable to Beethoven's entire creative life, although it did contain those labile and unfixed elements which made possible the transformation that led to the third period.

Beethoven's three periods have been variously described and defined. Among the most satisfactory and illuminating definitions is that of Marion Scott.[1] There is, however, another though closely related way of looking at the matter. From this point of view the first period can be seen as concerned primarily with purely musical values and concepts; with, that is, music more or less for its own sake, not eschewing spiritual and emotional elements, but more thoroughly dedicated to the problems and developments of the art of composition as such. In the second period the roles are to some extent reversed. Although this period is remarkable for its quality of sheer musical achievement, its principal motivating force is expression. We have here to take pains to avoid a basic misconception—that of allowing the expressive power and personal content of the second-period music to obscure the inherent musicality of the compositions which comprise the bulk of it. But, on the other hand, it is impossible not to feel that throughout the second period Beethoven's main efforts went in the direction of expressing in musical terms the experiences and aspirations of his inner life, and that his musical style was to some extent carried along on the torrent of his immense vitality as a living and experiencing human being. Only a musical genius of the highest order could have kept pace with such a vitality and such a passion of heart and mind; but it is essential to remember that Beethoven's capacity for experiencing and spiritually developing from within was in itself a constituent part of his genius.

The reason why on a certain type of listener Beethoven's second-period music produces an uncomfortable impression derives from the tumult of the inner life it was called upon to express and which frequently left on it the scars of violence. In this respect W. J. Turner once described the second-period Beethoven as an artist 'over-engined'. It was not that he lacked the technique necessary to his task; but the sheer outgoing force of his personality tended to overwhelm the mechanics of composition and so to endanger that perfection of balance between form and content that lies at the heart of artistic creation. In the third period he solved that, the last aesthetic problem left to him, in a way that can only be called miraculous because it was achieved with no loss of essential creative power, but rather through an expansion and development of it.

It is generally speaking not difficult to achieve perfection in the smallest forms—in a song, a sonnet, or a short lyric, even though considerable gifts are first necessary even there; and it is not beyond

[1] *See* page 111.

L

the scope of genuine talent to achieve it on a slightly larger scale where the idea or spiritual state to be expressed is not of the most profound. The production of small exquisitely polished diamonds of art is, though still rare, not beyond the scope of genuine talent to contemplate. But only genius of the highest order can work towards such a perfection on the largest scale and in the expression of great spiritual truths. Only Beethoven, Shakespeare, Dante, or Michelangelo can even hint at a perfection within those exalted dimensions.

It would be useless to argue that all Beethoven's third-period music did in fact approximate to perfection. The Ninth Symphony and the Mass in D are, while entirely representative of the transformation of Beethoven's life and art, imperfect as wholes, even though they are as spiritual and artistic diamonds less rough-cut than many of the second-period works. However, the last quartets and sonatas, though not perhaps perfect in the miniature sense, do approach that perfect fusion and equability, an ideality in the matching of form to content unparalleled in music of genuine substance. In these late compositions Beethoven no longer used form formalistically; he no longer took the established structures and charged them with new and overwhelming content, which, despite the enormous modifications and expansions of the process entailed, was essentially what he had done in the second period. Now in the third period he gathered together all his accumulated experience of composition to achieve a freedom of form and style that were, and have remained, essentially unique, and to give release to such an organic fusion between thought and expression that the two become in the deepest sense indivisible. Form was sunk in thought, thought in form, so that no longer is there the sense of a particular form being used as a *vehicle* for thought; instead it becomes the thought itself. The 'Eroica' Symphony is an outstanding example of a profound musical mind thinking naturally and spontaneously in terms of sonata form; the C sharp minor Quartet, though the opposite of formless, is a unique example of a musical mind thinking in terms of pure and uncompounded music, with no division between ends and means.

These final compositions of Beethoven, although we know full well the devoted labour that went into their making, and notwithstanding the tremendous intellectual power behind them, often give the impression of a sort of spontaneous combustion on the part of the creative spirit. The barriers of material necessity are broken through, and the spirit itself speaks. From the outside this freedom is manifested in an endless liability and plasticity wherein the creative impulse is harnessed neither to a predetermined form nor to a prescribed order. Movements fan outwards in illimitable motion, or else revolve eternally round a still point; a two-movement sonata, a seven-movement quartet, the mystery of numbers itself takes on new significance. Sonata form, fugue, variation—these are not abandoned and replaced by amorphous groping: they are transfigured and made free. The forms of music are spiritualized from within: Beethoven is not the destroyer but the avenger of form in music.

It is common to refer to the essential quality of Beethoven's third-period music as 'mysticism'. But, although it is impossible to deny the validity of such a definition, sufficient thought is seldom given to the inner meaning of mysticism. Mysticism is a difficult and a dangerous word to use, particularly when applied to art. Too often what is merely insubstantial, imprecise, imperfectly assimilated, and essentially vapid is mistaken for the mystical spirit. But mysticism is not vapid or insubstantial; it is not an escape from or a failure to come to grips with reality, but the reverse. The Italian philosopher Leone Vivante, writing of the poetry of William Blake, says, concerning the 'central and distinctive feature of mysticism':

> Mysticism is characterized by a feeling of the infinite, conceived not only as an essential character of inner being in its transient realizations, but as a reality existing outside all single realizations, and in itself highly contradictory. For this reality is conceived, on the one hand, as fundamentally creative: it is a living unity, it is love, and value, and, most certainly, form and time; and, on the other hand, it is represented, or asserted, as formless, timeless, immobile, fixed. The inherent contradiction should baffle and defeat us in our very power of thinking, but it is not exactly so for the mystic. He gives the greatest prominence to the *unintelligible* character of the Divine Unity. His mental attitude is ethical and practical rather than cognitive.[1]

Mysticism is in fact a living consciousness of reality at its deepest and most fundamental level; it has nothing whatever to do with amorphous and insubstantial groping, with 'moonshine' and intellectual woolliness. Its apparent obscurity derives from its existing in a dimension of consciousness basically apart from the dimension of day-to-day living on this earth. It is thus that language has an almost insurmountable difficulty in expressing mysticism. Language erects

[1] *English Poetry.*

a barrier of conventional symbols around a fundamentally unconventional faculty of experience. Perhaps in the final reckoning only music can communicate mysticism untrammelled; for music is not necessarily and absolutely tied to conventional and associative symbols.

The quality of mind in mystical experience and communication is of great importance. Vivante continues:

> Blake does not minimize intellectual powers, rather he is their avenger. He vindicates thought in its true and deepest meaning, as the fundamental reality, and essentially one with life—*life* being intimately intelligible in and through it.[1]

These remarks, I think, throw considerable light on the later Beethoven. When I spoke of Beethoven as the avenger of form in music it amounted to much the same thing as Vivante's calling Blake the avenger of the intellectual powers, for form is the outward manifestation of thought in music. Beethoven's freeing of form is the symbol of his freeing of thought. Most of the third-period music is strikingly unviolent, in contradistinction to the second-period style which is frequently dependent on violent thematic and rhythmic opposition. Although the first movements of the Ninth Symphony and the C minor Piano Sonata, and the *Grosse Fugue* are instinct with overwhelming power, they do not produce the violent impression of much of the second-period music, because it is no longer a power thrown or exerted *against* something else.

The impression given by the 'Eroica', the Fourth, Fifth, and Seventh symphonies, the 'Appassionata' Sonata, and most other characteristic works of the second period, including the triptych of the 'Rasoumovsky' Quartets, is of singleness of the ideal and aspiration; that of the C minor, A flat and E major Sonatas, the A minor, B flat and C sharp minor Quartets of infinite richness and variety altogether defying definition. Beethoven, in these late works, resolves the inherent contradiction which Vivante notes at the core of mysticism by a total comprehensiveness. Or rather, he does not so much resolve it, for resolution is not what is required here, as give ultimate meaning to it. He does not oppose the intelligible to the unintelligible; he creates art-works which are compounded of both so perfectly blended that there is no longer a conflict, and which produce at one and the same time the effect of a living unity, of love and value, of form and time,

[1] Ibid.

and also of the formless, timeless, immobile and fixed. It is this totality which gives the latter works of Beethoven their uniqueness among the creative achievements of the human mind.

The change from the single, assertive idealism of the second period to the direct apprehension of reality of the third was arrived at, and could only be arrived at, by way of mysticism. Berdyaev says:

> In mystical experience man always escapes from the isolated sphere of the soul and comes into contact with the spiritual source of being and divine reality.   Our answer to a certain type of Protestant who gladly invests mysticism with the character of religious individualism is that mysticism is in fact an escape from individualism which it succeeds in overcoming.   Mysticism is the depth and height of the spiritual life; it is one of its qualities. It is intimate and hidden from the common view, but it is not individualistic.[1]

This passage is of some importance because of the manner in which it refutes the individualistic quality in mysticism. I suggested in discussing the 'Hammerklavier' Sonata and the creative silence which preceded it that Beethoven became gradually and tragically conscious that hitherto the Ego had been all too persistent and pervading in his music, and that the spiritual crisis through which he passed was intimately connected with transcending the Ego and emerging into the ultimate freedom of the spirit. That he did not, prior to 1812, realize the necessity of such a transcendence is suggested by the long period of virtual creative barrenness between 1812 and 1818, and the magnitude of it as a spiritual crisis is revealed in the tragic power of the 'Hammerklavier' Sonata. In short, Beethoven's earlier music was too individualistic. Certainly that individualism was profoundly idealistic and unselfishly motivated. It had in itself a powerful urge towards spirituality. But all individualism, whatever its source or nature, is by definition involved with egocentricity. Individualism is simply the obverse of collectivism: both are insolubly bound to materialism and determinism, and both are opposed to personality and spirituality.

Beethoven's earlier music is charged with individuality, both in the generic and the idealistic sense. It was an individuality of an exceptional quality, and it kept breaking over into personality and reaching out towards freedom. But then came the crisis when Beethoven realized that he was compelled to 'escape from the isolated sphere of the soul' and enter into direct contact with 'the spiritual source of being and

[1] *Freedom and the Spirit.*

divine reality.' Again, it is necessary to insist that only a man of Beethoven's capacity for thinking and experiencing, and for realizing that thought and that experience, could have achieved the essential transformation. Mysticism is not a course that can be taken by short cuts, and mystical experience cannot be achieved, let alone realized, without great effort and in default of great spiritual and intellectual powers.

Nor is mysticism a permanent state of consciousness. It is, to say the least, doubtful if Beethoven during the last years of his life was, any more than St John of the Cross, in a condition of permanent mystical experience. Indeed, with Beethoven's biography before us we know that up to the end he was on one side a man very much of this world, embroiled in its affairs and living its everyday life with energy if not always with enthusiasm. But as Berdyaev insists, mysticism is intimate and hidden from the common view.

In his private hours Beethoven was the true mystic, and the last quartets and sonatas are a living transcript of his mystical experience; they are perhaps the most eloquent and articulate expressions of mysticism ever to be uttered. The experience itself was not of one kind only; for the penetration of spiritual reality that is the essence of mysticism has many aspects. Sometimes it is serene and radiant in its contemplation of the divine unity; at others it takes on a fierce, stark aspect. For Beethoven it could mean either the beatification of the C sharp minor Quartet or the 'Holy Song of Thanksgiving' of the A minor; or it could mean the dramatic visions of the Mass in D and the Ninth Symphony, or the huge intellectuality of the *Grosse Fugue*, a vindication of the power of thought if ever such was uttered in music.

Mysticism, then, is essentially realistic and in no way concerned with phantasies and make-believe. It is in fact the penetration of the ultimate reality. The enigma in mysticism is that it brings us face to face with the mystery of the infinite, and therefore the realization of it is dependent on the possibility of expressing infinity in finite terms. The problem is obviously one of the greatest magnitude and undoubtedly accounts for the rarity of mystical writings and compositions which have the authentic ring and do not degenerate into chaotic symbolism. On the other hand, when such art-works do succeed in communicating mystical experience there are none other which produce so remarkable an impression. Perhaps the problem is in one sense insoluble; but Beethoven at the end of his life did show what can be done by way of revealing infinite order and reality without lapsing into finite chaos and obscurity. It has been said on occasions that Beethoven's last music is obscure; but if it is so it is because, as Shelley said of Plato, 'he is obscure only because he is profound'.

Interwoven with the mysticism of Beethoven's last period there is a definite though not dominant element of asceticism. Beethoven was not by nature or attainment an ascetic. But there are contradictions and conflicts even in the spiritual life, although they are not of the same kind as those in the material world. They exist, and because they exist they constitute a part of mystical experience—therefore they play some part in Beethoven's latter-period music.

Although a form of spiritual and aesthetic asceticism permeates the whole of Beethoven's third-period music, in that it eschews sensuality and aspires constantly towards a divine simplicity, unity, and identity, it is in certain fugal passages or complete movements that the ascetic principle is most clearly revealed. The Finale of the 'Hammerklavier', the Finale of the D major 'Cello Sonata, parts of the A major Piano Sonata, and the *Grosse Fugue* are outstanding examples. The *Grosse Fugue* is not only the most outstanding piece of musical intellectuality in existence; it is also the most intellectually austere music ever composed. It is, however, only in its context as the Finale of the B flat Quartet that its meaning and significance become clear. After the five preceding movements the Fugue comes as the vindication of the human mind in its aspiration towards the infinite. Performed as written, by a string quartet, the *Grosse Fugue* stands for all time as one of the supreme achievements of the human intellect. It makes no concession to normal experience or common understanding; it is a spiritual and aesthetic exercise of the most severe yet comprehensive kind.

Beethoven's asceticism was not a denial or dehumanization of the world, but another transfiguration of it. The *Grosse Fugue* alone makes that abundantly clear; for, unlike the fugue of the 'Hammerklavier', it has not the severity of infinite hopelessness, but of infinite fulfilment. The G flat major section represents not a relaxation but a change of direction essential to the overall totality, the key to which is to be found in the earlier sections of the Quartet.

Asceticism is not a characteristic of Beethoven's second-period style, and mysticism is only hinted at here and there, as in the slow movement of the 'Archduke' Trio. However, that a form of voluntarily accepted ascetic self-discipline was a necessary concomitant of the emergence of the third-period style is shown by its appearance in the D major 'Cello Sonata and the A major Piano Sonata. These are not true third-period works in that they precede the 'Hammerklavier' and stand more or less isolated in a period otherwise barren of major compositions. It is not accurate to describe these, or for that matter any other music of Beethoven, as altogether ascetic; rather it is the appearance of a new ascetic element that marks them out from his previous works. It is notable, too, that where the ascetic elements become most apparent is in the newly conceived and executed contrapuntal sections. It seems likely that Beethoven in fugue, as he came to see and understand it, late in his life, found the ideal medium for concentrated spiritual and artistic, though in no sense academic or pedantic, exercises, for again it was his achievement to free counterpoint from these qualities.

The Sonata in A major is in itself a remarkable forerunner of the matured third-period style, from which much can be learned about the origins of that style. Apart from the contrapuntal features of the trio of the 'alla marcia' and the Finale, there is also a new freedom and expressiveness of melodic phrase which is to reach its apex in music for the piano in the E major Sonata, Op. 109, and which is to become so marked a feature of the late quartets. In its lyric aspects the A major Sonata anticipates the E major no less definitely than in its fugal aspects it anticipates the 'Hammerklavier'. And it is to the new freedom of melodic line and curve that we must turn to find the key to the last sonatas and quartets, for, paradoxically perhaps, it is linked with the more severe contrapuntal features.

We have seen that while preparing for the composition of the Mass in D Beethoven undertook an intensive study of the old modal polyphonic church music. But in fact this study had been active in his creative mind for some years before work was begun on the Mass; the Mass itself only served to focus his creative faculties and channelize his mind in the direction of the old music. In 1818 he jotted down in his sketch-book some words relating to an '*Adagio cantique*; sacred song in a symphony in an old mode . . . either to stand alone, or as introduction to a fugue'. The words are significant in showing the real linkage between a new freedom of melody and a new freedom of counterpoint. For it was via the old modal music that Beethoven discovered the expressive freedom of melody that characterizes his final period. And in another sense it was through it that he discovered the 'new and truly poetic element' which he said must be introduced into the traditional forms of fugue.

Ever since the entrenchment of music in tonality melody had been in chains. The square-cut periods of sonata form with its dependence on major-minor key sequences confined melody and clipped its wings. In the older modal music such confinement and constriction was unknown. Melody was free and untrammelled by the domination of harmony. The subsequent dependence on tonality led to the growth of formality in both melody and counterpoint. But Beethoven, with his tremendous intellectual grasp of essential form, was able eventually to achieve a re-emergence of freedom of melody and voice-leading in a manner that, far from weakening, actually strengthened basic musical structures.

This melodic plasticity and subtlety of voice-leading is an outstanding quality of the third-period Beethoven. And it is one of the most fructifying influences for the subsequent development of the art of music. Growing out of the fusion of the melodic and contrapuntal freedom in modal music with the fundamentals of sonata form Beethoven gave to music a new release from formality and enormously increased its expressive powers. What Debussy sought and formulated in these words: 'We want free speech in music, infinite melody, infinite variation, and freedom of musical phrase. We want the triumph of natural, free, plastic, and rhythmical music'—Beethoven had already anticipated in his late sonatas and string quartets. Of all music the Quartet in C sharp minor is the most free, natural, plastic, and rhythmical. It gives new meaning to infinite melody, infinite variation, and freedom of musical phrase. And what is true of the C sharp minor is true of all his last music.

In the mature music of Wagner the influence of late Beethoven is strongly to be discerned. Particularly in *Tristan* and *Parsifal* Wagner was stretching out to free melody in opera from its previous formality. The long, weaving lines and immense melodic paragraphs stand in direct contrast to the classically moulded beauty of the operatic arias of Gluck and also of Mozart. And it is in Beethoven's third-period discoveries that the mature style of Wagner originated. Without the last compositions of Beethoven the characteristic Wagnerian *melos* and its handling would not have come into being.

Beethoven was the great liberator of musical form and line from the rigid straits into which it had fallen during the classical period. It is of course true that no musical form becomes rigid and inflexible in the hands of a genius; and the sonata form music, with its entrenchment in tonality, of Haydn, Mozart, and the earlier Beethoven himself, can hardly be described as the suffocated victim of formalism. None the less, the gains of classical sonata form were bought at some cost to the essential nature of music. What Beethoven in his third period did was to return to music the freedom and plasticity of the pre-harmonic periods without weakening or nullifying the inherent virtues of sonata form and tonality. Gone now is the broad tonic-dominant swing of the typical second-period music; instead there is a variety, richness, and subtlety of relationship which represents a transcendent musical reality, just as the mystical experience to which it gives expression is a direct apprehension of the ultimate spiritual reality. The two are inextricably linked. The musical reality is a direct corollary of the spiritual reality, and *vice versa*.

In the typical second-period compositions the directness and simplicity, the clear harmonic breadth and tonal swing across tonic and dominant, were entirely suited to the expression of the direct ethical idealism and robust single-mindedness of Beethoven himself during the middle years of his life. It is only after the crisis leading to the 'Hammerklavier' Sonata that the style changed radically, and an entirely new direction was taken.

It is significant that the last three piano sonatas were all produced during the composition of the Mass in D. Among the notable features of the Mass are the superhuman sections of fugue and the renewed appearance in liturgical music of modal harmony and polyphony; and both these elements go, in a certain sense, as off-shoots of the Mass, into the sonatas, to be subsequently carried to fulfilment in the last five quartets. It is impossible not to affirm that the new lyric expressiveness, the new freedom of melodic line and originality of voice-leading of the E major Sonata, much of the A flat, and the final variations of the C minor were a direct outcome of Beethoven's rediscovery of preharmonic music, just as the fugal Finale of the A flat and of the first movement of the C minor were the outcome of his studies in modal counterpoint.

Even a man who has attained to mystical experience of the spiritual life can still know pain and the face of suffering. The 'arioso dolente' of the A flat Sonata is the infinitely poignant utterance of one who has reached a comprehensive vision of the ultimate mysteries. It is not the tragedy of the life in this world that is the slow movement of the first

'Rasoumovsky' Quartet; nor is it the pain of hopeless resignation that is the Adagio of the 'Hammerklavier' Sonata. But the apprehension of reality to which Beethoven's last music gives expression does not turn its back on suffering or banish it by a renunciation of activity in which there must always be a constituent of pain: it simply transforms pain and suffering into elements of a new extension of the consciousness. The pain of the Arioso finally dissolves and is gathered up into the superabundant strength of the concluding Fugue.

Similarly, the power of the opening movement of the C minor Sonata has not the sheer elemental and single-minded passion of the second-period heroic style. It is strength exerted for its own fulfilment. It is not pitted against its opposite or hurled recklessly into the silence and in passionate defiance. It has nothing of the violence of dramatic conflict of, say, the first movement of the C minor Symphony. It does not *assert*, it quite simply *is* the power of the human spirit and creative fire. It is a strength of pure spirituality such as alone can lead to the stillness of infinite peace that is the Arietta.

That the piano ultimately failed to satisfy Beethoven as a medium for conveying his deepest thoughts is an integral part of the creative process which led to the last quartets. The piano had served him loyally throughout his creative career. He was indeed first and foremost a pianist, a practising one until deafness finally brought an end to his executant activities in all forms, and it was only natural that the music he composed while predominantly occupied with the Mass in D should have been for the piano—it was the most direct and immediate form available to him while his principal energies were engaged elsewhere.

The three last sonatas play the role during these years in Beethoven's creative life that was later to be taken over by the string quartet. Already the elements of the late quartet style are to be discerned in the sonatas, in terms of keyboard music. There is the same improvisatory tendency, the same sense of 'sketch treatment', the same freedom of form, flexibility of melody and freshness of voice-leading. But in the end the piano revealed its inherent limitations. In the Arietta and variations of the C minor Sonata the clashing partials of equal temperament jar intolerably on the beatific vision of unearthly peace. In the 'Hammerklavier' these mechanical limitations could in one sense be seen as an advantage, the overcoming of which was symbolic of the gigantic conflict of the music. But the Arietta passes beyond all

limitations. Henceforth only the pure tones of four strings sufficed for
the expression of his most intimate experience. If Beethoven had lived
he might have composed more string quartets; he might have composed more for the orchestra and for voices; he would never again
have composed for the piano.

Beethoven's return to the string quartet was instigated in the first
place by a commission from Prince Galitzin to compose three quartets.
But his creative spirit was already moving inevitably towards this most
purely musical and untrammelled of media. The creative impulses of
the last sonatas could only be carried on in chamber music for strings.
The commission from Prince Galitzin came at the right moment: it
was another case of an igniting spark. But the quartets would have
been written one way or another even if circumstances had not
channelized already latent creative processes.

The commission, however, served also to add an element of external
confusion to the music of Beethoven's closing years. Galitzin had asked
for three quartets: consequently those in E flat, Op. 127, in A minor,
Op. 132, and in B flat, Op. 130, are dedicated to him, thus giving the
impression that these three are in some way related as the earlier
'Rasoumovskys' had been. Then, again, Beethoven himself did not
help towards clarification because the opus numbers themselves are
confusing and misleading. The true position is that the E flat stands
alone, as does the final work of all, the F major, Op. 135. The three
middle quartets, the A minor, the B flat, and the C sharp minor, form
a great interrelated triptych bound together spiritually by an internal
creative process of the most comprehensive and far-reaching kind, and
musically by a single thematic 'motif' which appears in its pure form
at the outset of the A minor. The transmigrations of this motif through
the three quartets is the musical testament to the spiritual and creative
freedom which Beethoven attained at the end of his life. To follow it
from the opening page of the A minor through the intellectual elevation of the *Grosse Fugue* which concludes and gives its full meaning to
the B flat, and thence to its further transformation into the essence of
the serenity which emerges out of the miraculously sustained fugue
which opens the C sharp minor, is to follow the naked and unadorned
creative spirit into the realm of eternal being itself. The transition from
the *Grosse Fugue* to the fugue of the C sharp minor Quartet is perhaps
the most purely inspired achievement of the human mind of which we
have direct recorded evidence.

These three quartets form the hard core of Beethoven's third period and are the ultimate justification of it. They may also be said to justify the works of man to God. Their individual characters are quite different; yet the overall unity is more comprehensive even than the unity of each single work. For cogency and coherence they stand alone among expressions of profound mystical experience in terms of created art.

The flanking quartets, in E flat and F major, are hardly less exalted examples of creativity, but they do not form a part of the unity of the central three. The Quartet in E flat is in three of its four movements remarkable for a serene, composed strength and a sort of radiant lyrical beauty new to the string quartet style. It is an illuminating experience to trace the development of Beethoven in E flat via the single-minded Hellenic ideal of heroism of the 'Eroica' through the mature self-assurance and well-being of the 'Emperor' Concerto to the serenity and ideality of the E flat Quartet. The great *maestoso* pre-ludal bars, which recur twice more in the course of the movement, stand in direct contrast to the fierce staccato chords which act as a 'signal' to the Allegro for the 'Eroica' as representing the difference between the energy of finite action and the stillness of infinite action. The latter exists purely on a spiritual plane and is thus characteristic of the third-period music. And the spiritual and intellectual development made manifest through these three compositions in E flat is complemented by an identical musical development.

The slow movement of the E flat Quartet, 'adagio, ma non troppo e molto cantabile', is another direct consequence of the studies in modal music associated with the Mass in D. Here for the first time in the string quartet is that sustained polyphony which Beethoven learnt from the example of the sixteenth century and welded with creative genius to the modern chamber music style. This Adagio is of a piece with the variations of the E major and C minor Sonatas and the Ninth Symphony, and is related to the *Benedictus* of the Mass. The most direct distillation of modal polyphony comes, however, in the slow movement of the A minor—the 'Sacred Song of Thanksgiving to God from one healed in sickness, in the Lydian mode'. The modal sections, set against passages in D major, surcharged with renewed life form the king-pin of the whole composition. It is thus strange, to say the least, that Sullivan saw fit to call the A minor the most pessimistic of all Beethoven's quartets. I cannot see how any composition which includes the 'heiliger Dankgesang' can be called pessimistic in any sense, even the superficial and popular one. The truth is that the A minor is the first step in the spiritual and creative process which came to fulfilment in the C sharp minor, and is thus conscious still of the world and its fallibility which the latter quartet will in its turn overcome. This sense of lingering mortal frailty was emphasized by the illness which preceded the A minor and which all but cost Beethoven his life.

The last quartet of all, the F major, and the last composition that Beethoven lived to complete, is in many ways unlike any of the others; yet it emerges recognizably from them. Lightly constructed, transparent, capricious, fantastical, and humorous as it is, the F major is anything but trivial and insignificant. It is one of the most economical quartets in existence, even from the pen of Beethoven, who wasted nothing. To the eye, especially the conventional eye, the score looks more like a sketch for a quartet. It is suggested that its brevity and concision were the result of Beethoven's irritation with a publisher who drove a hard bargain; but it is more likely that he simply used a quartet which was inherently brief and concise as a convenient means of causing annoyance to the recalcitrant business man. Certainly the brevity and concision of the F major Quartet are part and parcel of the creative process which lies behind it.

Much play has been made with the fact that this was indeed Beethoven's last completed composition. Only the new Finale for the B flat Quartet, a piece which differs fundamentally from the F major Quartet because it really is trivial, followed. This Finale was produced to replace the *Grosse Fugue* which was found too difficult and too exhausting by Beethoven's contemporaries. He obliged with a charming and fanciful piece which denied the B flat Quartet, just as his expressed permission to alter the order of movements, and even to omit some, in the 'Hammerklavier' Sonata denied that gigantic work. In both cases Beethoven was prepared to temporize with society for material reasons, knowing full well that the justification of both works lay not even in posterity but in eternity.

The F major Quartet, and especially the Finale with its 'difficult resolution', is an enigmatic composition. Whether it was enigmatic because Beethoven knew it was the end, or simply because it was just another aspect of the totality of his experience, is something that cannot be definitely settled one way or the other. No doubt Beethoven had his presentiments, if not his certain knowledge, of approaching death.

There is, however, no reason to suppose that he deliberately wrote the F major Quartet as his farewell to the world. When he died he was full of new plans for composition; he was anything but 'written out' and had some expectation of completing great new works. The question we have to ask is, would Beethoven have written the F major Quartet as in fact he did whether or not he had been conscious of the proximity of mortal death? The internal evidence and the characteristic manner in which Beethoven went to work at the end of his life suggest strongly that it would have been written exactly as in fact it was.

The key to the F major is probably to be found in the variations Andante and the Scherzo of the C sharp minor. The playful, boisterous humour and sparseness of ornament derive from the latter, while the Lento in D flat, which falls like petals of thought from the four instruments, attains to a peace and heart's ease which seem like something made possible through the multitudinous life that springs spontaneously from those heaven-inspired variations. The Finale too shows how far Beethoven had travelled from earthly problems and tribulations. Gravely the question is asked: 'Muss es sein?' (Must it be?): then jocosely comes the retort: 'Es muss sein! Es muss sein!' (It must be! It must be!) Is this another of Beethoven's little jokes?— or is it the final question and answer to approaching death? It is supposed to have originated as a jest, relating to an unpaid laundry bill or a performing right subscription or something—authorities are not unanimous on the subject, except that apparently the canon was originally written down in a moment of frivolous good humour. Others, not to be put off so easily, exert themselves to the full to load the resolution with metaphysical significance.

We need not concern ourselves long with the argument. The solution is not a case of either-or, but quite simply—both. Beethoven at the end of his life had attained to such a grasp of the ultimate mysteries and realities that for him a tiresome little incident on this earth and the greatest problem of all could quite easily be seen to revolve around the same axis. The two are only separated and put on different planes when a wedge is driven between 'this life' and 'the next'. But in mystical penetration this separation is shown to be artificial and meaningless. The spiritual world transforms the material world and gives new life to it. That Beethoven had reached to such penetration is revealed in the C sharp minor Quartet, the work above all in which he found the ultimate freedom. After it he could, as it were, toss the greatest and the smallest of problems from hand to hand as one at play with a ball; and when the final question was asked of him he could return a jocular answer, not by way of evasion, but simply because he had in the depths of his spiritual experience already passed beyond it.

In his farthest flights of spirit and imagination Beethoven remained to the end a true active subject. It is another illusion concerning the character of mysticism to suppose that it consists principally in passive contemplation. Mysticism is essentially active. Passive mysticism is a contradiction of terms. Mysticism cannot be passive because it pre-supposes creative activity on the part of personality. And Beethoven was the most active personality who ever lived. The radiant beauty of his late music is essentially an active principle; it is a beauty of free activity, of ultimate liberation and of infinite life. It transcends the conditioned freedom of a Bach or a Goethe and reaches out beyond the symbols to the realities of the spirit.

In the history of the development of the human mind Beethoven stands as the antithesis of the passivism of the East. Activism is par-ticularly a quality of the western or European mind; but it is not a necessity of that mind. Passivism has throughout history claimed the mind of western man in one form or another. Even the Christian religion, which is at bottom profoundly active, has been frequently projected into the body social as a passive and objective principle. None the less, activism is the distinguishing quality of the western mind and that which differentiates it most clearly from the eastern mind. It was Kant's theory of the active subject which dominated European philosophical thought during Beethoven's lifetime. Kant liberated the human mind from the inherent determinism of the objectivist philosophies. Beethoven for his part gave decisive meaning to positive activity, and in the end revealed nothing less than the reality of ultimate freedom.

It is true that the active subject existed before Kant discovered and propounded it, just as the structure of the mind and its psychological make-up and conditions existed before Freud adumbrated them. Thus it is not true to suppose that Beethoven could not have existed in a previous age before the active subject of which he is the outstanding example had been 'discovered'. All the same Beethoven was born into the age which was most ready for him and which, due to a variety of circumstances, in a real but wholly mysterious sense, stimulated his creative faculties.

It is not going too far to assert that Beethoven's greatest gift to that humanity he himself wished to serve was the living evidence of the power, the perdurable strength and the essential value of the human mind and spirit. So long as the world continues to be loyal to the music of Beethoven there is little danger of its acquiescing in the obliteration of personality in materialist, determinist, or collectivist philosophies, policies, economies, and theories of science, let alone of naïve scientism. Beethoven is the living example of what the individual human being can achieve by persistent endeavour. In times good or ill he cannot but inspire and fortify all who attend to him; for in his music is to be found the justification of the life of mankind. What one individual has done another can aspire to; the destiny that one man has challenged and finally mastered another has it in his power to confront courageously also. In its externals Beethoven's destiny was his own; seen from within it is the destiny of man made manifest in one individual.

The great and enduring potency of Beethoven's creative life lay not only in its courage, its heroism, its idealism—there have been brave men and heroes and idealists before and will be again. What marks Beethoven out is that he possessed on the one hand the capacity for experiencing the whole of life right through to the ultimate realities, and on the other the creative genius to realize that experience to the full. It is the coincidence of the twin capacities for experiencing and realization that gives Beethoven his unique quality as man and artist. There have been those in the course of history who have been capable of the profoundest experience but who have lacked the creative faculty to realize it; and there have been those possessed of fertile artistic talents but with little to communicate. In Beethoven alone among musicians there has been combined the capacity to follow both out to the limits. Because of the strength of the principle of positive activity in Beethoven's genius he could not rest or accept a finite solution to the mysteries of this life. He was obliged by the nature of his genius to go ever forward until at last he came face to face with the Divine Unity itself. It was his destiny that he should do so; but the cost to himself as a human being compounded of mortal flesh as well as transcendent spirituality was heavy in the extreme. His great value lies precisely in the fact that had he been a man of less stature he could have declined the challenge of destiny and remained something still fine and

M

upstanding but less than supreme. The little lump leaveneth the whole, and because one man, if only one man, has stormed the height and matched himself, spirit and sinew, with the Godhead the whole of life on this earth is made richer, deeper, and more potent for all mankind.

No man more than Beethoven has revealed and expanded the boundaries of human consciousness and human potentiality. He threw light and illumination into the darkest corridors of existence, and he brought a new essence to the concept of reality. In the profoundest sense he vindicated the idea of man as a creature bearing within him the living image of God the Creator. He provided the justification of the principle of activity on the part of the human personality and established beyond all doubt the meaning of personal responsibility. He once said: 'Whoever understands my music will henceforth be free of the misery of the world'. For nearly a century after his death his last music was misconstrued and regarded as enigmatic and more or less incomprehensible. Its simplicity was mistaken for complexity; its freedom for chaos; its aspiration for blind striving; its vital power for unyielding and unnecessary severity. But, as he himself knew, the time would come when it would be understood, and today it is honoured perhaps above all other creations of the human mind. The applications of science have made possible that familiarity through constant study which alone can make it yield up its secrets. Even now we cannot without vanity say that we understand to the full and are at one with Beethoven. For that we should ourselves need to attain Beethoven's own spiritual stature. But his claim to liberate us from the miseries of this world remains valid. We do not have to claim for Beethoven perfection and infallibility either as man or artist, for he was in all his parts a man like us and subject to the same temptations of the flesh and aspirations of the spirit. He does not fulfil our destiny for us, but he shows how we in our turn may fulfil it. We know, with certainty and beyond all more comfortable allurements to the contrary, that his claim to liberate us is true. And in that knowledge may lie the first step on the road to our own salvation and the transfiguration of the world.

Appendix

I GIVE BELOW a few of the most important Beethoven documents. Well known though most of them are, and familiar in detail to all students of the composer, I think it desirable to quote them once again because of the light they throw on Beethoven's state of mind at various stages of his life, and because they are directly relevant to the arguments in the main chapters of this book. There are of course literally hundreds more, many of them supremely illuminating. But I confine myself here to the minimum which throw particular light on some aspect of Beethoven's mind and personality and which thus appear as complementary to his music.

THE HEILIGENSTADT TESTAMENT

For my brothers Karl and —— Beethoven.

O ye men who regard or declare me to be malignant, stubborn, or cynical, how unjust are ye towards me. You do not know the secret cause of my seeming so. From childhood onward, my heart and mind prompted me to be kind and tender, and I was ever inclined to accomplish great deeds. But only think that during the last six years I have been in a wretched condition, rendered worse by unintelligent physicians. Deceived from year to year with hopes of improvement, and then finally forced to the prospect of *lasting infirmity* (it may last for years, or even be totally incurable). Born with a fiery active temperament, even susceptible to the diversions of society, I had soon to retire from the world to live a solitary life. At times, even, I endeavoured to forget all this, but how harshly was I driven back by the redoubled experience of my bad hearing. Yet it was not possible for me to say to men : 'Speak louder, shout, for I am deaf'. Alas, how could I declare the weakness of a *sense* which in me *ought to be* more acute than in others—a sense which *formerly* I possessed in the highest perfection, a perfection such as few in my profession enjoy, or ever have enjoyed; no, I cannot do it. Forgive, therefore, if you see me withdraw, when I would willingly mix with you. My misfortune pains me doubly in that I am certain to be misunderstood. For me there can be no re-creation in the society of my fellow creatures, no refined conversation, no interchange of thought. Almost alone, and only mixing in society when absolutely necessary, I am compelled to live as an exile. If I approach too near to people, a feeling of hot anxiety comes over me lest my condition should be noticed—for so it was during these past six months which I spent in the country. Ordered by my intelligent physician to spare my hearing as much as possible, he at least fell in with my present frame of mind, although many a time I was carried away by sociable inclinations. But how humiliating was it, when some-one standing close to me heard a distant flute, and I heard *nothing*, or a *shepherd singing*, and again I heard nothing. Such incidents drove me almost to despair; at times I was on the point of putting an end to my life—*art* alone restrained my hand. Oh! it seemed as if I could not quit this earth until I had produced all I felt within me; and so I continued this wretched life—wretched indeed, with so sensitive a body, that a somewhat sudden change can throw me from the best into the worst state. *Patience*, I am told, I must choose for my guide. I have done so—lasting, I hope, will be my resolution to bear up until it pleases the inexorable Parcae to break the thread. Forced already in my twenty-eighth year [Beethoven was actually thirty-two but was mistaken about the date of his birth] to become a philosopher, it is not easy; for an artist more difficult than for anyone else. O Divine Being, Thou who lookest down into my inmost soul, Thou understandest; Thou knowest that love for mankind and a desire to do good dwell therein. Oh, my fellow men, when one day you read this, remember that you were unjust to me, and let the unfortunate one console himself if he can find one like himself, who in spite of all obstacles which nature has thrown in his way, has still done everything in his power to be received into the ranks of worthy artists and men. You, my brothers, Karl and ——, as soon as I am dead, beg Professor Schmidt, if he still be living, to describe my malady; and annex this written account to that of my illness, so that at least the world, as far as possible, may become re-conciled to me after my death. And now I declare you both heirs to my small fortune (if such it can be called). Divide it honourably and dwell in peace, and help each other. What you have done against me, has, as you know, long been forgiven. And you, brother Karl, I especially thank you for the attachment you have shown towards me of late. My prayer is that your life may be better, less troubled by cares, than mine. Recommend to your children *virtue*; it alone can bring happiness, not money. I speak from experience. It was virtue which bore me up in time of trouble; to her next to my art I owe thanks for my not having laid violent hands on myself. Farewell, and love one another. My thanks to all friends, especially *Prince Lichnowsky and Professor Schmidt*. I should much like one of you to keep, as an heirloom, the instruments, given to me by Prince Lichnowsky, but let no strife arise between you concerning them; if money should be of more service to you, just sell them. How happy I feel that, even lying in my grave, I may be useful to you.

So let it be. I joyfully hasten to meet death. If it come before I have had opportunity to develop all my artistic faculties, it will come, my hard fate notwithstanding, too soon, and I should probably wish it later—yet even then I shall be happy, for will it not deliver me from a state of endless suffering? Come when thou wilt, I shall face thee courageously—farewell, and, when I am dead, do not entirely forget me. This I deserve of you, for during my lifetime I often thought of you, and how to make you happy. Be ye so.

Ludwig van Beethoven.

Heiligenstadt, the 6th October 1802.

(Codicil, on the fourth side of the Testament)

Heiligenstadt, October 1802. Thus I take my farewell of thee— and indeed sadly—yes, that fond hope which I entertained when I came here, of being at any rate healed up to a certain point, must be entirely abandoned. As the leaves of autumn fall and fade, so it has withered away for me; almost the same as when I came here do I go away—even the high courage which often in the beautiful summer days gladdened me, that has vanished. O Providence, let me have just one pure day of *joy*; so long it is since joy filled my heart. Oh, when, oh, when, O Divine Being, shall I be able once again to feel in the temple of nature and of men.

Never—no—that would be too hard.

For my brothers Karl and ―― to execute after my death.

Letters to the 'Immortal Beloved'

(Date of writing conjectural as to year)

On the 6th July in the morning.

My angel, my all, my very self,

A few words only today and in pencil (with your pencil). Not until tomorrow will my room be definitely engaged. What unworthy waste of time. Why this deep sorrow where necessity speaks? Can our love endure otherwise than through sacrifices, except through restraint in our demands. Can you help not being wholly mine? Can I not being wholly yours? Oh, gaze at nature in all its beauty and comfort yourself with that which is inevitable—love demands everything and that rightly. *Thus it is with me as far as concerns you and you with me.* Only you forget that I must live for myself and for you. If we were wholly united you would feel the pain of it as little as I should. My journey here was terrible. I did not arrive until four o'clock yesterday morning, and as horses were short, the mail post went by another route, but what an awful one. At the last stage but one I was warned against night travelling and in an alarming forest; but that only encouraged me, and I was wrong. The coach, of course, must break down on the dreadful road—a bottomless mud swamp. Without the postillions with me I should have been stuck in the road. Esterházy, travelling by the usual road, had the same fate with eight horses as I had with four—yet I got some pleasure from it, as I always do from successfully overcoming difficulties. Now a quick change from without to within. We shall probably soon see each other; beside, I cannot tell you all that has passed through my mind during the last few days about my life—were our hearts closely united I should not have thoughts of this kind. My heart is full of many things to say to you—ah, there are times when I feel that speech is powerless. Be cheerful—remain my true, my only treasure, my all, as I am yours. The gods must send the rest. What they say is and must be.

Your faithful

Ludwig.

Monday evening, July 6th.

You are suffering, my dearest love. I have only just found out that letters must be posted very early on Mondays and Thursdays—the only days when the post goes from here to K. You suffer. Ah, wherever I am you are there also with me. I will arrange for both of us so that I shall live—and with you. What a life!!!! Such it is!!!! without you. Pursued by the kindness of men, which I little deserve and as little care to deserve. Humility of man towards man—it pains me—and when I consider myself and the Universe, what I am and what is he whom we call the greatest; and again this shows the divine in man. I weep when I think that you will probably not get the first news from me until Saturday evening. Much as you love me, my love for you is stronger; but never conceal your thoughts from me. Good night. As I am taking the baths I must go to bed ***** ***** [two words crossed out]. Oh, God, so near, so far. Is not our life a truly celestial edifice, firm as the vault of heaven.

Good morning, on July 7th.

While still in bed my thoughts go out to you, my Beloved One, sometimes joyful and sometimes sorrowful, waiting to learn whether fate will take pity on us. For I must live wholly with you or not at all. Yes, I have made up my mind to wander into distant lands until I can fly to your arms and say that there I am really at home. With you about me I can send my soul into the realm of the spirits. Yes, unhappily it must be so. You will be all the more calm and resolved as soon as you know my faithfulness towards you. No one else can ever possess my heart—never—never—— Oh, God, why must one part from what one so loves. And yet life in V.[ienna] is a wretched one at present. Your love has made me one of the happiest and yet the most miserable of men—at my age I need a steady quiet life. Is that possible in our situation? My angel, I have just heard that the mail post goes every day, and I must stop at once so that you may receive the letter immediately. Only by calm consideration of our existence can we attain our purpose to live together—be calm—love me—today— yesterday—what tearful longings for you—you—you—my life— my all—farewell—and continue to love me—never misjudge the faithful heart

of your beloved

L.

Ever yours,
Ever mine,
Ever each other's.

BEETHOVEN, BETTINA BRENTANO, and GOETHE

Transcript of Bettina Brentano's Conversations with Beethoven, in a Letter to Goethe

Vienna, May 28th 1810.

When I saw him of whom I shall now speak to you I forgot the whole world, as it vanishes again when I recall the scene. . . . It is Beethoven of whom I wish to speak to you now, and in whose presence I forgot the world. I am still juvenile, I know; but I am not mistaken when I declare what no one yet perhaps believes and understands, that he is far in advance of the general culture of mankind, and whether we shall ever overtake him is doubtful. May it be granted that he shall live until the mighty and sublime riddle which lies in his spirit has been developed to its fullest expression. May he reach his highest goal so that he can leave the key to a divine knowledge in our hands, that we may advance a further step towards true happiness.

To you I can confess that I believe in a heavenly magic which is the element of intellectual life. This magic Beethoven practises in his art; all that he can tell you is pure magic, every attitude is the organization of a higher existence, and so Beethoven feels himself to be the founder of a new sensuous basis in the life of the spirit. You indeed will gather from this what I want to say and what the truth is. Who could replace this mind for us? From whom else can we expect so much? All mankind's activities buzz around him like clockwork, he alone creates freely out of himself the unexpected, uncreated. What to him is intercourse with the world, who is at his daily task before sunrise and who, after sunset, scarcely looks about him, forgets his bodily sustenance and is carried by the stream of his inspiration beyond the shores of superficial daily mechanism. He, himself, said: 'When I open my eyes I must sigh for what I see, it is contrary to my religion, and I must despise the world which does not suspect that music is a higher revelation than all wisdom and philosophy, it is the wine which inspires to new procreation, and I am the Bacchus who presses out this glorious wine for men, and makes them drunk with the spirit. When they are sober again, then they have fished up everything they can bring to dry land. I have no friend, I must live alone with myself. But I know well that God is nearer to me than to others in my art. I go fearlessly

with him, I have always perceived and understood him, and I have no
fear for my music, which can have no evil fate. Those to whom it
makes itself understood will be free from all the misery with which
others are enchained.'

All this Beethoven said to me the first time I saw him. A feeling of
awe filled me as he expressed himself to me with such open friendliness,
for I must have seemed quite insignificant to him. Also, I was surprised,
for I had been told that he was very shy of intercourse with people and
would talk with no one. They were afraid of introducing me to him.
I was obliged to seek him out alone. He has three lodgings in which he
conceals himself alternatively—one in the country, one in the town
and the third on the bastion. I found him in the last on third floor. . . .

He accompanied me home, and on the way spoke many beautiful
things about art, but speaking so loud and standing stock still in the
street so that it took courage to listen to him. He spoke with great
passion and much too surprisingly for me not to forget that we were in
the street. People were very surprised to see him go in with me to a
large company who were dining with us. After dinner, without being
asked, he sat down at the pianoforte and played long and wonderfully,
his pride fermenting with his genius. When he is in such a state of
exaltation he attempts the incomprehensible and his fingers accomplish
the impossible. . . .

Yesterday I went with him into a beautiful garden in full bloom. . . .
Beethoven remained standing in the oppressive heat of the sun and
said: 'Goethe's poems make a great impression on me, not only by
their content but by the rhythm. . . . From the vocal point of inspiration I must discharge melody in all directions. I pursue it, I capture it
again passionately, I see it elude me, disappearing in the mass of various
experiments. Soon I seize it again with renewed passion. I cannot
separate myself from it, I must with immediate rapture multiply it in
all modulations and at length triumph over the first musical thought—
that is a symphony. Music is the mediation between the intellectual and
the sensuous life. I should like to speak about this with Goethe. I
wonder if he would understand me? . . . Speak to Goethe of me. Tell
him to hear my symphonies and he will then agree that music is the
only bodiless entry into a higher world of knowledge which comprehends mankind, but which is not comprehended by it.

'Rhythm belongs to the spiritual, creating music in its substance, it
gives a foreboding, an inspiration of heavenly knowledge, and what

the spirit in sense perceives of itself, that is the incorporation of spiritual knowledge. If spirits live by that as man lives by air then to grasp them with this intellect is quite another matter. But the more the soul creates this sensuous nourishment out of itself, the richer the spirit will be in happy understanding of itself. But few succeed in this, for thousands wish to wed with love, and love in these thousands does not reveal itself although they all carry on the handiwork of love, so thousands carry on an intercourse with music but nevertheless have no revelation. Here is the basis of mortality as of all art. All pure invention is a moral progress. To be able to bring itself into subjection to these undiscoverable laws, to bind and guide the intellect to these laws so that the revelations stream forth, that is the isolating principle of art.

'To be loosened or dissolved from appearance, that is the devotion to the godlike which practises in quietness its dominion over the untamed spirit of rage and so gives to the fancy its highest efficaciousness. So art supplies the godlike and man's relation to it is religion, which we acquire through art, which is the divine gift of God. It gives a goal to man's capacity which he attains.

'We do not know what knowledge brings us. The seed sealed in its case needs the moist, electrical, warm soil to sprout, to think, to express itself. Music is the electrical soil in which the spirit lives, thinks, invents. Philosophy is a deposit of the mind's electrical spirit. Its necessity which will base everything on one primeval principle is elevated by it, and although the mind is not supreme over what it generates through it, yet it is happy in this generation and so every real creation of art is independent, more powerful than the artist himself, and returns to the divine through its manifestation and belongs to mankind only in that it is a sign of the mediation of the divine in him. Music gives to the mind its relation to harmony. A thought abstracted has nevertheless the feeling of the whole, and the relationship in spirit; so is every thought in music which is in inward decisive relationship with the whole the kernel of harmony. Everything electrical moves the spirit to fluid, streaming musical manifestation. I am an electrical nature. I must interrupt the flow of my undemonstrable wisdom otherwise I shall neglect my rehearsal. Write to Goethe from me if you understand what I have said; but I can be answerable for nothing and will gladly let myself be instructed by him.'

I promised him to write to you what he said so far as I understood it. He took me to a general rehearsal with full orchestra. I sat there in a box quite alone. . . . So I then saw this immeasurable genius lead his regiment. Oh, Goethe! No kaiser and no king has such knowledge of his power and how it proceeds from him as this Beethoven. . . . If I understood him as I feel him, then I should know everything. . . . Yesterday evening I wrote down all he had said and this morning I showed it to him. He said: 'Did I say that? Then I must have had a Raptus.' He read it through again carefully and struck out the above and wrote between the lines, for he is anxious that you should understand him.

Make me happy with a speedy answer which will show Beethoven that you appreciate him. It was always our plan to discuss music, I wished to do so; but I feel now for the first time through Beethoven that I am not equal to the task.

Bettina.

GOETHE'S REPLY TO THE ABOVE

6th June 1810.

Your letter, heartily beloved child, came to me at a fortunate hour. You have done well to portray to me a great and fine nature in its achievements and strivings, in its needs and in the superabundance of its gifts. It has given me great pleasure to receive this picture of a truly great spirit. Without wishing to classify him it requires a psychological feat to extract the true measure of agreement; however, I feel no desire to contradict what I have understood of your hurried explosion. On the contrary, I should like for once to admit to you a certain inner agreement of my nature with what I have been able to grasp from your varied expressions. The ordinary mind may perhaps find contradictions there; but a layman must have reverence for what is spoken by one possessed of such a daemon, and it is all the same whether he speaks from feeling or from knowledge, for here the gods are at work and scatter the seeds for future discernment, and we must wish that they may proceed to an undisturbed development. But before they become general, the clouds which veil mankind's spirit must part. Give Beethoven my heartiest greetings and say that I would willingly make his personal acquaintance, by which we could have a happy exchange of thoughts and feelings. Perhaps you may be able to persuade him to take a trip to Karlsbad, where I go almost every year and would have the most leisure to hear him and get to know him. The thought of teaching him would indeed be an impertinence even from anyone with more insight than myself, since his genius lights the way for him and often illumines him with a lightning stroke, while we sit in darkness and scarcely suspect from which side day will break.

It would give me great pleasure if Beethoven would send me the two songs of mine which he has composed—but clearly written. I am very curious to hear them. It is one of my greatest pleasures, for which I am very grateful, to have the old mood of a poem renewed again through a melody (as Beethoven very correctly says).

G.

BETTINA'S REPLY TO THE ABOVE

Dearest friend,

I communicated your beautiful letter to Beethoven so far as it concerned him. He was greatly pleased and exclaimed, 'If anyone can bring him to understand music I am he.' The idea of visiting you at Karlsbad filled him with enthusiasm. He struck his forehead and said, 'Why could I not have done that before? In truth I did think of it, but was stopped by timidity which affects me frequently, as though I were no real man, but I shall now fear Goethe no longer.' You may reckon therefore on seeing him next year.

Bettina.

EXTRACTS FROM BEETHOVEN'S LETTERS TO BETTINA

Vienna, 11th August 1810.

Dearest Bettina,

No finer spring than the present one, I say that and also feel it, because I have made your acquaintance. You, yourself, have probably seen that in society I am like a fish out of water, which turns round and round, and cannot get away until a benevolent Galatea puts him again into the mighty sea. Yes, I was quite out of my element, dearest Bettina, I was surprised by you at a moment when ill-humour was quite master of me, but it actually disappeared at the sight of you. I at once perceived that you belong to a different world from this absurd one, to which with the best will one cannot open one's ears. I, myself, am a wretched man and yet complain others!—You will surely forgive me, with your good heart, which is seen in your eyes, and with your intelligence, which lies in your ears—at least your ears know how to flatter when they listen. My ears, unfortunately, are a barrier wall through which I cannot easily hold friendly communication with men. Else!—perhaps—I should have more confidence in you. So I could only understand the great, intelligent look of your eyes, which so impressed me that I can never forget it. Dear Bettina, beloved maiden! —art!—Who understands it, with whom can one speak concerning this great goddess!—How dear to me were the few days when we gossiped or rather corresponded together; I have kept all the little notes on which stand your clever, dear, very dear, answers. So I have at any rate to thank my bad hearing that the best part of these fleeting conversations has been noted down. Since you went away I have had vexatious hours, hours of darkness, in which one can do nothing; after your departure I roamed about for full three hours in the Schön-brunner Alley, also on the ramparts; but no angel met me who could take such hold on me as you, angel—forgive, dearest Bettina, this digression from key; I must have such intervals in order to give vent to my feelings. Then you have written, have you not, to Goethe about me?—I would willingly hide my head in a sack, so as to hear and see nothing of what is going on in the world, because you, dearest angel, will not meet me. But I shall surely receive a letter from you? Hope nourishes me, it nourishes indeed half the world, and I have had it as my neighbour half my life; what otherwise would have become of me? . . .

Vienna, February 10th, 1811.

Dear Bettina, you are gong to be, or are already married, and I have not been able to see you once beforehand. May all good wishes where-with marriage blesses folk attend you and your husband. What then shall I say for myself: 'Pity my fate', I exclaim with Johanna; if I live still a few years, also for this and for all other weal and woe, will I thank the Highest who encompasses all things. When you write to Goethe about me, select all the words which will express to him my inmost reverence and admiration. I am just on the point of writing to him about *Egmont*, to which I have written the music, and indeed purely out of love for his poems which cause me happiness. Who can be sufficiently thankful for a great poet, the richest jewel of a nation? And now no more, dear good B.; I only came back from a bacchanalian festival at four o'clock this morning, at which, indeed, I was forced to laugh a great deal, with the result that I have to weep almost as much today. Noisy joy often drives me powerfully back into myself. . . .

Teplitz, August 1812.

Dearest, Good Bettina!

Kings and princes can certainly create professors, privy councillors and titles, and hang on ribbons of various orders, but they cannot create great men, master-minds which tower above the rabble; this is beyond them. Such men must therefore be held in respect. When two such as I and Goethe meet together, these grand gentlemen are forced to note what greatness, in such as we are, means. . . .

If God grant me yet a few years, then I must see you again dear, dear Bettina; so calls the voice within me which never errs. Even minds can love one another. I shall always court yours; your approval is dearer to me than anything in the whole world. I gave my opinion to Goethe, that approval affects such men as ourselves, and that we wish to be listened to with the intellect by those who are our equals. Emotion is only for women (excuse this); the flame of music must burst forth from the mind of man. Ah! my dearest child, we have now for a long time been in perfect agreement about everything!!! The only good thing is a beautiful, good soul, which is recognized in everything, and in presence of which there need be no concealment. *One must be somebody if one wishes to appear so.* The world is bound to recognize one; it is not always unjust. To me, however, that is a matter of no importance: for I have a higher aim. I hope when I get back to Vienna to receive a letter from you. Write soon, soon, and a very long one; in eight days from now I shall be there; and the court goes tomorrow; there will be one more performance today. The Empress rehearsed her part with him. His duke and he both wish me to play some of my music, but to both I made refusal. They are mad on Chinese procelain, hence there is need for indulgence; for intellect has lost the whip hand. I will not play to these silly folk, who never get over that mania nor write at public cost any stupid stuff for princes. Adieu, adieu, dearest; your last letter lay on my heart for a whole night, and comforted me. *Everything* is allowed to musicians. Great Heavens, how I love you!

Your sincerest friend and deaf brother,

Beethoven.

THE CREATIVE PROCESS

BEETHOVEN TO LOUIS SCHLÖSSER

I carry my thoughts about me for a long time, before I write them down. Meanwhile my memory is so tenacious that I am sure never to forget, not even in years, a theme that has once occurred to me. I change many things, discard and try again until I am satisfied. Then, however, there begins in my head the development in every direction and, in so much as I know exactly what I want, the fundamental idea never deserts me—it arises before me, grows—I see and hear the picture in all its extent and dimensions stand before my mind like a cast, and there remains for me nothing but the labour of writing it down, which is quickly accomplished when I have the time, for I sometimes take up other work, but never to the confusion of one with the other.

You will ask where my ideas come from. I cannot say for certain. They come uncalled, sometimes independently, sometimes in association with other things. It seems to me that I could wrest them from Nature herself with my own hands, as I go walking in the woods. They come to me in the silence of the night or in the early morning, stirred into being by moods which the poet would translate into words, but which I put into sounds; and these go through my head ringing and singing and storming until at last I have them before me as notes.

TO BREITKOPF AND HARTEL

Both are handled in an entirely new manner [the Variations for Pianoforte, Op. 34 and Op. 35] . . . usually I hardly realize when my ideas are new, and hear of it first from others; but in this instance I can myself assure you that I have done nothing in the same manner before.

SCHINDLER'S ACCOUNT OF BEETHOVEN AT WORK

I arrived at the master's home in Mödling. It was four o'clock in the afternoon. As soon as we entered we learnt that in the morning both servants had gone away and that there had been a quarrel at midnight which had disturbed all the neighbours because, as a consequence of a long vigil, both had gone to sleep and the food which had been prepared had become uneatable. In the living-room behind a locked door we heard the master singing parts of the fugue and the Credo [of the Mass in D]—singing, howling, stamping. After we had been listening a long time to this most awful scene and were about to go away, the door opened and Beethoven stood before us with distorted features calculated to excite fear. He looked as if he had been in mortal combat with a whole host of contrapuntists, his everlasting enemies. His movements were confused as if he had been disagreeably surprised at our having overheard him. Then he spoke of the day's happenings, and with obvious restraint said: 'Pretty goings on these! Everyone has run away. I have not had anything to eat since yesterday afternoon' —I tried to calm him and helped him to make his toilet. My companion hurried on in advance to the restaurant of the bathing establishment to have something made ready for the famished master.

BEETHOVEN TO VON KONNERITZ

Look upon me kindly and not unfavourably. I live only for my art and to fulfil my duties as a man; but alas it cannot always be done without the help of the subterrestrial powers. (July 1823.)

FROM BEETHOVEN'S SKETCH-BOOKS AND JOURNAL

Devotion—the deepest devotion to your destiny can alone bring you to the sacrifice of . . . and to the endurance of your daily toil. Oh! hard struggle! to accomplish all which remains to be done from the daily drudgery of necessity work to the longest journey, the highest flight. Now all this must be hewn out of myself. You may no longer be a man . . . for you there is no longer happiness except that which you find in yourself, in your art. O God, give me strength to conquer myself. I dare no longer chain myself to life—in that way everything connected with A. will go to destruction. (1812.)

Submission—submission! Thus we may win something even in the deepest misery, and make ourselves worthy to have God forgive our shortcomings.

Fate, show your force! We are not lords of ourselves. What is determined must be, and so let it be!

He who is burdened with an ill which he cannot alter, which is bringing him closer and closer to death and without which his life would have lasted longer, must remember that he might have been killed even sooner by assassination or other causes.

Live in your art alone. Limited as you now are by your hearing, this is the only existence for you.

Follow the counsel of others only in the rarest instances. In a matter that has already been considered, to whom can all the circumstances be as clear in consciousness as to oneself?

Just as the State must have a constitution, so must the individual have one of his own. (1816.)

Peace and freedom are the best of all things. True friendship can be founded only on the union of similar natures. (1817.)

TO ZMESKALL

I am often in despair and would like to end my life. . . . God have mercy on me, I regard myself as good as lost. If the condition does not change I shall next year be not in London but in the grave.—Thank God the role will soon be played out.

BEETHOVEN'S CREDO

Only by hard, persistent labour through such powers as are bestowed on a man can the work of art be made worthy of the Creator and Preserver of everlasting Nature!

WRITTEN OUT BY BEETHOVEN AND KEPT FRAMED ON HIS DESK

I am that which is.

I am all that is, that was, and that shall be.

No mortal man hath lifted my veil.

He is alone by Himself, and to Him alone do all things owe their being.

N

Bibliography

BEETHOVEN literature alone is of immense size and scope; a complete listing would fill a large volume. And in a book such as the present one, which covers material outside that devoted solely to Beethoven's biography and the direct musical analysis of his works, it is clear that bibliographical reference must extend over a correspondingly wider field. It is therefore only possible to append a short-list of books which impinge, in one way or another, on the principal arguments advanced in the main chapters. The volumes catalogued below can only be regarded as a starting point. The subject itself is inexhaustible.

Although the text of my book was substantially completed in 1957, I have before going to press added one or two volumes published since then which may help to throw further light on the ideas advanced in it.

I

Books Devoted to Beethoven Himself

BEKKER, PAUL, *Beethoven*, Berlin, 1911. English translation by M. M. Bozman, J. M. Dent & Sons, London, 1925.

BERLIOZ, HECTOR, *Beethoven's Nine Symphonies*. Translated by Edwin Evans, W. Reeves, London.

BLOM, ERIC, *Beethoven's Pianoforte Sonatas Discussed*, J. M. Dent & Sons, London, 1938.

BURK, JOHN, *The Life and Works of Beethoven*, New York, 1942.

EVANS, EDWIN, *Beethoven's Nine Symphonies*, 2 vols., W. Reeves, London, 1923.

FISCHER, EDWIN, *Beethoven's Piano Sonatas*, Faber & Faber, London, 1959.

FISKE, ROGER, *Beethoven's Last Quartets*, Oxford University Press, 1940.

GROVE, GEORGE, *Beethoven and his Nine Symphonies*, Novello & Co., London, 1906.

Beethoven—Schubert—Mendelssohn. Reprints of original articles in Grove's *Dictionary*, Macmillan & Co., London, 1951.

HADOW, W. H., *Beethoven's Op. 78 Quartets*, Oxford University Press, 1926.

HOWES, FRANK, *Beethoven*, Oxford University Press, 1933.

MARLIAVE, JOSEPH DE, *Beethoven's Quartets*. Translated by Hilda Andrews, Oxford University Press, 1928.

MASON, DANIEL GREGORY, *The Quartets of Beethoven*, New York, 1947.

NEWMAN, ERNEST, *The Unconscious Beethoven*, Parsons, London, 1927.

ROLLAND, ROMAIN, *Beethoven the Creator*, vol. i. Translated by Ernest Newman, Gollancz, London, 1929.

SCHAUFFLER, ROBERT HAVEN, *Beethoven, the Man who Freed Music*, Doubleday, New York, 1929.

SCOTT, MARION M., *Beethoven*, J. M. Dent & Sons, London, 1943.

SHEDLOCK, J. S. (trans.), *Beethoven's Letters*, J. M. Dent & Sons, London, 1909.

SULLIVAN, J. W. N., *Beethoven: His Spiritual Development*, Jonathan Cape, London, 1927. Also Penguin and Mentor Books editions.

THAYER, A. W., *The Life of Ludwig van Beethoven*. Edited and translated by H. E. Krehbiel, 3 vols., New York and London, 1921–5. New edition, Centaur Press, London, 1960.

TOVEY, DONALD FRANCIS, *Beethoven*, Oxford University Press, 1944.
Essays in Musical Analysis, vols. i–vi, Oxford University Press, 1934.
Essays in Musical Analysis: Chamber Music, Oxford University Press, 1944.

TURNER, W. J., *Beethoven: The Search for Reality*, Benn, London, 1927. New edition, 1933.

WAGNER, RICHARD, *Beethoven*. Translated by E. Dannreuther, W. Reeves, London, 1893.

WEINGARTNER, FELIX, *On the Performance of Beethoven's Symphonies*. Translated by Jessie Crosland, London, 1907.

II

Books on Other Composers and on Music in General

COOKE, DERYCK, *The Language of Music*, Oxford University Press, 1959.

DUNHILL, THOMAS, *Chamber Music*, Macmillan & Co., London, 1913.

GROVE, GEORGE, *Dictionary of Music and Musicians*, fifth edition, Macmillan & Co., London, 1954.

HOWES, FRANK, *Man, Mind and Music*, Secker & Warburg, London, 1948.

KATZ, ADELE, *Challenge to Musical Tradition*, Putnam & Co., London, 1947. Original edition, New York, 1945.

LANGFORD, SAMUEL, *Musical Criticisms*. Edited Neville Cardus, Oxford University Press, 1939.

MACHLIS, JOSEPH, *The Enjoyment of Music*, Dobson Books Ltd, London, 1958. Original edition, New York, 1955.

NEWMAN, ERNEST, *A Musical Critic's Holiday*, Cassell & Co. Ltd, London, 1925.

SCHUMANN, ROBERT, *Music and Musicians*, 2 vols. Translated by Fanny Raymond Ritter, W. Reeves, London.

SCHWEITZER, ALBERT, *J. S. Bach*, 2 vols. Translated by Ernest Newman, A. & C. Black Ltd, London, 1923.

TERRY, C. S., *Bach: a Biography*, Oxford University Press, 1933. *See also* Terry's other books on Bach.

TOVEY, DONALD FRANCIS, *Essays and Lectures on Music*, Oxford University Press, 1949.

ULRICH, HOMER, *Chamber Music*, Columbia University Press, New York, 1948.

WAGNER, RICHARD, *Prose Works*, 8 vols. Translated by William Ashton Ellis, Kegan Paul, London, 1900.

WEINGARTNER, FELIX, *Symphony Writers since Beethoven*. Translated by Arthur Bles, W. Reeves, London.

III

Literature and Philosophy [1]

BERDYAEV, NICHOLAS, *Works*. Published in English translation by Geoffrey Bles: The Centenary Press, London.

BERGSON, HENRI, *Creative Evolution*, Macmillan, 1911.

CARLYLE, THOMAS, *Sartor Resartus, Past and Present, On Heroes and Hero-worship*, etc.

FREUD, SIGMUND, *Collected Papers*. Published in English translation by The Hogarth Press Ltd.

KANT, IMMANUEL, *Critique of Pure Reason, Critique of Aesthetic Judgement, Natural History of the Firmament* (found in Beethoven's private library after his death).

KRAUS, OSKAR, *Albert Schweitzer: His Work and His Philosophy*, A. & C. Black Ltd, London, 1944.

LOCKE, JOHN, *Essay on Human Understanding*.

MANN, THOMAS, *Freud, Goethe, Wagner*, New York, 1937.
Essays of Three Decades, Secker & Warburg, London, 1948.

NIETZSCHE, F. W., *Thus Spake Zarathustra, The Will to Power*, etc.

RUSSELL, BERTRAND, *A History of Western Philosophy*, George Allen & Unwin Ltd, London, 1940.

SCHOPENHAUER, ARTHUR, *The World as Will and Idea*.

SCHWEITZER, ALBERT, *Civilization and Ethics*, A. & C. Black Ltd, London, 1946.

SHAW, GEORGE BERNARD, *The Perfect Wagnerite*, London, 1903.

SPINOZA, BENEDICTUS DE, *Ethics*.

VIVANTE, LEONE, *English Poetry*, Faber & Faber Ltd, London, 1950.

WILSON, COLIN, *The Age of Defeat*, Gollancz Ltd, London, 1959.

[1] The works of the classic philosophers (Kant, Spinoza, Nietzsche) are available in various popular editions. Therefore I have indicated no specific publisher. I need hardly reiterate that this third list is inevitably incomplete. Indeed, it is, by the very nature of its subject, the most inadequate of all.

Index

Active subject (*see also* Kant), 60,
61, 63
Acton, Lord, 91
Adler, A., 1, 2, 3
An die ferne Geliebte, 113–14
Apollo, 95 ff., 104–7
Arnold, Matthew, 5, 42
Asceticism, 155–7

Bach, Johann Sebastian (1685–1750),
93, 124, 126, 127–9, 144, 164
Mass in B minor, 126, 128–9
Balzac, Honoré de, 69
Beethoven, Johanna van (mother),
10–11
Beethoven, Johann van (father), 10,
11
Beethoven, Johann van (brother), 4
Beethoven, Karl van (nephew), 7,
51, 113
Beethoven, Ludwig van (1770–
1827). Influence of heredity on,
1–4, 9–10; psychological characteristics, 1–8, 77–9, 91; 'The
Spaniard', 10; family responsibilities, 4; word portraits of, 5;
deafness, 6, 13, 34, 76; relationship between life and art, 6–9;
relationship to his times, 8–9;
musical environment of youth, 1,
9, 11; unenviable childhood, 10–
11; death of mother, 11; early
social life, 11–12; first visit to
Vienna, 11; leaves Bonn for
Vienna, 12; 'a fresh start', 13;
revolution and revelation distinguished, 14–15; simplicity and
directness of his music, 18–19;
religious convictions, 19, 123,
126–30; Greek affinities, 28–31,
95 ff.; unconscious element in
composition, 30, 58; relations
with women, 32–4, 36; syphilis
theory discussed, 34–6; effect of
French occupation of Vienna, 39;
visit to Martonvasar, 39–40;
purity and chastity of his music,
41, 91–2; love music, 44; psychology of love, 46–9; relationship
between love and heroism, 40;
identity of 'Immortal Beloved',
49–52; Josephine von Brunswick's child possibly his, 51–2;
celibacy, 34, 52; psychological
truthfulness, 50–1, 70; influence
of commissions and suggestions,
55, 121–2, 160; 'I will take Fate
by the throat . . .', 55; meaning
of 'Fate' for him, 56–8, 63;
nature of knowledge and experience, 58 ff.; positive activity
as characteristic, 60–3, 65–6, 164–
165; 'fate' motif, 64–5; sketch
books, 68, 132, 141; example of
grotesque in music, 68–9; relationship between orchestral and
chamber works, 70–1; Russian
influence, 72–4, 80–1; consciousness of his powers, 82–3, 85;
personal character in 1812, 86–91;
unity of his music, 88; lightning
strokes of genius, 94; Dionysian
and Apollonian elements, 95 ff.;
attitude to Nature, 99–102; uniqueness of third-period music,
109–10; three 'periods' analysed,
111–15, 146–50; a developing
personality, 119; studies old
music, 123, 156–7; idea of human

187